THE UNION FIRST

COMMUNITY AND COMMITMENT IN THE FIRST IOWA INFANTRY

RANDEE FIESELMANN

The Union First: Community and Commitment in the First Iowa Infantry
Published by RocketGirl Press
Iowa City, IA

Copyright © 2025 by Randee Fieselmann. All rights reserved.

No part of this book may be reproduced in any form or by any mechanical means, including information storage and retrieval systems without permission in writing from the publisher/author, except by a reviewer who may quote passages in a review.

All images, logos, quotes, and trademarks included in this book are subject to use according to trademark and copyright laws of the United States of America.

ISBN: 979-8-218-51073-2

HISTORY / United States / Civil War Period

Cover design by Benson & Hepker Design
Interior design by Asya Blue Design, copyright owned by Randee Fieselmann.

This book presents a historical analysis of the Civil War in Missouri based on available records and interpretations. While every effort has been made to ensure accuracy, perspectives and interpretations may vary. The views expressed are those of the author and do not necessarily reflect all historical opinions or accounts.

QUANTITY PURCHASES: Schools, professional groups, clubs, and other organizations may qualify for special terms when ordering quantities of this title. For information, visit theunionfirst.com.

All rights reserved by Randee Fieselmann and RocketGirl Press.

CONTENTS

Preface 1
Introduction 9
    Local Community 15
    Company Community. 18
Part I: Iowa
Chapter One: Seedbeds of Conviction. 23
    George Burmeister 26
    Eugene Ware. 27
    Stephen A. Douglas and Abraham Lincoln in Burlington 29
    Iowa's "First Born" 31
    Company K Cedar Rapids 33
    Company E Burlington 34
    Iowa citizens prepared to put down the Southern
    rebellion but were not prepared to finance a war. 36
Chapter Two: Mid-May to June 13, 1861 39
    Honorary Funeral for Stephen A. Douglas 42
    "Pleasure, Complaint and Drill" 43
    Outdated Muskets 44
    General Nathaniel Lyon orders Iowa troops to Missouri. 46
Part II: Combustible Missouri and the Men Who Lit Matches
Chapter Three: Nathaniel Lyon and the "Epoch-Making Event" . . . 51
    Nathaniel Lyon and William S. Harney in Kansas. 54
    St. Louis 58
    Abraham Lincoln and Missouri 60

  The Election of Delegates to Missouri's Secession Convention. 62
  General Harney's Recall and Curious Kidnapping 68
  The Camp Jackson Affair. 68
  The Price-Harney Agreement 76
Chapter Four: Claiborne Fox Jackson 80
  What happened in Kansas in the 1850s
  did not stay in Kansas. 82
  First Commissioner of Missouri Banking 84
  The Great Pretender 86
  Secession Momentum. 87
  Governor of Missouri 88
  The Planters' House Showdown 91
  Governor Jackson Declares War 95

Part III: The First Iowa Infantry in Lyon's Missouri Campaign

Chapter Five: June 14 to July 3, 1861 103
  Railroad Guard Duty 104
  "The Happy Land of Canaan" 108
  Through the Spotting Glass General Lyon
  meets the First Iowa, and they meet him 113
  "The Motley Crew". 120
Chapter Six: From Boonville to Springfield. 125
  Rivalry. 131
  Major Samuel D. Sturgis and the Kansas
  soldiers from Fort Leavenworth 132
  U.S. Commander of the West General John C. Frémont 134
  Accidents and Casualties 135
  Extreme Marching 138
  "Running a race with hunger as well as with

  Price and Claib Jackson" 140
  All for Naught....................................... 140
Chapter Seven: July 13 to 28, 1861 143
  "Hard Times" 147
  Lyon in a Peck of Trouble 149
  Expedition to Forsyth................................ 150
  "We swallowed our scruples" 154
Chapter Eight: "Too late" 159
  Dug Springs and the Rebel Camp near McCulla's Store 161
  Butternut Confusion 163
  "We know not at what moment." 165
  Truth or Rumor? 166
Chapter Nine: A Storm was Brewing 169
  Lyon's Bit of Luck 173
  The Battle of Wilson's Creek.......................... 174
  The Union Retreat 181
Conclusion 186
  Leadership... 190
Acknowledgments 195
Afterword 198
  Appendix A 203
  Appendix B 208
  Appendix C 214
  Appendix D 220
  Appendix E 224
  Bibliography 227
  Index 239

PREFACE

In the months after Abraham Lincoln was narrowly elected president in November 1860, Southern states followed through with their earlier threats to secede, leading to the opening salvos of the Civil War. Opinions and politics in the North remained divided, with fragile support for and ample criticism of President-Elect Lincoln. The South took advantage of a slow, disorderly transition by the new administration and prepared for war, and believing they had an edge, on April 12, 1861, South Carolina shelled Fort Sumter for thirty-three hours.[1] Following the bombardment and the surrender of the fort, there was an inexplicable and unforeseen reaction: an "epidemic of war fever" spread through the Union.[2] Iowans, like many northerners from different political parties and beliefs believed in one America, not two, and the Union mattered more than politics.[3] They supported Lincoln's decision to go to war and prioritized the value that united them: the Union first.

---

1 David. M. Potter, *The Impending Crisis: America Before the Civil War 1848–1861*, ed. Don. E. Fehrenbacher (New York: Harper Perennial, 2011), 555–583. Chapter 20 "Fort Sumter: End and Beginning" describes the complicated series of events that preceded the April 12 bombardment.

2 Brian Matthew Jordan, *A Thousand May Fall: Life, Death, and Survival in the Union Army* (New York: Liveright Publishing Corporation, 2021), 28.

3 Thomas R. Baker, *The Sacred Cause of the Union: Iowa in the Civil War* (Iowa City: The University of Iowa Press, 2016), 32, 60. "One night of heavy artillery fire in Charleston Harbor unleashed all of the anger at once... incited Iowans to turn out en masse and demand reintegration by any means necessary," and "They reacted as if they themselves had been guarding Fort Sumter."

Eugene Ware of Company E Burlington Zouaves and George Burmeister of Company K Cedar Rapids were among the first boys and men to form Iowa militias, drill, and to enlist in the First Iowa Infantry. The first Civil War volunteers enlisted for only ninety days. When I stumbled across Burmeister's remarkable unpublished diary, I was stunned by his polished handwriting and the story it told. I am unaware of other references to his diary. Although there were three companies of German-speaking men in the First Iowa Infantry, George is one of dozens of German Americans who enlisted in other companies.[4] I wanted to learn all that I could about the First Iowa Infantry and soon read Eugene Ware's memoir, which is often cited in Civil War literature for its descriptions of the regiment and the Battle of Wilson's Creek. The Burmeister and Ware diaries depict the uncertain conditions which were, in many ways, similar for other northern soldiers who entered early into the Civil War. [5]

The diaries tell of boys enlisting in the First Iowa Infantry in the few weeks after Fort Sumter, the unpredictable nature of war with General Nathaniel Lyon in Missouri, and the importance of community with fellow soldiers. The diaries and newspaperman Franc B. Wilkie's accounts document Lyon's Missouri campaign in the Civil War. Wilkie was assigned by the Dubuque *Herald* to travel with and report on the experiences of First Iowa Infantry and he was on hand for the Battle of Wilson's Creek.[6] These first-hand sources allow for a richer retelling than can a single

---

[4] See Jordan, 7–8, for a discussion of German-American soldiers.

[5] Eugene Fitch Ware, *The Lyon Campaign in Missouri, Being a History of the First Iowa Infantry* (Iowa City: Camp Pope Bookshop, 1991) iii. The book was originally published in 1907; George C. Burmeister Diaries 1861–1862. Civil War Collection, Special Collections and Archives. The University of Iowa Libraries. Collection-MsC0906 (Digital.lib.uiowa.edu). I quote and paraphrase material at length from Burmeister's and Ware's diaries, including Ware's descriptions of the pre-war Burlington community.

[6] Michael E. Banasik, *Missouri in 1861: The Civil War Letters of Franc B. Wilkie, Newspaper Correspondent*. (Iowa City: Camp Pope Publishing, 2001). Hereafter cited as Banasik (Wilkie). Wilkie first published his newspaper reports in 1861 as *The Iowa First: Letters from the War*. His accounts sew together many otherwise absent details that are missing in the diaries about circumstances.

account and, together, provide a case study for a glimpse of community evolving around the everyday interactions of the ninety-day enlistees in the summer of 1861.

Eugene Ware wrote that any history of 1850s, pre-Civil War America, attempts to explain the wildly conflicting values and politics of the times so that "the reader may understand what was done and why it was done."[7] The Fugitive Slave Act (part of the Congressional Compromise of 1850), the Kansas-Nebraska Act of 1854, and the Dred Scott case of 1857, were salient for Iowans who were, literally, surrounded by concerns created by the acts. Territorial Nebraska was on Iowa's western border and the Territory of ("bleeding") Kansas was just a few miles to the southwest. Missouri, a slave state, bordered Iowa to the south. Iowans were not like-minded about the political issues of their day. In many ways, Iowa is a microcosm of the turmoil that gripped the North before the Civil War began.

In 1860, most of Iowa's population was concentrated in towns near the Mississippi River, Iowa's eastern border, where opinions were heavily influenced by riverboat traffic, secessionist ideas, or Southern ancestry. Contrasting opinions came from local ministers who had been sent early to eastern Iowa by the American Home Missionary Society and other denominations, and who strongly influenced the Iowa settlers.[8] There were also anti-slavery feelings carried by a surge of American migrants, thousands having moved west from eastern and southern states during the 1850s. Eugene observed this phenomenon from river crossings near his town on the Mississippi: "Miles and miles of covered wagons poured

---

[7] Ware, iii.
[8] Truman Orville Douglas, *The Pilgrims of Iowa* (Concord: The Rumford Press, 1911); The early efforts of American Home Missionaries in southeast Iowa strongly influenced the state's education, civic, and political progress; Daniel Matson, Company E, described the presence of several churches in his small rural community. An 1873 Atlas lists 10 churches and 20 school houses in the area with population of 1,752. "Map of Yellow Springs Township Kossuth, Northfield, Pleasant Grove, Mediapolis, Danville, and Middletown Cities," 49-50. Cadastral Maps. *An Illustrated Historical Atlas of Des Moines Country, Iowa, 1873*. https://digital.lib.uiowa.edu/node/436504, accessed April 12, 2025.

through from Illinois...one group coming as another passed on."[9] In addition, there were many immigrants (who came mostly from Europe, principally Germany) who did not want to live in America with an aristocratic class who profited from enslaved workers. Eugene Ware's memoir captures an atmosphere of incompatible viewpoints with examples from newspaper articles, political arguments, sermons, Lincoln-Douglas debates, and street fights.

The Iowa soldiers were ordered to brigade under one of the most controversial, if little known, generals in the Civil War. The diaries describe how soldiers in the First Iowa Infantry endured more than what might seem humanly possible, then followed General Lyon into battle knowing that they might die. I asked a question that plagues many who research the Civil War: what kept soldiers together and committed to their cause? Much has been written in the Civil War literature about the significance of community to address the question, using a variety of terms such as brotherhood, comradeship, family, bonding, or solidarity. The notion of community is generally based on the concept of personal ties, a type of solidarity based on common will, where each individual feels part of an empowering whole.[10]

Eugene wrote that "the story of the First Iowa Infantry is typical." The First Iowa Infantry was also atypical, making it both representative and rare. But admittedly, two selected diaries offer a limited range of soldiers' experiences. Two Iowa soldiers from Companies K and E cannot fairly represent other three-month Civil War volunteer soldiers, nor can their observations speak for the trained, professional U.S. Army Regulars, or the Missouri and Kansas volunteers who marched and fought along-

---

9 Ware, 30.
10 John Urry, "Sociology of Time and Space," *The Blackwell Companion to Social Theory*, ed. Bryan S. Turner (Malden, MA: Blackwell Publishers, 2000), 423–424; Gordon Marshall, "Community," *A Dictionary of Sociology* (New York: Oxford University Press, 1998), 249. Talcott Parsons, *The Social System* (Glencoe, IL: Free Press, 1964) 91, 96–97. According to Parsons, community is formed by people performing daily activities together and who share some commonness of value orientation; Baker, 85, refers to "unit cohesion" of the regiment.

side them. Neither can we expect the soldiers to have fully revealed their feelings in the diaries; even personal diaries are filtered by cultural modes, written for an unacknowledged audience. Many of the Iowa enlistees in the first regiment of volunteers were young, aged eighteen to twenty-one. The boy-soldiers came into the First Iowa Infantry infused with presumptions of manly honor and duty.

Like many accounts, Eugene Ware's memoir was published years after the Civil War, and some historians have noted that Ware rewrote parts of his original diary. He kept a dated, detailed diary and sent it home just before the Battle of Wilson's Creek. Surely, to complete his memoir later for publication, he added memories of growing up in Iowa, the Missouri campaign, maps of routes taken by soldiers in the First Iowa Infantry, officers, and the Battle of Wilson's Creek. There is little doubt, however, that he could have written such an exceptional memoir without having drawn from his recorded first-hand observations.[11]

There are more broadly representative studies of community written by Civil War scholars, as discussed in the following introduction. There are diaries written by other soldiers in the First Iowa Infantry and are referenced here to emphasize, enrich, or validate significant moments in the Missouri campaign.[12] However, none are as abundantly complete as are the Ware

---

11 See Clark Kenyon's "Introduction to the Camp Pope Bookshop Edition" of Ware's *The Lyon Campaign*, xxvii–xxxv. Ware continued to write and publish throughout his later career as a lawyer and legislator in Kansas.

12 I reference the diaries of: William Branson, 24, Muscatine Company C (recorded as Bransom in the Guy Logan Roster and Record of Iowa Civil War soldiers). Branson, from Ohio, enlisted in First Iowa Infantry Company C while visiting Cedar and Muscatine counties.; Henry O'Connor, 40, Muscatine Company A; Jacob Ritner, 33, Mount Pleasant Company F; John (James) S. Clark, 19, Henry County Company F; Daniel Matson, 20, Burlington Company E. Sources: William W. Branson Diary (C0218), The State Historical Society of Missouri Research Center-Columbia; Henry O' Connor, "With the First Iowa Infantry" *The Palimpsest* 3, no. 2 (February 1922); Charles F. Larimer, Ed., *Love and Valor: Intimate Civil War Letters Between Captain Jacob and Emiline Ritner* (Western Springs, Ill.: Sigourney Press, 2000); *Life in the Middle West: Reminiscences of J.S. Clark*. (Chicago: Advance Publishing Company, n.d.). Much of Clark's *Life in the Middle West* is taken from Ware's memoir, as noted by C. Kenyon, "Introduction," xxv; Daniel Matson, *The Life Experiences of Daniel Matson* (Mary H. Matson, March 18, 1924). His memoir, published posthumously by his wife, mostly tells of his early life and of pioneer times in Iowa. https://books.google.com

and Burmeister diaries. These are no ordinary, hum-drum records of daily routine: they give us in-depth access to their authors' daily struggles, hopes, and disappointments. I try to keep the soldiers' voices present and alive and use their first names to help capture bits of their very different personalities. Eugene Ware was young, boastful, and always eager to join in a fight. George Burmeister was three years older, contemplative, and industrious. I hope my efforts reanimate these young Civil War soldiers, who marched into manhood to ensure that our country was reunited.

Although the pulse of this story comes from a close-range perspective, it isn't meaningful without the important background story. Full appreciation of the diaries includes learning why General Nathaniel Lyon ordered the First Iowa Infantry to join his forces, and this necessarily involves events which take place in Missouri. The history of the Civil War in Missouri is dramatic. It tells of a tinderbox Union slave state, under siege by opposing parties. When researching the so-called Camp Jackson Affair and the Planters' House Meeting which led up to the Wilson's Creek battle, William Piston and Richard Hatcher write, "no summary can do justice to the complex events in St. Louis between January and June, 1861. Nor do historians agree on all the details."[13] Those events triggered hostilities in Missouri. Differing perspectives, as well as deception by political leaders and in the press in 1861, made it difficult then and now to comprehend the truth. It is important to describe Nathaniel Lyon and Missouri Governor Claiborne Jackson, the men responsible for the Camp Jackson Affair and the Planters' House Meeting.

The oft-repeated narrative was that General Lyon declared war as the Planters' House meeting ended and was responsible for driving the governor and his followers into exile from the state. At least 14 historical sources repeat the account written immediately after the forum by

---

13 William Garrett Piston and Richard W. Hatcher II, *Wilson's Creek: The Second Battle of the Civil War and the Men Who Fought It* (Chapel Hill: University of North Carolina Press, 2000), 343, n18.

the editor of a secessionist newspaper, Thomas L. Snead, who served as Governor Jackson's secretary.[14] A different version with fuller context and a different conclusion was published a day later by Major Horace Conant, who served that day as General Lyon's secretary.[15] As I found differing accounts of those events, they seemed to constitute a story in themselves.

A biography of Nathaniel Lyon portrays him much like John Brown, as a self-righteous zealot who "plunged...Missouri into war."[16] The same author, in a biography of Claiborne Fox Jackson, shares how the governor had a domineering personality and a long history of using secret politics and inflammatory rhetoric to get what he wanted. Abraham Lincoln and loyal Unionists believed secession was a mass movement resulting from the conspiratorial action of a minority whose true purpose was blackmail. Claiborne Fox Jackson provides an example for how this process took place in Missouri. "Minority coercion" almost worked.[17]

Sorting out "truths" is a challenge. I can only touch on the tangled history of how "The Lyon and the Fox" ignited an explosive state.[18] Although secondary sources include a variety of historical perspectives, and Missouri sentiments before the Civil War (and after) were heavily influenced by secessionist sympathies, I try to view events from Nathaniel

---

14 See Chapter 4 footnote 266, for a list of authors who rely on Confederate Thomas L. Snead's account written for Governor Jackson and reprinted in Snead's book written twenty-five years later: *The Fight for Missouri: From the Election of Lincoln to the Death of Lyon* (New York: Charles Scribner's Sons, 1886),199–200.

15 John McElroy, *The Struggle for Missouri* (Washington, D.C.: The National Tribune Company,1909), 109–115. McElroy provides both the full account published for newspapers by Major Horace Conant as well as the one written by Snead. Importantly, Conant's account is not Lyon's declaration of war as stated by Snead and gives fuller details of the discussion; "Meeting at the Planters House," www.civilwarstlouis.com/articles/meeting-at-the-planters-house/ This website provides excerpts from McElroy's book noting that it gives fuller details than other accounts and warns that the author is notably anti-Confederate.

16 Christopher Phillips, *Damned Yankee: The Life of General Nathaniel Lyon* (Baton Rouge: Louisiana State University Press, 1996), xiv, xv, xviii.

17 Potter, 558; Baker, 60–61. A Mount Pleasant, Iowa, newspaper blamed the war on the "seventy-five thousand negro drivers" who were trying to force five million white men to abandon the principles of democracy.

18 James M. McPherson, *Battle Cry of Freedom* (New York: Oxford University Press, 1988), 290.

Lyon's perspective. Before his assignment to St. Louis, his political transformation from Democrat to a Lincoln Republican was much like that of many Iowans described by Kenneth Lyftogt and Thomas Baker, as noted in Chapter One.[19] This point of view unavoidably creates a quarrel with the historians who agree with Governor Jackson's repeated claims that Nathaniel Lyon and the federal government were aggressors in the "neutral" Union state of Missouri and responsible for the deaths at the Camp Jackson Affair. It may seem contradictory that those same authors have also been vital sources for much of my reference material. While I argue with facts and footnotes, I hold deep appreciation for those who have given attention to these same Missouri events. Their research legacies are invaluable.

What matters most is the story that tells of the soldiers in the First Iowa Infantry as they marched unrelenting miles, camped near Springfield in southwestern Missouri, and hoped to fight a battle. I try to fairly interpret the perspectives of the Iowa soldiers, their mentors, and officers as I search for how they formed community. Nathaniel Lyon and soldiers of the First Iowa Infantry believed absolutely in preserving the Union. They went into the Battle of Wilson's Creek to fight for their cause.

---

19 Baker, 40–41; Kenneth L. Lyftogt, *Iowa and the Civil War, Volume I: Free Child of the Missouri Compromise 1850–1862* (Iowa City: Camp Pope Publishing, 2018), 16, 20, 22–43.

INTRODUCTION

> The Civil War was a battle of ideas interrupted by artillery.   —Eugene Ware

Southern states began preparing for war even before their favored candidates lost the November 1860 election to Abraham Lincoln. Secretary of War John Buchanan Floyd guaranteed early advantages for the South by ordering 105,000 muskets and 10,000 rifles to be transferred from northern repositories to five arsenals in the South while they were still in federal hands. Within months, partisans captured those five arsenals and all their remaining arms.[20] Southern leaders used their sharp political skills and took advantage of a "period of intermittent paralysis" (the one hundred-twenty days before Lincoln took office).[21] They exploited the ineptitude or southern sentiments of the outgoing president (Buchanan) as well as newly elected Republicans who were inexperienced at holding power.

---

20 W.A. Swanberg, "Was the Secretary of War a Traitor?" *American Heritage*, February 1963, 2. Americanheritage.com. Floyd resigned December 29, 1860 and was soon appointed brig. general in the Confederate Army; Randy R. McGuire, "Solving the Mystery of the Arsenal Guns: The St. Louis Arsenal in the Years Leading up to the Civil War," Part I, http://www.civilwarstlouis.com/arsenal/. After reviewing correspondence from the War Department and the Ordnance Department held in *The Official Records of the Rebellion*, McGuire concludes that in 1859, Southern states and Secretary of War, Floyd, demonstrated their intention to diminish the Union's supply of arms.

21 Potter, 514–515.

President Lincoln understood the critical importance of Missouri to the war (its resources, access to the Mississippi River, and the largest federal arsenal in the slave states.) He did not want to lose it to the South. U.S. Army Captain Nathaniel Lyon was assigned to protect the St. Louis Arsenal and to help keep Missouri in the Union. The president gave significant support to U.S. Republican Congressman Francis Preston Blair, Lyon, and other Unionists in Missouri. Lincoln appointed two Missourians to his cabinet. The governor of Missouri, Claiborne Fox Jackson, and a powerful minority of Missouri slave owners, businessmen, bankers, politicians, and people whose families had come from the Deep South, were loyal to secession and fought hard to make it happen.

The South had out-maneuvered the North by preparing early for war. Ulysses S. Grant later described how Southerners were hard at work on strategies to paralyze the North's ability to respond.[22] As Eugene Ware wrote, they secured a "running start." On April 12–13, 1861, South Carolina bombarded federal Fort Sumter, and everything quickly changed. President Lincoln, who was not an extremist on slavery as portrayed by the South and rival politicians, was indeed a radical for preserving the Union.[23] In a previously unimagined patriotic response, Northern boys and men eager to join Lincoln's war to save the Union, surged forward to enlist.

After the blasting of Fort Sumter, President Lincoln believed the war would be over quickly. Soldiers in the First Iowa Infantry were first to respond to President Abraham Lincoln's and Iowa Governor Kirkwood's requests to enlist in the Civil War. They were the only Iowa regiment to be enlisted for ninety days and the first to go into a Civil War battle. Wilson's Creek was the first battle following the humiliating Confederate victory at Bull Run and the first battle fought west of the Mississippi.[24]

---

22 Ulysses S. Grant, *Personal Memoirs of U.S. Grant* (New York: Charles L. Webster & Co., 1885), 1:226. Grant described how Floyd, the Secretary of War, transferred soldiers and cannon and small arms from Northern arsenals to the South so that many could be captured when hostilities began.
23 Potter, 558.
24 Piston and Hatcher, xiii-xiv.

INTRODUCTION

The First Iowa was commanded by the first Union general to be killed in the Civil War, in the first and only state with a governor who attempted to take it into secession without the support of a vote by representatives or elected state delegates. The soldiers in the First Iowa gave their best quick-march when needed to help another regiment or whenever there was a chance to catch the enemy. Although they were resilient and resourceful, and there are remarkably few complaints in the diaries used here as sources, the story of the First Iowa Infantry is often one of disappointment and buzzing confusion.

On August 10, 1861, General Nathaniel Lyon went into battle at Wilson's Creek near Springfield, Missouri. General Sterling Price, leading the Missouri State Guard Troops, and Governor Jackson had pressured the Confederacy and General Benjamin McCulloch, commanding troops from Arkansas, Texas, and Louisiana, to invade Missouri from Arkansas.[25] They fought Lyon and his Union troops, including soldiers of the First Iowa Infantry who followed and bravely fought for him. Lyon acknowledged their unique strengths before he died on the battlefield. Historians consider the Wilson's Creek battle a Confederate victory. However, because the larger Confederate and Missouri State secessionist forces left the field and did not follow the Union soldiers, the result fulfilled Lyon's goal for a safe withdrawal.[26] Within a few weeks of the battle, New York newspapers, *Frank Leslie's Illustrated Newspaper*, and *Harper's Weekly* published at least five images of the Wilson's Creek Battle and Lyon's death.[27] The media sent special artists to the scenes who

---

25 Thomas W. Cutrer, *Theater of a Separate War: The Civil War West of the Mississippi 1861–1865* (Chapel Hill: The University of North Carolina Press, 2017), 28, 36, 41.

26 Lyftogt, 209; William Riley Brooksher, *Bloody Hill: The Civil War Battle of Wilson's Creek* (Washington: Brassey's, 1995), 173; See Piston and Hatcher, 280–286, for details of how the Battle of Wilson's Creek ended. As Lyon's troops retreated, the Southerners were "fought out" and glad to see them go.

27 Joan Stack, 2012. "The Hat, the Horse, and the Hero," Paper presented at the Proceedings of the Mid-America Conference on History.https://www.academia.edu/122938192/The_Hat_the_Horse_and_the_Hero_The_Impact_of_the_Battle_of_Wilson_s_Creek_on_the_Legacy_of_General_Nathaniel_Lyon?email_work-cards=view-paper. Retrieved September 9, 2024.

attempted to draw accurate representations of the battle. Their drawings were later edited to make the newspapers' preferred points, using a process which converted them into prints for publication. Henri Lovie's onsite sketch of the Battle of Wilson's Creek shows soldiers from the First Iowa Infantry fighting alongside General Lyon. The engraved version, published in Frank Leslie's Illustrated, portrayed General Lyon as a martyr who died for the Union cause.[28] Although Lyon's decisions were controversial and often criticized, the Northern news coverage praised triumphs of the battle: the surprise strike against the odds and the courageous, prolonged standoff by much smaller numbers before their retreat. Soldiers in Lyon's army were celebrated as heroes in St. Louis and in every Iowa community that had sent a company into the First Iowa Infantry.

HENRI LOVIE SKETCH: The Miram and Ira D. Wallach Division of Art, Prints and Photographs: Print Collection, The New York Public Library. "Death of General Lyon, August 10, 1861," The New York Public Library Digital Collections. https://digitalcollections.nypl.org/items/6eaed3cc-756d-1df6-e040-e00a18065bf1.

---

28 "Artist-Journalists of the Civil War," 02/17/1961.https://TIME.com/archive/6623040/the-press-artist-jounalists-of-the-civil-war; Joshua Brown, *Beyond the Lines: Pictorial Reporting, Everyday Life, and the Crisis of Gilded Age America* (Berkeley: University of California Press, 2006), 32, 55, 56.

INTRODUCTION

The charge of the First Iowa Regiment under General Lyon at the Battle of Wilson's Creek near Springfield, Missouri August 10, 1861.
Licensed from Alamy.com (April 5, 2024).

General Lyon's Charge at the Battle of Springfield, Harper's Weekly, August 31, 1861 Missouri Historical Society Photographs and Prints Collection (P0084-1266) (Accessed 02-24-2025)

Eugene Ware was especially proud of the Congressional resolution of recognition which was ordered by President Lincoln and Army Commander General George B. McClellan, to be read aloud to every regiment in the U.S. Army across America: "Thanks of Congress are hereby given to the brave officers and soldiers who, under the command of the late General Lyon, sustained the honor of the flag...against overwhelming numbers at the battle of Springfield" (referring to the nearby Battle of Wilson's Creek).[29]

Perhaps surprising for a story about such heroic efforts is that, just days before the Wilson's Creek battle, the Iowa soldiers had expressed hatred for General Lyon. And Lyon had voiced disgust at seeing such a ragtag bunch of men, many of whom had no shoes and wore aprons or whatever they could find to cover their backsides, exposed by worn-out uniforms. Lyon had complained about the "gypsies" mingling on marches with his finely uniformed and disciplined Regular U.S. Army soldiers. The Iowa volunteers had the impression that Lyon didn't like them.[30] After repeatedly pleading for food, supplies, and more soldiers, Lyon had received no support from his commanders. Soldiers in the First Iowa had little information about why they weren't getting their promised and sorely needed new uniforms, shoes, enough food, or better arms.[31] The boys were disappointed and they were hungry, unfairly blaming Lyon

---

[29] Ware, xvii, 354. The First Iowa Infantry was the only Iowa Civil War regiment to be enlisted for ninety days. Lyftogt, 212. Governor Samuel Kirkwood, "to keep its glory undiluted," honored the regiment by retiring their title; "Alexander Clark Organizes African Americans in Iowa to Fight in the Civil War," www.iowapbs.org. Retrieved 01/19/2021. "The First Iowa" was not used again for Civil War units until the formation the First Regiment Iowa Volunteer Infantry (African Descent) in 1863, Iowa's first and only all-black unit .

[30] H.W. Lathrop, *The Life and Times of Samuel J. Kirkwood, Iowa's War Governor* (Iowa City: Published by Author, 1893), 117. This seems to be the original use of "tatterdemalion" to describe the ragged appearance of the First Iowa soldiers; Wilkie wrote, "The Iowa troops were ragged and dirty enough to beat Falstaff's (sic) recruits all to 'fits.'" Banasik (Wilkie), 102. Burmeister and Ware do not mention either tatterdemalion or gypsies.

[31] Cyril B. Upham, "Uniforms of the Iowa Troops in Civil War, "*Iowa Journal of History and Politics* 16 (January 1918). https://iagenweb.org/history/IJPH/IJPHMainPage.htm. The First Iowa Infantry soldiers did not know, for example, that replacement uniforms had been made and shipped, but were first delayed in transit for lack of freight payment, and later in Rolla for unknown reasons. Retrieved 1/20/2020.

and other officers. The expected systems of government and military support had failed and created frustration for Lyon and his soldiers. Either information, troops, and supplies were not readily available, or military leaders and supply chains were dysfunctional or corrupt. System failures created a context of "booming, buzzing confusion" that summer of 1861.[32]

Given the stressful, confusing context, the question must be asked, how was social order in the regiment possible? How did soldiers remain committed to the war effort? Historian James M. McPherson used hundreds of soldiers' letters and diaries to learn what motivated soldiers to remain dedicated in the Civil War. His conclusions fueled my desire to understand the fabric of community as it formed in the soldiers' daily activities. The Ware and Burmeister diaries fuse with Wilke's reports to tell us about the boys' comrades, singing, honoring the death of Illinois Senator Stephen A. Douglas, witnessing their first execution, mischief, impressions of President Lincoln and officers, times of utter discouragement and fear, and pondering the stars at night while trying to sleep outdoors on the rocky ground.

Local Community

In the title of McPherson's award-winning 1997 study *For Cause and Comrades,* "and" refers to the nearly complete bonding of men who share a mission to fight for a just cause *and* who are closely bound in a primary group.[33] Both primary groups and soldiers' commitments to cause began during enlistments in hometown communities. The Ware and Burmeister

---

32 Gary Alan Fine, "Agency, Structure, and Comparative Contexts: Toward a Synthetic Interactionism," *Symbolic Interaction* 15(1) (1992) 87–107, 101. Fine uses the catchy notion of "booming, buzzing, confusion," adapted from William James's phrase "blooming, buzzing, confusion," *Principles of Psychology* (New York: Henry Holt, 1890), 462. James referred to the sensory experiences of infants. *Stanford Encyclopedia of Philosophy.* https://plato.stanford.edu/entries/james/. Retrieved 4/6/2020.

33 James M. McPherson, *For Cause and Comrades: Why Men Fought in the Civil War* (New York: Oxford University Press, 1997), 82, 85–91, 114–115. McPherson concluded that primary groups were the source of melding for Civil War soldiers. Primary groups are men closest to a soldier with whom he interacts every day in camp, on the march and in combat.

diaries chronicle two types of community, beginning with local support, which inspired these young men and were the roots of enlistment.

William G. Piston studied soldiers in the First Iowa Infantry and found that each company felt strong identity with its hometown and wanted to uphold its honor.[34] In *The Bonds of War*, Diana Dretske studied a group of men who had immigrated from Scotland, Ireland, and England. They lived as rural neighbors in northeastern Illinois and enlisted together in the second summer of the war "to preserve the Union."[35] She found that the soldiers' families had built a meaningful local farming community before they entered the war together.

In 1887, Ferdinand Tönnies introduced terms which became fundamental concepts for studying society. *Gemeinschaft* describes the close social relationships found in small rural villages where people know each other and work together, bonded by sharing the basic conditions of life. Tönnies noted a sense of belonging as essential for community. *Gesellschaft* refers to larger, more diverse societies which hold fewer personal contacts, less social solidarity, and rely more on interdependence for building community.[36] According to Gordon Marshall's *Oxford Dictionary of Sociology* one study analyzed ninety-four definitions of the concept.[37] The exact content and meaning of community have been under endless dispute but remain important for understanding soldiers' commitments in the Civil War.

Wilson's Creek historians Piston and Hatcher conclude that Northern and Southern soldiers closely identified with their local communities and

---

34 William Garrett Piston, "The 1st Iowa Volunteers: Honor and Community in a Ninety Day Regiment." *Civil War History* 44 (March 1998) 3, 34. Militias and companies were formed with very localized identities.

35 Diana L. Dretske, *The Bonds of War: A Story of Immigrants and Esprit de Corps in Company C, 96th Illinois Volunteer Infantry* (Carbondale, IL: Southern Illinois University Press, 2021), 2, 188

36 Ferdinand Tönnies, *Fundamental Concepts of Sociology, Gemeinschaft und Gesellschaft,* Charles Loomis, editor, (East Lansing: Michigan State University Press, 1957), 223–231. Max Weber, Emile Durkheim, and later sociologists explored how social arrangements developed in diverse societies. They theorized that community bonding in modern society requires interdependence and some form of collective conscience.

37 Marshall, 97.

their respective company units. They found that, for volunteer soldiers, "company level identities" were strong and lasted much longer than historians have granted.³⁸ Dretske explains how, by dealing with severe hardships together, soldiers built "esprit de corps" that forged them into a determined family.³⁹ Peter S. Carmichael has examined how, by solving challenges, soldiers used hard-nosed pragmatism to form "extended military families" which helped them traverse harsh conditions. Their use of situational thinking for adaptation was empowering.⁴⁰ Brian M. Jordan studied German American soldiers who fought together near the end of the war. He found that although soldiers were "whipsawed" between conviction and disappointment, they formed strong bonds of comradeship "powerful enough to persist across generations."⁴¹

People who are working together in a place with common purpose create community. Professor Gary Alan Fine reminds us that the heart of social order takes place in "group space," or "tiny publics." Civic action is found wherever citizens are bound together in shared activities.⁴² The diaries tell us about the soldiers' shared activities in military companies. The First Iowa soldiers connected with each other in their hometowns because of their common commitments to the Union and local enlistments. Those close connections stretched wider whenever they completed tasks with each other.

---

38 Piston and Hatcher, xv, xx, 333,334. Soldiers continued to think of themselves as members of their old units. I refer to the authors' term "identity" as the sense of belonging to a cohesive group; Baker, 85, refers to "unit cohesion" of the regiment.

39 Dretske, 154, 188, 190.

40 Peter S. Carmichael, *The War for the Common Soldier: How Men Thought, Fought, and Survived in Civil War Armies* (Chapel Hill: The University of North Carolina Press, 2018), 7, 8, 43.

41 Jordan, 15, 233, 241.

42 Gary Alan Fine, *Tiny Publics: A Theory of Group Action and Culture* (New York: Russel Sage Foundation, 2012); Fine, "The Sociology of the Local: Action and its Publics," *Sociological Theory* 28, no. 4 (December 2010): 355–376. G. A. Fine is the James E. Professor of Sociology at Northwestern University; Talcott Parsons, *The Social System* (Glencoe, IL: Free Press, 1964) 91, 96–97. According to Parsons, community is formed by people performing daily activities together and who share some commonness of value orientation.

Company Community

Although community is an elusive term which often refers to home communities, I suggest that company community refers to the bonds formed within a clearly defined military unit of about 78 to 100 men. Soldiers who enlisted together also cooked, ate, drilled, marched, slept, and fought together side by side within the boundaries of those same enlistment companies. Borrowing from the research of Civil War historians and concepts from classical sociologists, I ask if local community continues to develop from the combined forces of soldiers' face-to-face relationships and pragmatic duties within a common base of operation (military company); strong feelings of group-belonging; mutual concern, interdependence; and overriding all, shared cause. Given the stressful buzzing confusion that characterized the First Iowa Infantry's official days of duty, were the soldiers able to weave community anew in their companies as they negotiated social order each day? If so, the challenges and experiences of military life as described by Burmeister and Ware, interlock with the prevailing bonds formed in local communities to create company community and commitment to the cause of the Union.

Eugene and George wrote in their diaries whenever they could throughout their training and Lyon's Missouri campaign. Most of the soldiers' days in Missouri were spent marching and camping within assigned military companies and waiting to go to into battle. Although the Wilson's Creek Battle was the culmination of Lyon's campaign, community was formed before soldiers faced the reality of battle. Going into battle tested its existence.

The first part of this book introduces George and Eugene, their local enlistments, and time in training camp before they were ordered to Missouri. Chapter One begins with a brief description of a rapidly changing Iowa. Iowa citizens reluctantly considered civil war before Fort Sumter and were propelled into it immediately after the bombardment.

Chapter Two continues as ten companies in the First Iowa Infantry drill and train in Camp Ellsworth, just outside Keokuk, Iowa.

Part II of the book characterizes the men who instigated the Civil War in Missouri. A complex series of events surrounded the actions of General Lyon, Governor Claiborne Jackson, and General William S. Harney, Lyon's superior and the U.S. Army's head of the Department of the West. Chapter Three is an effort to understand Lyon and why he felt forced into war in Missouri. It includes Lyon's time as an officer in Kansas before he went to St. Louis to defend the arsenal. Much tension followed Lyon's assignment to protect the arsenal. His rash reactions to the plans of secessionists often transformed into significant clashes and led to the Camp Jackson Affair. This pivotal event intensified divisions between secessionists and Unionists in Missouri.

Chapter Four assesses Governor Claiborne Jackson. The governor forcefully plotted for secession without the support of a majority of Missourians, while he consistently asserted that the federal government were the aggressors in the state. It details the failed truce meeting held at the Planters' House Hotel on June 11, 1861, and the governor's sudden declaration of war early the next morning. The actions of these men led to the Civil War in Missouri and determined, in part, the routes taken by the First Iowa soldiers. On June 12, 1861, Lyon ordered the First and Second Iowa Infantries to leave training camp and come by steamboat down the Mississippi River into Missouri.

Part III retells Eugene Ware's, George Burmeister's, and Franc Wilkie's accounts of the First Iowa Infantry in the summer of 1861. The abrasive, outspoken General Lyon ordered the First Iowa Infantry to Missouri and directed the soldiers' lives as they completed their ninety-day enlistments. The core of this steely story reveals how soldiers connected with each other as they endured Lyon's campaign. Chapter Five describes their arrival in Hannibal, and the surprisingly dangerous march to join Lyon in Camp Cameron, near Boonville. Chapter Six continues as the troops marched long miles to Springfield, Missouri. George and Eugene describe marching, hunger, foraging, high-water river crossings, anger, and fears. Chapter Seven tells of excursions and soldiers expecting to fight.

Chapter Eight tells of poorly equipped soldiers called out to march to phantom battles, false alarms, and disappointments. The diaries disclose how the soldiers equivocated but remained committed to the cause of the Union. Chapter Nine brings this story to its end in the early hours of August 10, 1861, as the First Iowa soldiers, alongside General Lyon and his diminished troops, quietly marched into a dark night towards a battle at Wilson's Creek.

In the Conclusion, I layer summaries about company community with thoughts about remaining puzzles. In the Acknowledgments, I attempt to give due credit to the people and sources that were critical in this project. In the Afterword I ask why people followed the "Fire-Eaters" (Southern extremist politicians) who led our nation into the Civil War. It provides an opportunity to comment on the continuing scuffle over whose stories are "for the record" and why it matters, as facts remain combustible.

PART I

IOWA

CHAPTER ONE

SEEDBEDS OF CONVICTION

Madness seemed to have taken over. Nothing appeared to go according to reason or as it was planned.
—C. Van Woodward

By 1860, many Iowans viewed slavery as an aristocratic institution, which was not the way their country was meant to be. But what concerned them more was the throat-gripping political domination by Southerners and supporters of slavery who had for years controlled the presidency, legislative branches, the Supreme Court, high military posts, cabinet posts, and the federal bureaucracy for nearly three-quarters of a century.[43] Powerful and persuasive supporters of slavery demanded its extension and permanent protection as an American institution. Most Iowans, like other northerners, were willing to put up with slavery according to the 1820 Missouri Compromise as necessary to maintain the Union. They acquiesced to compromise but were angry about the acts which had been

---

[43] Lyftogt, 12–21; Jordan, 9; Geoffrey C. Ward, Ric Burns, and Ken Burns, *The Civil War: An Illustrated History* (New York: Alfred A. Knopf, 1992), 87. Hereafter cited as Ward, *The Civil War*.

created to ensure slavery's permanent expansion. Resistance grew stronger against policies which favored the South and insulted the North until Iowans felt empowered to change their political alliances. Their bitterness spread and soon toppled the long-dominant power of the Democratic Party in the state. Southern-dominated politics at the national level ignited citizen action in Iowa until the state was ready to fight.

The harsh Fugitive Slave Act, Part 5 of the Compromise Bill of 1850, made catching escaped and freed slaves profitable. Although the 1850 Bill was approved by Iowa's long-powerful Democratic congressional senators and representatives, and endorsed by the Iowa General Assembly, it horrified growing numbers of people. Then, the 1854 Nebraska-Kansas Act repealed the long-standing agreements held in the Compromise of 1820 which had allowed Missouri to join the Union as a slave state, allowed no other slave states north of the Ohio River dividing line, and had kept the fragile Union together for nearly forty years. Southern politicians wanted more. They declared unrestricted rights to take their property (including slaves) into any new territory and were winning in Congress.[44] Popular Sovereignty meant the possibility of slavery moving into new states north of that long-standing dividing line. By reversing the Missouri Compromise, the 1854 Act gave popular sovereignty to settlers of new territories, who would have the right to decide about slavery. This especially troubled Iowans as the slave statuses of neighboring Nebraska and Kansas territories were no longer guaranteed by the Missouri Compromise.

Iowans were not fooled by the popular claim of states' rights, understanding that the claim was important only as it applied to Southerners' rights to expand slavery. As citizens in northern states began to revolt against the new Compromise bills and the Fugitive Slave Act, Iowans voted for James W. Grimes, a Whig governor who, in 1854, broke through

---

[44] Cutrer, 26.

the solid Democratic grip on state politics. He was committed to "Free Soil", which meant that new territories would be free from slavery as defined by the Missouri Compromise. He organized citizens for a new Republican party in Iowa.[45] By 1856 Republicans had won every state office in Iowa and taken control of the state legislature.[46] The Fugitive Slave Act and the Kansas-Nebraska Acts kindled heated debate and anger, and there were more sparks ahead.

Soon came the surreal 1857 Dred Scott v Sanford decision which refused citizenship to blacks, enslaved or not, and declared the early Missouri Compromise of 1820 unconstitutional. Although the Dred Scott decision was intended to settle the slavery debate by the power and authority of the Supreme Court, it is considered by most constitutional scholars as its worst decision ever. It is characterized as a "self-inflicted wound" which had far-reaching, unintended consequences.[47] Eugene Ware described how everybody in his community discussed the ruling: "It was talked up by the press, the church, the prayer-meeting, and the sewing-society."[48] "Slavocrats" were angry that many Northerners did not agree with their demands and blamed northerners for the country's troubles, calling them abolitionist fanatics, disunionists, advocates of miscegenation, black republicans, and worse.[49]

While Southern politicians threatened secession against opposition, President James Buchanan blamed secessionist threats on the incessant "agitation of the slavery question throughout the North."[50] He didn't blame the acts, but the North's resistance to them. Southern

---

45 Baker, 9. The Free Soil platform did not ask for existing slavery to be abolished, but was called radical by many.
46 Lyftogt, 29.
47 Urofsky, Melvin I. "Dred Scott decision," *Encyclopedia Britannica*, https://www.britannica.com/event/Dred-Scott-decision. Accessed 29 March 2022; Potter, 277–281, 291–293.
48 Ware, 56.
49 See Appendix B, "Lyon's Letters." Lyon used "their superior elixir pharmacy" to describe secessionists' slander and threats; Robert Cook, "The Political Culture of Antebellum Iowa: An Overview." *The Annals of Iowa* 52(1993), 233.
50 Ward, *The Civil War*, 87. Buchanan's term of office was March 4, 1857 to March 4, 1861.

political power, gag rules, ballot box frauds in Kansas, and the activist Supreme Court decision, intended to settle the matter by power and control, demonstrated to many northerners that self-government was under assault.[51]

George Burmeister

George was the son of John and Marie (Groth) Burmeister who emigrated from Dömitz, in the northern state of Mecklenburg, Germany, in 1847. When George was nine, he and three siblings and parents came to the U.S. and settled in St. Louis before moving to a farm in Iowa County in 1856. George worked in a bookstore in Alton, Illinois, before joining his parents on the farm. He and his brothers did much of the farm work, and their father practiced his trade as a cabinet and furniture maker. George was a hardworking, accomplished farm boy and earnest student. He became the first teacher in the community-built "old Excelsior School."[52] He established both a Sunday school and a debating society before he left home to enter Western College in Shueyville.[53]

The college had been established in 1857 by a German denomination, United Brethren in Christ. It had a farm which paid students for their labor, to help offset expenses. It was coeducational, open to all races and creeds, and was characterized by a serious religious atmosphere.[54] George began writing his diary in January of 1861. He wrote of his close connections to church and school. He described attending the Easter ser-

---

51 Jordan, 9.

52 Biographical information is from a personal interview with Dolores Rawson, George Burmeister's great-niece, on April 12, 2024, and from her copy of an informal biography written by family genealogist, Eugene Burmeister. Mrs. Rawson explained that for a short time, George's parents were part of Jasper Colony, an early German communal colony in Iowa County.

53 John Davis, "Complete List of Civil War Veterans of German Descent of Muscatine County." *IA GenWeb Project*, https://iagenweb.org/muscatine/CivilWar/civilwar2.htm. Retrieved 4/10/2020.

54 Henry Winfield Ward, *Western-Leander Clark College, 1856–1911* (Dayton: Otterbein Press 1911),. Available on https//archive.org/details/westernleanderc100ward. Retrieved 02/02/2021. Ward provides an overview of the college.

vice: "Today is the great day our savior rose from the dead, a day strictly observed by Germans as a day sacred to this event." And, on another Sunday, "listened to an old pioneer preacher, eccentric, about value of the soul."[55] George was trying to make sense of the times.

Eugene Ware

Nineteen-year-old Eugene Ware, the son of a harness maker in Burlington, Iowa, wrote how they were aware of the stakes, understanding that if Lincoln was elected the South would secede. Ware said it was impossible to have a political parade in his town because the southern sympathizers were "full of fight."[56] He described a community with some violence, more volatile than the Linn County enlistment area as described by George Burmeister. In 1860, Burlington's population was 6,706 compared to Cedar Rapids' 1,830.[57] Most of Iowa's population clustered in towns not far from the Mississippi River, where Iowa citizens were more likely to live among people from the South and be exposed to southern attitudes. The bustling Mississippi river town was different from Cedar Rapids, which had just acquired a railroad line and had little steamboat traffic on its Cedar River. George was part of an even smaller community at Western College.

Eugene and George grew up disgusted by the Fugitive Slave Law. U.S. Marshalls had to send fugitive slaves back to their masters and there were people in their communities who assisted the Marshalls. Eugene remembered how even manumitted (freed) slaves were not permitted to write or send off letters and were often kidnapped and sold back into slavery. He and George knew people who defied it, who believed in a higher law than those framed by powerful legislators. Some Iowans assisted fugitive

---

55 Burmeister, 03-31-1861, 04-14-1861.
56 Ware, 66, 67.
57 In 1860, early census estimates show the largest Iowa populations were in these towns along the Mississippi river: Dubuque, 13,000, Davenport, 11,267; Keokuk, 8,136; Muscatine, 6,000. iowadatacenter/datatables/Places All/population. Retrieved 3/23/2020; Baker, 5.

slaves, hiding them in attics, cellars, caves, wagons, or haymows. Others paid fines or were sent to prison for these actions.[58]

Neither Eugene nor George was an avowed abolitionist. Like President Lincoln, then Captain Lyon, Ulysses S. Grant, and many others, they agreed slavery was inhumane, but were willing to allow it to stand in the South as defined by Congress in the 1820 Missouri Compromise (which Congress had overturned). They were, however, strongly opposed to the extension of slavery. From Ware's perspective, much opposition to slavery was based on the fear among native-born and foreign-born workingmen from competition of unpaid (slave) labor, especially if slavery expanded. He said the strongest and most active recruits, such as the personnel in his company and regiment, came from among Northern workingmen.[59]

Eugene wrote about coming of age before the war in Burlington, where his family had moved from Connecticut when he was a young boy.[60] Although his father was an abolitionist, Eugene said being called an abolitionist was derogatory, meaning a crazed zealot (like John Brown), the worst kind of thief, and someone who might start an insurrection.[61] His observations and boyhood experiences were gelling into strong convictions. Eugene Ware lived in a river town alongside secessionists, where "everybody was trying to convince somebody else and somebody would rather fight than be convinced." Jacob Ritner, a thirty-three-year-old married school teacher and father of four, described nearby Ft. Madison as much the same: "It is the most pro-slavery hole I ever saw. Some have intimated to me that it would not be prudent to speak out very freely on

---

[58] Ware, 46–49; Henry William Elson, *History of the United States* (New York: The Macmillan Company, 1929), 550–552.

[59] Ware, 34.

[60] Eugene Ware was raised under the influence of Congregationalists, as were many other Civil War enlistees from southeast Iowa. "Turner, Asa," *The Biographical Dictionary of Iowa*. www.uipress.lib.uiowa.edu.

[61] Ware, 46, 47.

that subject."⁶² Like others, Eugene referred to the distinctly southern party as "Fire-eaters" because of their fiery push towards secession.⁶³ He became eager to join a militia in case of war, and ultimately did.

Money and jobs were scarce. Early Republican supporters like Ware's family were called "Wide-Awakes." California Senator John C. Frémont had run as the first Republican for president and lost the election in 1856. The following years were tough for Republican supporters, with gloomy forebodings. Because many in Iowa believed that war was inevitable, communities organized militia groups to prepare and drill, "to enjoy peace or encounter war." Notions of war had crept into everyday language, in phrases such as "fall in," "dig trenches," and "drill," references to plowing and planting; and wives on "commissary" duty.⁶⁴ Iowans had grown fighting mad.

Stephen A. Douglas and Abraham Lincoln in Burlington

Eugene described a steady transformation as the citizens heard and considered different political opinions. Most of the local Democrats supported Stephen A. Douglas and were called "Little Giants," after Douglas's nickname. Douglas came twice to Burlington to give speeches and got "full" (of liquor) both times. On the stand he was given a table to steady himself. "If oratory is the art of pleasing an audience, Mr. Douglas surely had it."⁶⁵ Douglas called Abraham Lincoln a warmonger because of his radical opinions. Lincoln also spoke on one occasion in Burlington in

---

62 Larimer, 13. The obituary for abolitionist Samuel A. Howe (the founder of Howe's Academy and Jacob Ritner's teacher) stated: "He suffered much from persecution, having property destroyed and was finally mobbed by pro-slavery ruffians on the streets of Mt. Pleasant." Appendix.

63 Mark Mayo Boatner, *The Civil War Dictionary* (New York: Vintage Books, 1991),280. "Fire-Eaters" was a term used for the extremist Southern politicians.

64 John E. Briggs, "Enlistment of Iowa Troops," *Iowa Journal of History and Politics* 3 (1917): 332–333. https://archive.org/stream/iowajournalofhis1917stat/iowajournalofhisstat_djvu.text. Retrieved 1/16/2020.

65 Ware, 41.

October of 1858. Ware said Lincoln's speech seemed to "shoot over the heads of his hearers," and Abe seemed ill at ease.[66] Even abolitionists, like Ware's father, had great respect for Douglas, but came to dislike his promotion of popular sovereignty, because the expansion of slavery could be stopped only if enough anti-slavery settlers voted against it, which often involved violence while fighting for fair elections.

Ware said that popular sovereignty was popular with some and unpopular with others, but the Dred Scott decision incited a tidal wave of opinion. More people began to pull away from the allure of popular sovereignty to become Republicans. As they began gaining in numbers, some of the strongest secessionists moved south, but those who remained were often vicious.[67] In Burlington, the increasing debates over slavery meant boys fighting each other was so common that parents "took little notice." Ware thought about a third of the northerners were Copperheads, people who wanted the South to win but wouldn't fight for it. Another third believed in peace at any price. The Democratic party broke apart.

Eugene estimated that just before Lincoln's election, two-thirds of the community had become anti-slavery: "In the end pacifists had to be held by the throat with one hand while northern armies coerced the Confederacy with the other."[68] In November 1860, white male citizens voted, and the deep resources and power of the United States government passed from President Buchanan's passively co-opting hands into Abraham Lincoln's control.[69] The national election moved political authority of the country into an anti-slavery-expansionist North, but southern Secessionists refused to yield their non-negotiable condition: the permanent right to extend slav-

---

66 Ware, 40; Herbert L. Moeller and Hugh C. Mueller, "Lincoln and Grant in Iowa," in *Our Iowa, It's Beginning and Growth*, (New York: Newsome and Company,1938), 272. https://archive.org/details/ouriowaitsbeginn00moel/page/n7/mode/2up.
67 Ware, 66–67.
68 Ware, 59, 66.
69 Snead, 74.

ery into new U.S. territories.[70] For years they had been using the threat of disunion to pressure northerners to vote for their bills.

The new compromise bills, the Dred Scott decision, and the South's secession threats nudged the North towards war. But after the attack on Fort Sumter, there was a "supernatural" response across political parties.[71] Eugene describes hearing the news about Ft. Sumter. Businesses stopped and everyone rushed onto the streets. In nearby Kossuth, Daniel Matson wrote: "On April 12th, like a flash of lightning out of a clear sky, came the news that Sumter was fired upon and the great conflict began."[72] There were rallies of patriotic frenzy. Iowa citizens unified to protect the Union at any cost and readied for war. Abraham Lincoln (on April 15, 1861) asked states for regiments of three-month volunteers.[73] On April 17, 1861, Iowa Governor Samuel Kirkwood, uncertain whether as many as one thousand Iowans would enlist, issued a proclamation calling for volunteers. He wrote to Secretary of War Simon Cameron: "Ten days ago…we had two parties in the state; today we have but one, and that is for the Constitution and the Union unconditionally."[74]

Iowa's "First Born" [75]

When the news was telegraphed that guns had fired on Fort Sumter,

---

70 William E. Parrish, *Turbulent Partnership: Missouri and the Union 1861–1865* (Columbia: University of Missouri Press, 1963), 7,13; "United States Presidential Election of 1860," *Britannica*, www.Britannica.com/event/united-states-presidential-election-of-1860. Southern Democrat presidential candidate Breckenridge wanted a guaranteed intervention so that slavery rights could not be altered in the future by Congress or state legislatures.

71 McPherson, *Battle Cry of Freedom*, 274.

72 Ware, 69; Matson, 54.

73 John D. Hicks, "Organization of the Volunteer Army in 1861 with Special Reference to Minnesota," *Minnesota History Bulletin* 2, no. 5 (February 1918) 326. Hicks describes the challenges of raising a Union army and the steps taken by Lincoln and an unprepared Congress to do so when there were few troops stationed east of the Mississippi. A restrictive 1795 Congressional Law gave authority to the president to call out the militias of any portions of states to suppress a resurrection or to react to an emergency. Congress used the act to carry out the intent of the Constitution as an immediate means to raise a temporary army until it could officially mobilize an army.

74 Dan Elbert Clark, *Samuel Jordan Kirkwood* (Iowa City: The State Historical Society of Iowa, 1917),182. https://archive.org/details/samueljordankirkooclar.

75 Wilkie (Banasik) uses the phrase, "First Born" to describe the First Iowa Infantry (46).

Ware's volunteer militia group telegraphed the governor, believing the war would be short.[76] Seven out of the ten First Infantry companies were organized before war began. The governor ordered Iowa's First regiment to be ready by May 20. Ten companies, nearly 1000 volunteers of the First Iowa Infantry Regiment, were ready by April 24, 1861.[77]

Just a few months after his arrival at Western College, George wrote, "I'm astonished to learn that U.S.A. and C.S.A. (Confederate States of America) are going to battle...Northern sons of liberty, rouse for the protection and defense of your union...I called a meeting in response to a call made by a committee from Cedar Rapids to solicit volunteers for the northern army."[78] Recruiters of volunteer soldiers were often influential citizens or men who wanted a military commission.[79] They recruited soldiers in home communities which surrounded potential enlistees with reminders of their patriotic duty and honor. The April 18, 1861, issue of the *Cedar Valley Times* patriotically claimed:

> Now more than ever, it is the duty of every true man to respond to the call of this country. Party ties are broken, party divisions forgotten, in the common necessity which summons every true American to the standard of his country – to the defense of our Union, our Constitution, our liberty, our rights. Every man to his post, that post the support of the Administration.[80]

---

76 Ware, 69

77 *Roster and Record of Iowa Soldiers in the War of Rebellion, Together with Historical Sketches of Volunteer Organizations*, 1861–1866, 6 vols. (Des Moines: Iowa General Assembly 1908–1911), 1:4. https://archive.org/details/aby1249.0001.001.umich.edu/page/n3/mode/2up.

78 Burmeister, 04-15-1861 and 04-19-1861.

79 Lyftogt, 145.

80 Luther A. Brewer and Barthinius L. Wick, "Linn County in War," in *History of Linn County Iowa* (Cedar Rapids: The Torch Press, 1911), 2. Transcribed for IaGenweb Project by Terry Carlson, February, 2004. Iagenweb.org/linn/military/LinnCoWar1.htm. Retrieved 4/19/2020.

A crowd gathered in the Western College chapel, where young men were urged to enroll for the honor of Linn County and the cause of the Union.[81] George Burmeister was elected the president of the Western Light Guards, a volunteer militia. On April 20, 1861, he held a meeting for six other boys who intended to volunteer.[82] The locals contributed five dollars to aid in purchasing Bibles for the company. Attended by prayers and well-wishes, the boys headed out in a farm wagon with boards across the seats, hoping to enlist. It was eight miles to Cedar Rapids.[83]

Company K Cedar Rapids

After taking the eight-mile wagon ride to Cedar Rapids and enlisting in Company K, the boys elected officers and immediately began to drill. A company of enlistees would usually include 78–100 men from a cluster of neighboring towns. The boys who enlisted in Company K were from Cedar Rapids, Marion, Mount Vernon, Vinton, Kingston, Bertram, Western College, and nearby settlements. They elected as captain Thomas Z. Cook, age twenty-six, from Cedar Rapids. First Lieutenant John C. Marvin (Marven) was twenty-four. The enlistees did not know their departure date or destination. News was meager and based mostly on rumor. Thirty-seven enlistees were ages 18–20, and thirty-seven were ages 21–24. Fourteen men were 25 or older.[84] For uniforms they were given pants, two short-sleeved shirts, a hat, and socks.

Enthusiastic local citizens presented the Cedar Rapids company with a flag and a Bible before the boys took the train to Clinton and waited for their steamer to arrive. The very young soldiers of Company K were headed for training camp in Keokuk, Iowa, on the Mississippi river next to the Missouri border. On May 7 George wrote, "with thundering cheers and booming cannon" they departed on the *William L. Erving*.

---

81 Ibid.
82 Burmeister, 04-24-1861.
83 Ward, *Western-Leander Clark College*, 112. Retrieved 02/02/2021.
84 *Roster and Record*, 1:12-88. Tabulations are based on this source.

He described passing safely under the "dangerous" Rock Island bridge and at Davenport took on company B from Iowa City, including several boys who were former students at Western College. At Burlington they stopped for company F, the Mt. Pleasant Grays.[85] They crowded together, played euchre, sang, and danced until arriving at Keokuk at midnight. They were given blankets and slept in a building on hay-softened boards.

Company E Burlington

In Burlington, Ware's Zouave militia company wore red French "colonial" style military uniforms, elected officers, drilled, and paraded in front of spectators, relatives, and sweethearts. Burlington also had a militia of German speaking men called the German Rifles.[86] The "twin" militias drilled together, camped, received muskets, and learned fencing with bayonets. Eugene and the boys had to swim across the Mississippi river, which was about half a mile wide. Eugene swam the wide river several times "with a platoon of boys, accompanied by a skiff."[87] They also held boxing matches in the armory which "was a good deal like a barnyard, where it was necessary for each of us roosters to know who was who."[88] There were hundreds of southern sympathizers attempting to talk men out of enlisting. Some asked if we really were going to fight for "Ape Lincoln."[89] A few boys changed their minds and became secesh. Eugene felt it was very important to be an enlistee, and he worried because not all could be accepted. Ware's militia group, which had been drilling

---

85 Burmeister, 05-7 to 05-8-1861. George refers to the dangerous bridge, which was the first to cross the Mississippi, connecting the Chicago and Rock Island Railroad to Davenport, Iowa. After a steamboat crashed into it, Abraham Lincoln represented the railroad in the lawsuit Hurd vs Rock Island Bridge Company; Larimer (Ritner), 16–17. Jacob Ritner Company F, describes joining Cedar Rapids company K in Burlington onboard the William L. Ewing. His Mt. Pleasant company was outfitted in Burlington. For the first several nights in training camp, companies Cedar Rapids Company K and Mt. Pleasant Company F bivouacked together with Burlington companies D and E.
86 Lyftogt, 126, Ware 76.
87 Ware, 65.
88 Ibid., 71.
89 Ibid., 81.

"constantly day and night" enlisted as the core of Company E.

After enlistment, the Burlington community gave the Zouaves (Company E) a flag which read, "The Union as Our Fathers Made It." As McPherson notes, the most meaningful symbols of pride in the cause were the colors, the flags which "bonded men's loyalty to unit, state, and nation."[90] Company E's twin unit, the Burlington Rifles (Company D) of all German-American men with Captain Matthies at the lead, was also given a flag, reading, "We Defend the Flag of our Adopted Land."[91] Wilkie described Captain Matthies as one of the most soldierly men in the regiment and his company was one of the best drilled.[92]

Ware's Company elected as captain George F. Streaper, twenty-six, and John C. Abercrombie, thirty-six, as first lieutenant.[93] Sixty-one of those enlisted in Company E reported their residence as Des Moines County; three were from Louisa County, two from Wapello County, one Van Buren County, one Kossuth County, one from Danville, and the remainder stated they were from Burlington.[94] The Company E muster roll recorded place of birth of both foreign-born and native-born.[95] The muster roles reflect the rapid growth and immigration in Iowa during the mid-nineteenth century. Of the 90 mustered soldiers, only 11 had been born in the young state of Iowa. Twenty-four had come from other Midwestern states, 19 were born in Pennsylvania, 15 in New England and the northeast, six from the southeast or southern states, 11 were

---

90 McPherson, *For Cause and Comrades*, 84.

91 Lyftogt, 133.

92 Banasik (Wilkie), 39, 29n56. This reflects on Ware's company, because many men in his company E had drilled with the German American men in company D. Charles Leopold Matthies left the First Iowa Regiment on July 25, 1861, when he was appointed lieutenant colonel of the Fifth Iowa Infantry.

93 Ware, 69. Eugene thought that Captain Streaper, a cigar maker, falsely claimed to have spent five years in the Regular Army. The election of company officers appears to have been based on the status of age, which indirectly reflects experience and occupational expertise. Ware, 96, 97, comments on the election of regimental officers by political favoritism or relationships, but not military ability.

94 *Roster and Record*, 1:12–88. Tabulations based on Company E Roster.

95 *Roster and Record*, 1:12–88. Tabulations based on Company K muster role which did not record birth states, it notes if a soldier was born in the U.S.

from Germany or Prussia, and five were from other European countries. Nineteen boys were "veal," aged 18–20, forty-eight were 21–24, and twenty-three were 25 and older. [96] At nineteen, Eugene Ware was "veal."[97]

Iowa citizens prepared to put down the Southern rebellion but were not prepared to finance a war.

The state was expected to enroll, clothe, arm, transport, subsist, and pay its troops until they were mustered into federal service. But the financial panic of 1857–58 had drained the treasury. When Governor Kirkwood asked the Iowa General Assembly on May 15, 1861, to get a war loan through the sale of state bonds, he was strongly opposed by some senators.[98] The General Assembly eventually gave permission, with the expectation of strong sales in eastern states, but the bonds failed, even in Iowa. Governor Kirkwood obtained an advance of credit from the federal government, but when state agents were sent to purchase fabric for uniforms and guns, they found that the supplies they needed were no longer on the market. Regiments from other states had already secured the available stock. Some of the purchased shoes were of decent quality, but some were very poor, with soles that came off easily. The governor asked Ezekial Clark, his brother-in-law and business partner who was an Iowa City banker, to find material for uniforms in Chicago. Clark came home with light-weight cloth he hoped might hold up for three months; it didn't. The uniforms had to be sewn by volunteers in the hometown communities, resulting in a variety of different outfits for companies in the First Iowa Regiment with the exception of the uniforms

---

[96] *Roster and Record*. Tabulations are based on this source. Between the two companies, 141 (nearly 80 percent) of enlistees were ages twenty-four or under, compared to 37 (20.8 percent) enlistees over the age of twenty-four. The elected lieutenants in Company E were aged 36 and 32. In Company K, 74 of the enlistees were ages 24 or under, the elected lieutenants were aged 24 and 23;
[97] Ware, 74, 80.
[98] Ivan L. Pollock, "Iowa Civil War Loan," *Iowa and War* 3 (September 1917), 4–5.

patterned after Captain Wentz's Davenport company.[99]

The fancy Zouave militia outfits worn by the Burlington company were replaced by uniforms made the way the women in the community wanted to make them with the fabric purchased by the state. Eugene depicts them as hunting frock coats of the Daniel Boone type, fitted closely at the neck, cuff and belt with "surplusage" everywhere else. They were made with "fluffy," loosely woven, blue-gray cloth with bold Venetian Red flannel trim. Trousers were like heavy buckskin, with a black felt hunting-hat sporting a red cockade. The boys felt proud to wear what the girls had made. However, as soon as they got to the field the officers ordered the target-red trim torn off, and the uniforms went to pieces fast.[100]

In their hometown communities, enlistees had learned principles and made pledges. They had internalized values of hard work, the importance of freedom, and a desire to fight for the Union. Before enlistments, many of the boys were friends, had been together in local militias, or soon came to know one another. Soldiers' identification with home communities remained essential.

On May 7, headed for training camp, the "twin" Companies D and E marched aboard the steamboat *Kate Cassel* while the fife and drum played "The Girl I Left Behind Me."[101] Eugene admitted to fear as angry southern sympathizers gathered to threaten violence and called them "Rats" and "Abolitionists." He and others would have fallen out for a fight if they hadn't been "drummed and drilled" by their first lieutenant to remain soldierly. Eugene marched off to fulfill a "promise and a prophecy." He carried a bag

---

99 Upham, 37–41; Banasik (Wilkie) 12n15. Clark and Governor Kirkwood made personal guarantees of borrowed money to support the volunteers; Larimer, 16; Wilkie described the uniforms made for the Davenport company: "It consists of a light blouse with green collar and patent leather belt, dark grey pants without stripe except in case of officers, a black felt hat turned up at one side and fastened by a tin bull's eye the size of a sauce plate which displays the red, white, and blue. The whole makes the soldier look not unlike a pauperized cartman. The same general style has been adopted by the Burlington Companies and that at Mt. Pleasant, except that the others revel in a profusion of bright red-flannel trimmings." Banasik (Wilkie), 21.
100 Ware, 79–80.
101 Ware, 80.

with a shaving mug, a Bible, socks, and photos.[102] As the boys left for Keokuk and began to sing "Dixie," some—but never all—their loyalties were shifting from their closest hometown friends to their enlistment companies.

*Burlington Companies D and E loading onto the
Kate Cassel, headed for training camp in Keokuk, 1861.*
From a photograph donated by Kenneth Weygant to the Des Moines County
Historical Society, Burlington, Iowa (Permission, February 22, 2024)

---

102 Ware, 80, 81.

CHAPTER TWO
MID-MAY TO JUNE 13, 1861

Flags— fly from all the principal buildings, decorate cart horses, are stuck up in every window, are seen everywhere. Patriotism is boiling over. Nothing is dreamed of but battles. —Franc B. Wilkie, April 25, 1861

After the ten companies arrived from towns across eastern Iowa, nearly eight hundred soldiers of the First Iowa Regiment were together in training camp with the following companies: Muscatine A; Iowa City B; Muscatine C; Burlington Rifles D; Burlington Zouaves E; Mt. Pleasant F; Davenport G; Dubuque Wilson Guards H; Dubuque Governor's Grays I; Cedar Rapids K. German-speaking Americans enlisted together in three of the companies: Burlington D, Davenport G, and Dubuque H. Many of the native German enlistees had previous military experience from the revolutions in European countries, and their captains were respected military leaders: Charles L. Matthies, Augustus Wentz, Frederick Gottschalk, respectively.[103]

---

[103] Banasik (Wilkie) 17–18, 39; Piston and Hatcher, 49. One in three Burlington adults was German, and they held strong ethnic identities.

Camp Ellsworth was about a mile north of Keokuk, and a half mile from the Mississippi River. It was two or three hundred acres of high ground, a spot for "magnificent" parade grounds. It was named after Colonel Elmer E. Ellsworth, a popular soldier who organized militia units in Chicago and New York and who was shot while removing a rebel flag from a hotel in Alexandria, Virginia.[104] Eugene said when his company arrived in Keokuk they were jeered, not cheered. They were told to be wary of rebel people connected to steamboats. Some boys were not used to the indifference shown by town citizens with southern sympathies. George said there were quarrels from the start as the boys were thrown together. He was shocked by the coarse behavior of some boys, "Some do more harm than good." He might have noticed Eugene and his friends who "were spoiling for a fight" with the boastful, defiant secessionists in town.[105]

The lives of enlistees were soon framed by daily duties structured by army regulations. The soldiers identified with their own company's captain, uniform, and flag. The outfits for Ware's Company E were a bit fancier than others. The company had learned to drill in the distinctive Zouave style, unlike other companies, and they liked to show it off. Eugene believed (or falsely assumed) their company had been picked as the color company to carry the Union and state flags for the regiment.[106]

Together, the ten companies elected regimental officers for the nearly one thousand soldiers in the First Iowa Infantry. For many Iowans after Fort Sumter, patriotism trumped long-standing loyalty to the Democratic party. People from opposing political parties had unified to save the Union. It was not just a Republican war, as shown in the voting results. The elected regimental officers were all War Democrats: Colonel John Francis Bates; Lieutenant Colonel William Merritt; Major Asbury B.

---

[104] Banasik (Wilkie) 44, 39.
[105] Ware, 87, 88.
[106] Ware, 70; Piston and Hatcher, 53. According to Henry O'Connor, Company C was the color company.

Porter. These men had political clout but no military skills.[107] With few exceptions, the officers were soon learning from manuals their first lessons in army regulations and soldiering. Wilkie reported to the newspapers how the soldiers, with difficulty, tried numerous times to erect the newly arrived tents in a proper formation until it was decided to follow Hardee's *Manual of Arms*, "It may seem remarkable that this brilliant idea did not occur earlier."[108]

Burmeister had close friends from Western College with him in Company K: Alfred Collier, 20; William Eckles, 20; Benjamin Whisler, 22, Edwin R. McKee, 18, and John M. VanArsdel, 21, and his circle of friends was growing. George described how they were assigned to barracks which were dirty and untidy, looking "better suited for bandits." They bathed and swam in the Mississippi. "It was fun to be one of about 100 boys swimming, some very good swimmers." He thought some boys very obscene, "shocking every moral and religious principle." They could attend church services in town, where he heard a sermon on cause of war. The Presbyterian preacher attributed it entirely to the system of slavery.[109]

George had the first of many wash days in the river, with a bath and laundry washing. Cleanliness was important to George, and throughout the campaign he refused to let the filthy conditions outweigh his personal standards. Rainy weather hit and some boys were getting sick.[110] Some founded a reading room and organized regular prayer meetings. They drilled about six hours a day, until an order was received to drill not less than two hours or more than four. George thought his company

---

107 Lyftogt, 133; Banasik (Wilkie), 280–346, in his roster reports that neither Bates or Merritt re-enlisted. Major Asbury Porter joined the Fourth Iowa Cavalry October 1, 1861.

108 Banasik (Wilkie), 44. The manual was the standard military guide for troops in the North and South.

109 *Roster and Record*, 1:12–88, Company K. There were two boys named Van Meter (Van Metre). Joseph was from Western College, but was rejected for illness (lung fever). Isaiah, 23, Sergeant Company K, was from Cedar Rapids; Burmeister, 04-12-1861 and 04-20-1861.

110 Baker, 71. Some of the early volunteers were infected with bacteria. Annie Wittenmeyer witnessed the death of the first Iowa soldier in the Keokuk camp May, 1861.

(K) had the worst appearance of any company, with no coats or jackets, just short-sleeved shirts. On Saturday, May 18, the arms arrived, reconditioned muskets, patented in 1827. Most of the boys had been shooting since young age and weren't happy with the arms. They drilled every day, while officers stood with Hardee's *Manual* in one hand and a musket in the other. Not all company officers or drill sergeants were familiar with the manual and made mistakes until they got it figured out. George hoped to learn some military tactics during training, but said it was impossible. Colonel Bates made several blunders. The soldiers had to "learn and unlearn at the same time."[111]

They drilled in rain or sunshine, the companies spending about four hours each day learning to march together in perfect order. They took turns standing guard to protect guns and ammunition, marched and paraded, and heard speeches by men of the state. When they left the barracks for tent camp, they had to sleep on bare, wet ground. George complained about low rations, sometimes a loaf of bread and piece of pork for eight boys. They sent a mess mate to a nearby farmhouse to see what he could buy or steal. Five men from each company were detailed to cook each day, while the other soldiers marched to the company kitchen for their rations.[112] On June 1, George was appointed to cook for his mess, but found little food other than coffee and bread.

Honorary Funeral for Stephen A. Douglas

The regiment received news that Senator Stephen A. Douglas had died (June 3, 1861) and had a parade to honor the great northern leader.[113] Eugene wrote details of the June 11 honorary funeral, telling how soldiers had become admirers of Douglas. After the attack on Fort Sumter, Senator

---

111 Burmeister, 05-12-1861 to 05-18-1861; Hardee's Manual for Civil War soldiers, demonstrated how to load a musket, secure a bayonet, and positions for holding arms. *Hardee's Rifle and Light Infantry Tactics*. (3rdusreenactors.com/home/drill/manual of arms).
112 Banasik (Wilkie), 57.
113 Burmeister, 05-29-1861, 06-10-1861.

Douglas immediately showed his support for President Lincoln and the war. Douglas had told a crowd in Chicago, "There are only two sides to the question. Every man must be for the United States or against it. There can be no neutrals in this war, only *patriots—or traitors.*"[114] Northerners respected Douglas by putting a principle, the Union first, above fierce political antagonism. An empty coffin was placed on an artillery caisson and draped with an American flag. The First Iowa Regiment marched all through the town, with drums playing a monotonous funeral dirge. They were followed by perhaps 10,000 citizens.[115]

"Pleasure, Complaint and Drill"[116]

George said it rained hard and they walked home in knee deep mud, making them feel mean and mad. They were soaked and dirty but had no change of clothes. A comrade poured water on his pants, so he returned the favor. At least, he said, they got their pants washed. There was friction between companies. Ware's Company E believed that the Dubuque Grays usurped their place during a dress parade and, refusing to give up, had to be sent off the field. It turned out to be a mistake made by their own Captain Streaper.[117]

The severest part of camp life was guard duty. The soldier, with heavy musket on his shoulder, walked along a designated guarded area for several hours while on constant alert. His job was to prevent unwanted

---

114 McPherson, *Battle Cry of Freedom*, 274.
115 Ware, 104; "Abraham Lincoln, Stephen Douglas, and the Election of 1860," Worldhistory.us. https://worldhistory.us/American-history/Abraham-lincoln-stephen-douglas-and-the-election-of-1860.php. Although Douglas and Lincoln, both from Illinois, were opposing candidates in the North during the 1860 presidential election, Douglas gave his support for newly elected President Lincoln to maintain the Union; He left a message to his sons to be true to the Union; Rombauer, 223. Stephan Douglas showed Lincoln great respect at his inaugural. On the podium Lincoln removed his hat to take the oath of office, and Douglas jumped forward to hold it.
116 "Pleasure, Complaint and Drill" is borrowed from Lurton Dunham Ingersoll's description of a Civil War training camp, in *Iowa and the Rebellion* (Philadelphia: Lippincott, 1866), 20. See also Wilkie's comments in Banasik (Wilkie), 47.
117 Banasik(Wilkie), 55.

people from coming in, or, just as hard, to keep soldiers from going beyond permitted areas.[118] Later, guard duty became even more dreaded when it meant protecting comrades from the enemy. Franc Wilkie described camp life as "plain, drudging, stupid reality."[119]

The Iowa boys were getting used to living with and cooperating with other enlistees. Burmeister wrote about the great continual noise in camp.[120] They were also building camaraderie. On Sunday June 9, George went with friends from his company, Charles Esgate (20), Michael Mentz (28), and Charles Stewart (21), on a strawberry hunt and were surprised to come across a group of Germans from a Catholic Benevolent Society who treated them to a picnic feast with beer. More often, the young troops expressed disappointment at being given old muskets, seemed surprised at the poorly performing commissary, and according to Ware, "came near mutiny." The boys thought the commissary was stealing and rations were being wasted. Careless cooks spoiled food and sickened men. There were reported attacks against "secesh" merchants suspected of selling poisoned food or overpriced goods. From the start, boys complained about scarce rations. Eugene and a few other men in his company E bought some utensils and formed a private mess. Somehow, they found Mace, a fugitive slave, or he found them, and Mace, who could cook, made food worth eating.[121]

Outdated Muskets

Eugene complained about the outdated, heavy muskets. They had to drill double-quick loading while on the run for several hours a day, jumping

---

118 Ibid., 51.
119 Banasik (Wilkie), 47.
120 Burmeister, 06-03-1861.
121 Ware, 99–100. Mason Johnson, a fugitive slave, wandered into camp and offered to cook. It seems there was an informal arrangement for "Mace" to cook for Company E in exchange for protection from slave hunters. Mace was free to leave and did so for a short time in Missouri. Later, when they met again in St. Louis, the company paid him for services; 252. Ware wrote that two or more years later, a man from his company ran into Mace in negro artillery regiment near Vicksburg; African American Civil War Memorial Museum. This website lists two entries "Johnson, Lot – 1st U.S.Colored Heavy Artillery" and "Johnson, Major – 8th U.S. Colored Heavy Artillery" both aged 30, enlisted 1864. https://afroamcivilwar.org

ditches, and climbing fences.[122] Boys called their guns after their gals back home, like Hannah. Eugene named his gun Silver Sue. They practiced taking down tents, hauling them around, and putting them up again. They washed clothes on the banks of the Mississippi.[123]

Eugene Ware was six feet tall in stockings and weighed 150 pounds. His new friends soon nick-named him "Lincoln" and "Link." Mace called him "Corpular Link," a mispronunciation of "corporal," although Ware was only a private. "Link" described the guns as smooth bores which could not be adjusted to shoot straight. He explained that the muskets were made in different years, refitted, that is, flintlocks altered into percussion caplocks, fitted with a bayonet. He was concerned that secesh soldiers were getting Springfield rifles fitted with fine sites. "The musket was an old-fashioned, long, big, sturdy weapon and nothing could outkick it but a government mule...But we understood guns and could get as close to it as anybody could."[124]

Jacob Ritner wrote: "(The gun) will kill both ways. The men do not like it much...All I am afraid of is we'll not have a chance to use them." Wilkie depicted them as more dangerous to friend than foe, as they could kick further than they could shoot. He thought that it would be a master stroke to let the enemy steal them.[125]

The boys did not seem to be aware of the state's empty treasury. Although conscious of immediate circumstances such as not enough food, funny-looking uniforms, and outdated muskets, the boys expressed little awareness of Iowa's system failures. Eugene tells how the boys felt impatient for war, sometimes shouting in the dark after bugle-call, making profane remarks about officers. Before taking oaths, they were given the chance to back out of duty. A few left and went home. Those who remained were mustered into

---

122 Ware, 86.
123 Ware, 87, 92.
124 Ware, 86.
125 Larimer, 21; Banasik (Wilkie), 35.

federal service on May 14, 1861, enlisted for ninety days.[126]

Eugene expressed disappointment that their uniforms were already wearing out, but was proud of the nearly perfect drill of Company E. The volunteers learned that not all officers were alike. Eugene thought Captain Streaper and Colonel Bates were "of no account whatsoever." They gained respect for conscientious officers, like those who stayed in camp and helped the boys take care of themselves.[127] It is important to grasp just how intensely the Union soldiers, like Ware and Burmeister, felt about secession. For loyal Unionists, secession was as egregious as slavery, or worse. When the southern states seceded from the Union, they rejected the still-fragile Constitution that created it. George Burmeister and many soldiers entered the war because of secession and the attack on Ft. Sumter. Enlistees described the "secesh" with words like "scheming," "treacherous," and "senseless." These vengeful feelings inflamed relentless angry determination. As the boys grew increasingly anxious to meet the enemy, they were restless and unruly.

Despite quarrels and disorder, the boys were starting to create mutuality. They participated together with members of their companies in daily duties and drills, swimming, fights, wrestling competitions, and pranks like dousing each other with water. The soldiers surely felt as if their haversacks carried shared hometown enlistment experiences, culture, or militia training, a sense of togetherness which would have easily transferred to their new, locally born companies. According to Eugene Ware, training camp made them learn how to take care of themselves and each other. They were in it together.

General Nathaniel Lyon orders Iowa troops to Missouri

On June 12, General Nathaniel Lyon sent word from Missouri that the

---

126 Lyftogt, 131, 132. They were mustered out August 21, 1861. (*Roster and Record*, 1:5).
127 Ware, 93, 98, 99. Ware wrote that they had elected their enthusiastic captain in part because of the lie he told them about having served in the army.

first two regiments from Iowa were needed in Missouri to protect railroads. The message first dispatched to Col. Samuel R. Curtis at Camp Ellsworth began, "A terrible secession movement headed by Gov. Jackson has commenced. I want you to come at once with all the force you can command, to Hannibal, Mo." He ordered Colonel Curtis and the Second Iowa Infantry to "move over the road (railroad) to St. Joseph, and put down traitors everywhere on both sides of the road."[128] Col. Curtis and his regiment were first to ship out from the Keokuk training camp on June 13. On that same day, George heard the news telling how Governor Jackson's Proclamation called for 50,000 enlistments to protect Missouri from an invasion by U.S. troops, and that Jackson had left for Boonville to make a stand. George told of boy-soldiers ready to leave for battle where they could distinguish themselves.

Eugene evoked the excitement of getting called into action, the "howling" troops, and leaving Keokuk for duty in Missouri. They were starting to think that the First Iowa Infantry would never be called to duty but when they were called up, nearly a thousand men united as a regiment of ten companies. They unloaded personal items and let their Bibles go, but kept the poker decks. Eugene wrote: "As I never expect to be young again, I never expect to see and feel again such enthusiasm." [129]

The Second Iowa Regiment shipped out first and later that day when the *Jennie Deane* returned, the First Iowa soldiers boarded her. They took the riverboat to Hannibal, Missouri, and then a train to Macon City, where General Nathaniel Lyon had assigned them to guard railroad bridges. The boys did not seem to know much aside from rumors, of the

---

128 Banasik (Wilkie),60. (re: Curtis) Col. Samuel Curtis was an 1831 graduate of the military academy at West Point and a civil engineer,13n20. He was elected as a Republican congressman from Iowa in 1856 and appointed by Governor Kirkwood to lead the Second Iowa Infantry. He was successful in his duties to guard the northern Missouri railroads and later led the Union victory at the Battle of Pea Ridge, Arkansas. (https://Iagenweb.org/civil-war/biographies/biographies_c.htm).

129 Ware, 105.

important events in Missouri that prompted Lyon's orders. They would soon learn how the new U. S. Commander of the Western Army was engaged in war against Missouri Governor Jackson's secessionist troops.

PART II

COMBUSTIBLE MISSOURI AND THE MEN WHO LIT MATCHES

CHAPTER THREE

NATHANIEL LYON AND THE "EPOCH-MAKING EVENT"

In dealing with known events, I have tried to cleave to historical fact where such fact was ascertainable. For certain thoughts and feelings attributed to historical characters...I alone must be held responsible.
—Stephen Vincent Benet (*John Brown's Body*)

The North, the South, and Abraham Lincoln understood the critical value of Missouri in the Civil War. It was a gateway to the West bordered by the Mississippi River, and St. Louis, with a larger population than Chicago, was a valuable trading port for goods coming from and going to the North and the South. St. Louis was also home to the largest federal arsenal in the slave states. President Lincoln worried that if Missouri (as a border state) seceded, it could "cost the Union the whole game."[130] Efforts by Unionists in St. Louis, before and during the Civil War, were

---

[130] "1860 Census: Population of the United States," www.census.gov; Mark W. Geiger, "Missouri's Hidden Civil War: Financial Conspiracy and the Decline of the Planter Elite, 1861–1865," 2006 PhD Dissertation, University of Missouri, Columbia. Valuable trading goods included horses and mules, which were critical in the war effort; Phillips, *Damned Yankee*, xiv; Walter Barlow Stevens, "Lincoln and Missouri" *Missouri Historical Review,* 10 (January 1916):80.

critical in securing Missouri for the Union. Those efforts were led by then Captain Nathaniel Lyon and his strong political ally, Francis P. Blair.[131] Their Missouri antagonists were Governor Jackson, his legal strategist Lieutenant Governor Thomas C. Reynolds, and the former Missouri governor appointed by Jackson to lead the Missouri State Guard troops, General Sterling Price. In early 1861, pleading for federal support, the Union supporters struggled against the nearly successful secessionists.

Before the First Iowa Infantry joined him in Boonville, Brigadier General Nathaniel Lyon had played a significant role in bringing the Civil War to Missouri. Then Captain Lyon was a center of controversy as of February 6, 1861, when he arrived to protect the St. Louis Arsenal. Lyon quickly understood the vulnerability of the federal arsenal to plots of secessionists and did whatever it took to cut through intended and unintended bureaucratic red tape to demand protection for the Arsenal. Lyon caught the rebels in Camp Jackson with the arms and siege guns secretly ordered from the South by Governor Jackson for the purpose of assaulting the St. Louis Arsenal. But when Lyon marched the prisoners through the city where his mostly German troops fired in reaction to the mob violence of secessionists, it was not the governor or the secessionist commander of Camp Jackson, General Daniel Frost, nor was it the street mob who fired the first shots, who would take the blame. The historical record has assigned the onus for what was called an "epoch-making" affair to Nathaniel Lyon.[132]

A few weeks later, following his appointment as a brigadier general and Commander of the U.S. Army Department of the West, Lyon made the decision to chase Governor Claiborne Fox Jackson after he declared

---

[131] Phillips, *Damned Yankee*, 134; Banasik (Wilkie) 85; Stevens, 64. Francis Preston Blair was a prominent Free-Soil Republican politician in St. Louis. He helped Lyon organize the First Missouri Volunteer Infantry and the Home Guards to protect the arsenal; Francis Blair developed a close relationship with Abraham Lincoln before and after Lincoln was elected president. Frank's brother, Montgomery, was Postmaster General in President Lincoln's cabinet. Their father, Francis Blair Sr., ran the *Globe* newspaper in Washington, DC.

[132] John McElroy, *The Struggle for Missouri*, 88.

war and fled with General Sterling Price from St. Louis. Lyon has often been depicted as "too" duty-bound. General Sherman recalled that as a young soldier, Lyon's earnestness might have outstripped his discretion, and there were many features in his character "very few understood."[133] However, Lyon's actions in St. Louis were most often countermoves to the information he learned about the schemes of Governor Jackson and the Missouri secessionists. It is helpful to examine a timeline of facts. [Appendix A, Timeline]

Perhaps, as suggested by his biographer, Lyon developed rigid convictions when raised in Connecticut, with community and family guided by Congregationalists.[134] Although Puritan spirit helped guide the founding of America, it is true that some "New Englanders" had little tolerance for other religious convictions. Their ancestors had been subjected to severe persecutions in Europe and the early Puritans demanded rigid obedience. That image too often remains a lasting stereotype. Many are surprised to learn that "The American Puritans were the most progressive population on earth."[135] The polity of church self-governance (authority by the congregation) endures today. Before and during the Civil War, having a Congregational background could have seemed radical, because of many of the country's radical abolitionists were Congregationalists.

Actually, we know little about Lyon's religious beliefs. When stationed at Sackets Harbor, N.Y., he attended church, studied military law, moral philosophy, and different systems of belief. During his time

---

133 James Peckham, *Gen. Nathaniel Lyon and Missouri, 1861: A Monograph of the Great Rebellion* (New York: American News Company, 1866), 390, 392. Peckham's book was one of the first written on the Missouri events which led to the Civil War. Although he was a first hand observer of many events, he had to often rely on newspaper accounts which were not always accurate.

134 Phillips, *Damned Yankee*, xiv, xv.

135 Marilynne Robinson, "One Manner of Law, the Religious Origins of American Liberalism," *Harpers*, 08/2022. https://harpers.org/archive/2022/08; "The Congregational Christian Tradition" *Congregational Library and Archives*, https://www.congregationallibrary.org/congregational-christian-tradition.The Puritans highly valued religious freedom. It is a Calvinist-based denomination based on principles of scripture-based justice with emphasis on democratic governance by the congregation and education. The earliest Puritans (and Hugenots) in Europe were persecuted, in part, because they believed in the right of an individual to read the Bible.

in the Mexican War (1846-1848), he observed links between corrupt priests and the aristocracy and developed contempt for institutionalized religion. Lyon valued American efforts to separate church and state and a "healthful state of religion." Although he knew the Bible very well, he later did not often attend church. Lyon's faith was not bound to a literal interpretation of the Bible, but to the cause of human dignity and freedom, the Union, and its rare opportunity for the growth of human progress.[136] After his death, the coffin was held in the Congregational church in Eastford, Connecticut. Rev. Williams, the former pastor of the church, gave the prayer at Lyon's very notable funeral service, and Methodist Episcopal pastor, Rev. C.C. Adams, presided over his burial. Nathaniel Lyon had faith, even if unorthodox, in the ultimate triumph of good. He was zealous and uncompromising in his principles, but there is little evidence that he was a religious zealot determined to punish enemies.

Nathaniel Lyon and William S. Harney in Kansas

Lyon was an experienced Army soldier when he was assigned in spring of 1854 to the new settlements in Kansas, and by 1855 had to deal with the consequences of free-state sovereignty and the Kansas-Nebraska Act. He developed strong personal opinions about slavery versus freedom. While stationed as a captain at Fort Riley, Kansas, although a long-time Democrat, Lyon became an advocate of the Free-Soil movement, opposed to the expansion of slavery.[137]

---

136 Ashbel Woodward, *The Life of General Nathaniel Lyon* (Hartford, CT: Case, Lockwood and Company, 1862), 61–62, 92, 341; *The Last Political Writings of Gen. Nathaniel Lyon: With a Sketch of his Life and Military Services* (New York: Rudd and Carleton, 1861), 257; Peckham, 332; Lyon was transferred to Madison Barracks (Sackets Harbor, N.Y.) after fighting in the second Seminole War. https://historicmissourians.shsmo.org/nathaniel-lyon

137 *The Last Political Writings*, 22–24; James McElroy, *The Struggle for Missouri*, 51; Christopher Phillips, *Damned Yankee*, 83–85.

At Fort Riley, Lyon became a friend of William A. Hammond, the assistant surgeon, who later described Lyon's mental characteristics: "intensity and conscientiousness...Whatever he felt, he felt with a force that carried everything before it. There was no middle ground with him... and it was his duty to enforce his doctrines upon all...to the extent of being offensive." Hammond characterized Lyon as eccentric, unpredictable, and with "a vein of cruelty...for those he thought behaved badly."[138] Fort Riley had a strong pro-slavery atmosphere. Lyon and Hammond were the only anti-slavery officers. Yet, Lyon boldly voiced hatred for all advocates of the Kansas-Nebraska Act.

Lyon also hated the tendency of southerners to call anyone opposed to their acts "abolitionists." He considered radical abolitionists to be "irresponsible rabble-rousers."[139] Lyon was irritated by people who didn't comprehend the difference, but he understood that secessionists vilified anyone who opposed their policies. Dr. Hammond described an odd, truthful man with forceful will, who strongly believed in his principles and expressed them in nearly any setting. Nathaniel Lyon did not seem to care if he was unpopular, even with his superiors. He was honest and transparent about his beliefs. We know from the letters Lyon wrote to the *Manhattan Express* that his convictions grew bolder during his time as a first-hand observer of "bleeding Kansas."[140] (See Appendix B for the titles of and extracts from his letters to the press.)

The border wars (violent confrontations along the Missouri and Kansas border) grew worse in 1857 and 1858. Lyon observed fraudulent territorial elections and the power of slaveocracy. The elections in

---

138 William Hammond, "Recollections of General Nathaniel Lyon," *Annals of Iowa* 4, no. 6 (1900): 434.

139 Phillips, *Damned Yankee*, 105.

140 Peckham, 372–431, 418; *The Last Political Writings*,111–229. Lyon's letters were written to the *Manhattan Express* (Kansas) newspaper in 1860 and January of 1861.The series of essays begins with a discussion of morality, then moves to his harsh grievances against pro-slavery politicians and their schemes. After severely criticizing the other presidential candidates, Lyon promoted Abraham Lincoln. Many secessionists would have hated Lyon's published rants and concluded that he was a religious zealot.

Kansas were embroiled in violence. From Lyon's view, President Franklin Pierce's government, with Jefferson Davis as Secretary of War, took an immoral, compliant approach in the unremitting brutalities in Kansas, except to protect pro-slavery interests. Captain Lyon considered resigning the Army rather than carrying out orders to enforce a proslavery Kansas legislature.[141]

William Selby Harney was assigned to Fort Leavenworth where he commanded the U.S. Army troops stationed in the territory of Kansas. He was asked to "quiet the difficulties," and in May 1857, Nathaniel Lyon, a West Point graduate, was under his orders. As experienced U.S. Army officers and veterans of warfare against Native Americans and the Mexican war, both men been had trained to kill and had followed orders to do so, sometimes savagely.[142] Captain Lyon demanded harsh disciplines for U. S. Army soldiers under his command and was court- marshalled for excessive punishment.

The Southern control over federal government positions, especially positions in the Army, provoked Lyon.[143] For example, he wrote about the U.S. Army's quartermaster position after long-term quartermaster Thomas S. Jesup died in the summer of 1860, when John Buchanan Floyd was Secretary of War. Instead of the appointment going to the next in command, it was given to Floyd's relative, Joseph E. Johnston,

---

[141] William E. Parrish, "General Nathaniel Lyon, A Portrait," in *The Civil War in Missouri: Essays from the Missouri Historical Review, 1906–2006* (Columbia, MO: The State Historical Society of Missouri, 2006), 15.

[142] George Rollie Adams, *General William S. Harney: Prince of Dragoons* (Lincoln: University of Nebraska Press, 2001). See pages 80 and 102 for descriptions of Harney's brutal treatment of soldiers and the hanging of thirty soldiers who had deserted in the Mexican War; See Phillips, *Damned Yankee*, 67–69, and Woodward, 35, 60, and 218, for descriptions of Lyon's fighting in the Seminole wars and his later participation in the annihilation of Indian villages.

[143] Buchanan's Vice President was Southern Rights Democrat John C. Breckenridge; Secretary of War was John B. Floyd; Secretary of Interior was secessionist Jacob Thompson; Albert Sidney Johnston was head of the U.S. Army and later became a Confederate General. There is no simple way to summarize how the brutal conflicts in Kansas became an undeclared Civil War.

who became the famous Confederate general.[144]

Lyon believed that President Buchanan could prevent southern states from seceding but was not capable, or was unwilling, to take the actions necessary to do so. In one of his letters, Lyon asked how disunion could possibly make Northerners more eager to return escaped slaves to their owners. He believed that national sovereignty mattered more to the country than state sovereignty. Lyon also described how disunion would leave the Southern Confederacy without an inch of territory to extend slavery, as all possibilities for slave expansion into new territories would be held by the Union. It was perplexing that southerners threatened the North that if it would not agree to the extension of slavery the South would secede, when secession itself would leave no future for slavery expansion in the U.S. It was a striking incongruity. Lyon withdrew his support from Stephen Douglas and transferred his loyalty to Abraham Lincoln.[145]

When William Harney was made brigadier general in 1858, his duty was to comply with his superiors, prevent bloodshed, uphold civil law and federal authority under Presidents Pierce and Buchanan.[146] In 1860, Harney ordered Lyon and his company to Fort Scott, Kansas, to drive off James Montgomery, a radical leader of Free-Soil fighters.[147] Lyon had earlier met Montgomery, who told him that he would give himself up before a proper county court, but would not submit himself to court under Judge Williams at Fort Scott who gave power to U.S. Marshalls to

---

144 *Encyclopedia Virginia*," John B Floyd" (1806-1863). https://encyclopediavirgina.org. Johnston was Floyd's cousin through marriage.

145 Peckham, 372–431, 418; *The Last Political Writings*, 24–25, 186. Lyon wrote anonymous letters to the *Manhattan Express* newspaper from June 1860 to January of 1861, 111–213. See Appendix B for titles of and extracts from his letters to the press.

146 Adams, 181. Harney was at times peace-loving, but he was also called rude, brutal, and careless.

147 Adams, 218–219; "Montgomery, James," www.civilwaronthewesternborder.org/encyclopedia. Retrieved 1/06/2021. The Missouri governor sent six hundred militia troops to the western border to suppress Montgomery's raids. Daniel Frost, a strong supporter of extending slavery into Kansas, was part of this expedition. He and Lyon became adversaries at Camp Jackson.

summon jurors who would not do justice. Several times troops had been ordered to Fort Scott to arrest Montgomery. Lyon believed in the right of Kansas citizens to self-defense when it was necessary. Although Lyon understood that not all people in Lawrence were innocent of bloodshed, he knew that Ft. Scott had been sold by 1857 to pro-slavery men and he was no longer willing to serve the wishes of slavocrats.[148] Lyon was suspected of side-stepping Harney's orders. After serving several years in "bleeding" Kansas, he concluded that pro-slavery strangleholds would never end without war, that it would be the only solution to the haggling political clang, coercing, maneuvering, playing favorites, and neglecting responsibility for all citizens.[149] He held hatred for slave power. General Harney, his superiors, and close associates were supporters of slavery and would have considered Lyon an annoying abolitionist opponent.

After years of struggle and bloody civil warfare, Kansas entered the U.S. as a free state on January 29, 1861, just before Captain Nathaniel Lyon and his Company B, Second U.S. Infantry, received orders to protect the U.S. Army's federal arsenal in St. Louis.[150] St. Louis was also the hometown for General William Selby Harney, who, in November 1860, was headquartered there as Commander of the Army Department of the West. A few months later, Captain Lyon arrived nearby in Jefferson barracks. He was again under General Harney's mandate and remained a burr under his saddle.

St. Louis

General Harney knew that the state's slave owners were a small percentage of the state's population but understood that slavery was a key source of labor, wealth, and identity for a powerful group. Harney believed secessionists were not a threat in Missouri because they were a minority. The majority of citizens in the state had voted for moder-

---

148 Woodward, 233–234, 236, 284.
149 Robert Julius Rombauer, *The Union Cause in St. Louis in 1861: An Historical Sketch* (St. Louis: Nixon Jones, 1909), 151; Peckham, 395–432.
150 Piston and Hatcher, 28.

ates in the recent presidential election and not for the Southern Rights' candidate John C. Breckenridge, and in February 1861, citizens elected no outright secessionists as convention delegates to vote on the state's relationship with the Union.[151] The degree of secessionist threat, however, was a matter of opinion. Two of the state's most ardent secessionists led Missouri's General Assembly.[152] Secessionists were aggressive in counties which bordered the Missouri River, an area of strong support for Governor Jackson, and supported an overthrow of the federal system.[153] General Harney remained loyal to his Army superiors, but also held convictions similar to and had close connections to many slave-holding friends and relatives in his home city.[154] He did not seem as concerned about secessionist threats as were Lyon, Frank Blair, and other Unionist supporters.

Abraham Lincoln was president-elect, and President Buchanan was still in office when Captain Lyon arrived with eighty Regulars (February 6, 1861) to protect the St. Louis Arsenal:

> Lyon was well-knit but had a slender frame, long narrow face, full high forehead, keen deep-set blue eyes…manner quick and nervous; bore himself as rigid disciplinarian mingled with thoughtful kindness for all who knew duty and tried their best…Of old Puritan stock, 42 years old…He was well-informed in profession of arms, history, and general

---

[151] Parrish, *Turbulent Partnership*, 5. Missouri voted for Stephan Douglas as the presidential candidate, and the close second was John Bell, the Constitutional Unionist Candidate.

[152] Parrish, *Turbulent Partnership*, 6. Lieutenant Governor Thomas C. Reynolds was elected with Jackson under the guise of a popular Douglas moderate until after the election, when both revealed their true colors: they were ardent secessionists. Reynolds presided in the upper house of the Assembly, with a Breckinridge Southern Rights Democrat as Speaker of the House.

[153] Christopher Phillips, *Missouri's Confederate: Claiborne Fox Jackson and The Creation of Southern Identity in the Border West* (Columbia, MO: University of Missouri Press, 2000), 221– 222, 238; McGuire, "Solving the Mystery of Arsenal Guns" https://www.civilwarstlouis.com/articles/solving-mystery-arsenal-guns/ Retrieved October 16, 2024.

[154] Adams, 218, 376.

history and literature, a devoted student of the Bible and Shakespeare who wrote well and forcibly. Very outspoken in his views—abolitionist and national sovereignty—so to many, antagonistic: a weaker willed man would have been forced out of the army or acquiesced to prevailing sentiment...When sent to arsenal met Frank P. Blair.[155]

Captain Nathaniel Lyon was doggedly determined, singularly focused, and fortunately, very well-connected. When Lyon arrived in St. Louis, he and Frank Blair formed an immediate partnership. Lyon's success in St. Louis was possible because of his relationships with Blair, his brother Montgomery, and their personal connections to Abraham Lincoln. With the help of the Blair brothers, other hard-working Unionists in St. Louis, and President Lincoln, Lyon was able to keep the arsenal and the city under Union control. Lyon's actions, like those of his superiors and the Iowa soldiers, were always enmeshed in a web of social networks.

Abraham Lincoln and Missouri

Although citizens in the East and politicians in the nation's capital might not have recognized the significance of the Mississippi River Valley, Abraham Lincoln understood it long before his election as president. He lived in Illinois, with its long western border entirely defined by the Mississippi River with Missouri on the opposite bank. As president, he believed it was "the most strategically important corridor of the war."[156] Lincoln established close political relationships with the Missouri Blair family. While Abraham Lincoln and other anti-slavery interests were establishing the Republican party of Illinois, Francis Blair entered his first term in Congress at the national level (April 1857). When they met

---

155 McElroy, *The Struggle for Missouri*, 51. The author assumed that Lyon was an abolitionist because he hated the institution of slavery, but Lyon believed slavery should stand in the South as defined by the Missouri Compromise.

156 Cutrer, 3.

in Springfield, Illinois, Lincoln's platform was based on allowing slavery to stand as it existed according to the Missouri Compromise of 1820 but opposing its further expansion. Blair's manifesto was also "free-soil." Blair, Lincoln, and their supporters urged newspapers in border states to take a stand against the extension of slavery, but they did not promote abolition. The situation was delicate. There were slave-owners who supported the Union and Northerners who supported slavery. Lincoln did not want slavery issues to jeopardize Union supporters, especially in Missouri. He hoped to tread carefully on the matter.

Lincoln and Blair promoted the theme that slavery was a great concern that should be settled peaceably in Missouri, hopefully, with gradual emancipation by the citizens. Above all, the Union should stand. Blair's cousin B. Gratz Brown had become editor of the *Missouri Democrat* and began to give more attention to slavery. John Hay, the newspaper's correspondent in Springfield, Illinois, sent reports (often from Lincoln's office) about all the Lincoln-Douglas debates to the St. Louis newspaper.[157]

Frank Blair sometimes rode along with Lincoln on his campaigns. The Blairs hoped for Lincoln's success at the Chicago Republican Convention in 1860, where Missouri politician (and contender for the nomination) Edward Bates gave a convincing endorsement for Lincoln. Bates said how Lincoln especially cares for the great valley of the Mississippi which cannot be divided and how indivisibility is necessary for prosperity. Bates concluded, "He will use his mind and knowledge as his weapons."[158] Lincoln won the Republican nomination for president but lost the national November vote in Missouri where Democrat Stephen Douglas won one-third of the votes.[159] The fragmentation of other parties resulted

---

157 Stevens, 66. Other newspapers hoped to keep it quiet because papers which mentioned slavery were labeled "abolitionist."

158 Stevens, 71–72; Ora Williams, "Lincoln and Iowa," *The Annals of Iowa*, 34, no. 2, (Fall 1957): 145. John A. Kasson was head of the Iowa Republican party and a member of the resolutions committee at the Chicago Convention. Kasson wrote much of Lincoln's platform for the campaign. Lincoln appointed him assistant postmaster general.

159 Phillips, *Missouri's Confederate*, 231. Missouri was the only state to declare for Stephan Douglas in the 1860 election.

in divided votes, and Lincoln won the national election. He appointed two Missourians to his cabinet, Montgomery Blair as Postmaster-General, and Edward Bates as Attorney General, and he hired John Hay, the Missouri newspaper correspondent, as one of his personal secretaries.

After President Lincoln's inauguration, March 4, 1861, it took time for him to assemble a cabinet, gain trust, and establish authority before South Carolina made the bold first war strike at Fort Sumter.[160] It was common knowledge in Missouri that control of the St. Louis Arsenal was critical for control over the city and the state. President Lincoln and Francis Blair feared loss of the St. Louis Arsenal would carry Missouri into the Confederacy. Lincoln trusted Francis Blair absolutely and closely relied on him for updates on St. Louis affairs, especially concerning the arsenal. The president strongly supported his (and Lyon's) efforts.[161]

In St. Louis, Blair and Lyon had to counter the efforts of Claiborne Jackson, who in the summer of 1860, knowing that Stephen Douglas was the most popular Democratic presidential candidate in Missouri, strategically ran for governor as a Douglas Democrat with a (false) promise of neutrality for the state. After his August election, which was successful under a cloak of pretense, Jackson soon made his true secession intentions clear. As governor, he continued to claim a politically popular "Peace Policy" while aggressively working with the Confederacy for rebellion.[162]

The Election of Delegates to Missouri's Secession Convention

By February 13, 1861, the governor had successfully implemented a new

---

160 Senategov/artandhistory/historycommon/expulsion_cases; Fergus M. Borderwich, "Congress Fights the Civil War," *American Heritage*, Spring 2020. Americanheritage.com. congress-fights-civil-war. After resignations and expulsions of secessionists, Democrats held less than twenty five percent of the House in the 37th Congress which included pro-Unionists and anti-war Democrats. In 1861 eleven Senators were expelled for support of the Confederate rebellion. Stronger, more willful Republicans were left in control who pushed President Lincoln into increasing activism.

161 Stevens, 76.

162 Phillips, *Missouri's Confederate*, 248.

law banning any recruitment of troops outside his authority. Jackson knew the established legal pathway for secession would come from a Convention of Delegates elected from around the state for that purpose. Like governors in the Southern states, he called for an election of state delegates to consider secession and assumed they would do so. But on February 18, Missouri voters overwhelmingly chose Union delegates from the three men elected from each of the thirty-three senatorial districts. Some delegates held unconditional support for the Union, and most supported the Union only with conditions, but on March 19 those representatives voted to remain neutral and in the Union.[163] After the delegates voted against secession, the disappointed governor disregarded the convention outcome and went to plan B, taking control of the St. Louis Arsenal so that he could arm troops and prepare to fight.

The U.S. Army had ordered Captain Nathaniel Lyon into a derecho of Missouri turbulence. Lyon's assignment was to protect a critically important United States arsenal in a slave state governed by a vehement secessionist who was pretending to be neutral. It was a formidable task. Lyon knew that during the preceding November, South Carolina had seized a federal arsenal, and in the months of January and February, Georgia, Alabama, Florida, Louisiana, and Arkansas had done the same.[164] On February 16, when Texas took federal arsenals and property, Lyon would

---

163 Piston and Hatcher, 26; Jason Roe, "Missouri Rejects Secession," The Kansas City Public Library and Missouri State Library. http//civilwarwesternborder.org. Although it was a slave state, Missouri was also a border state with strong Union ties, and the elected delegates hoped to maintain neutrality. This would not be possible as hostilities mounted; Phillips, *Missouri's Confederate,* 241. The unsuccessful secession convention didn't dismay the governor, "he was encouraged by it."

164 Rachel Katlyn Deale, " 'Acts of War,' the Seizure of Federal Property, 1860-1861" . 2017 Dissertation Tuscaloosa, University of Alabama. https://ir.ua.eu/handle/123456789/3446; David C. Keohn, 2/24/2017, "Avowed Enemies of the Country: Knights of the Golden Circle," HistoryNet. https://www.historynet.com/avowed-enemies-country-knights-golden-circle/. These states had seized arsenals before each of the states had seceded.

have learned more about how it happened. [165] He hated hearing news of the surrenders and was skeptical of the army officers who had been forced to submit the U.S. federal properties. Lyon would learn to trust two of those officers who came under his command, but he continued to loathe the idea of capitulation.

Lyon, Blair, and President Lincoln understood that Missouri secessionists would follow suit and try to take the arsenal. If successful, it would severely threaten Union efforts. Lyon, duty-bound, found ways to protect it. He had been court-marshalled as a young officer and was obnoxiously outspoken. He called politicians who complained about the election of Lincoln "bugaboo screechers."[166] Lyon swiveled around army rules when trying to get what he needed. He indirectly criticized superior officers using terms like "imbeciles," "villains," or "allies of the enemy" whenever he believed they were negligent.[167] It is easy to see why many hated Lyon, even superiors and those with only small allegiance to the secession. But as he dealt with politicians' lies, secret aid from Confederates, and even Union leaders who obstructed his mission, he pre-empted the governor's insurrection.

Based on considerable evidence that Governor Jackson was not to be trusted, Lyon and Blair never believed his ongoing popular pledge to the people that he wanted Missouri to remain neutral. Immediately after his inauguration, Jackson revealed his southern allegiance with covert and overt actions. On January 8, Lieutenant Governor Reynolds held a proslavery

---

165 "Texas Civil War History." http://www.thomaslegion.net/americancivilwar/texascivilwarhistory.html Retrieved 1/10/2021. Texas ratified the Ordinance of Secession February 1, 1861, and joined the Confederacy on March 2. The state took federal arsenals, outposts, and property on February 16. On February 8, 1861, land barons and representatives of the Texas government met with Brevet Major General David E. Twiggs. Twiggs (a friend and early mentor to General Harney), at the age of nearly seventy-one, was commander of U.S. Army's Department of Texas. A wealthy and powerful group of secessionists encouraged him to peacefully surrender his entire command of facilities and armaments, including the U.S. Army soldiers under his command and 10,000 rifled muskets. He did so before accepting commission as a Confederate general and died the following year.
166 Peckham, 418.
167 Rombauer, 154.

meeting in St. Louis to organize the paramilitary "Minute Men." Soon after, the governor requested Missouri's quota of state arms from Washington.[168] Jackson took control of the St. Louis Police Commission that demanded the removal of any U.S. troops outside the arsenal. When Lyon refused to comply, the issue was referred to the state legislature which alleged that such troops were against U.S. laws.[169] Lyon did not agree.

General Harney, Commander of the U.S. Army's Department of the West, became part of the Missouri controversy which led to war. After Lincoln's inauguration, Harney was no longer under the command of President Buchanan, a Southern sympathizer for whom achieving peace was mostly a matter of controlling the "Free-soilers." Harney's professed goal was to curb anything that might inflame violence. He viewed himself as peacekeeper of Missouri, much like his previous assignment in Kansas, but his bull's eye was now on Nathaniel Lyon, not on the governor. On January 24, and again February 13, U. S. Army General-in-Chief Winfield Scott wrote to Harney suggesting that he add more defensive troops and prepare the St. Louis Arsenal for an emergency, when "re-enforcements may be cut off." Scott's aide-de-camp added for clarification, that "it is best to move in advance of excitement." Harney's response was that such concerns are not well-founded and should not be seriously considered.

Brevet Major Peter V. Hagner, Chief of Ordnance in command of the St. Louis arsenal, wrote to his superior officer that "we are perfectly secure" and "watchful."[170] Lyon urged Hagner to strengthen defenses of the Arsenal, but he refused and used his authority to restrict Lyon's access.[171] Lyon

---

168 Phillips, *Missouri's Confederate*, 238.
169 The Last Political Writings, 26–27.
170 United States War Department, *The War of the Rebellion: A Compilation of the Official Records of the Union and Confederate Armies*, 70 volumes in 128 (Washington, DC: Government Printing Office, 1880–1901). Reprint Harrisburg, PA: National Historical Society, 1980. Series 1:482, 1:655, January 24, and February 21, 1861. There are two sources used here for the *Official Records*: "Series" refers to the original text and "Serial" notations refer to the Ohio State University digitalized eHistory site. https://ehistory.osu.edu>-books>war-rebellion-official-records-civil-war. Hereafter, both are cited as *OR*.
171 Snead, 131.

called Hagner's actions "imbecility or damned villany." Blair understood the susceptibility of the arsenal and was skeptical about U.S. army assignments made under Buchanan's administration. He wrote to the Secretary of War directing attention to Lyon's legitimate authority which was higher than Hagner's Brevet (honorary) rank, and suggested that Hagner be in charge only of the ordnance department. Col. Thomas responded in a clear directive: "Captain N. Lyon...the senior officer of the line present and on duty at St. Louis Arsenal, Mo., is assigned to the command of troops and defenses at that post."[172] In response, Harney immediately informed Lyon that the orders did not mean that he (Lyon) should exercise any control over the Ordnance Department, and a few days later sent the same interpretation to the Assistant Adj. General for verification. Col. Thomas replied with another clear directive for Hagner to transfer to Captain Lyon all requested mounted artillery and necessary supplies.[173] As of April 6, there were only a dozen pieces of mounted artillery protecting the arsenal.

Following the attack on Fort Sumter and one month after General Scott had ordered Harney to send more men to protect the arsenal, Harney admitted in his April 16 report that Governor Jackson intended to occupy the slopes and demand surrender. He then asked for urgent guidance, and in mid-April discreetly asked General Scott for reassignment, away from St. Louis, his home town.[174] There was just cause for Unionists to worry. On April 21, Major Nathaniel Grant reported that secessionists seized the small U.S. Army arsenal in Liberty, Missouri. Over the course of three days, a body of armed men removed the ordnance stores from the small arsenal. Grant, the facility commander, had felt secure that strong nearby Union sentiment prevented worry. Having no means of resistance against "forcible and unlawful seizure of public

---

172 *OR*, Serial 1:656, March 11, Frank Blair to Simon Cameron; Serial 1:656, March 13, Special Orders 74.
173 *OR*. Serial 1:658, 661. March 13, March 20, April 6, 1861.
174 Adams, 224.

property" he was powerless.[175] General Harney made no response. His lack of action caught the attention of the federals in Washington, D.C. [176]

Claiborne Jackson worked with Daniel Marsh Frost who was elected to the Missouri Senate in 1854 and was a strong supporter of the "Central Clique" in Missouri Democratic party politics. In 1858 Frost helped enact a law for creating the state militia and was appointed Brigadier General. He was the likely brains behind a plot to assault the arsenal. Frost wrote to Governor Jackson of his January 24 talk with Major Bell at the arsenal and how Bell agreed to make no resistance to a secessionist takeover.[177] The letter held plans for a plot. Frost recommended that the governor ask Jefferson Davis for assault weapons and explained the importance of acquiring the arms taken from the small Liberty Arsenal in western Missouri.[178] In April, Governor Jackson sent Colton Green and Basil Duke as secret emissaries to Jefferson Davis with his letter requesting arms for an attack on the arsenal.[179]

After Ft. Sumter, the U.S. War Department and President Lincoln understood the arsenal was at risk and became more decisive. The threats, combined with letters from loyal Unionists across the state, convinced the federal government and the War Department that Jackson was an enemy of the United States.[180] On April 21 they issued orders for Lyon and Blair to

---

175 *OR*, Series 1, Vol. 1:649, Report 5 by Nathaniel Grant; *History of Clay and Platte Counties*, (St. Louis: National Historic Company, 1885) 196–197; "April 20, 1861: The Capture of the Liberty Arsenal and the Service of Secessionist Col. Henry Routt," Extract from 1861 *Missouri Speaks*, Series 10, Vol 1, Article 3. Available thru link on Missouri Civil War Passport Program, A Google Doc.

176 Adams, 226.

177 Phillips *Missouri's Confederate,* 238, 239; Phillips, *Damned Yankee*, 140. Bell was soon reassigned to a different post, but decided to retire. He was replaced by Brev. Major Peter V. Hagner, who was reposted from his position at Ft. Leavenworth.

178 Adamson, 4–6; Snead, 150.

179 OR Serial 1:688, April 23 from Jefferson Davis agreeing to Jackson's request of April 17: "I concur with you as to the great importance of capturing the arsenal;" Piston and Hatcher, 33.

180 McElroy, 85–88. Lyon and Blair, having obtained clear evidence of Jackson's cooperation with the Confederacy, believed that his actions constituted treason against the U.S. government.

muster four regiments, arm loyal citizens, protect the peaceable Missourians, execute laws, and if necessary, proclaim martial law in St. Louis.[181]

General Harney's Recall and Curious Kidnapping

General Harney was recalled by the Secretary of War to Washington, and a peculiar thing happened. On April 25, he was "kidnapped," taken from the train by Confederate soldiers to Richmond, Virginia, where he was met by several old southern friends who tried to bring him to their cause. According to biographers, neither the Virginia governor nor Confederate Generals Robert E. Lee and Joseph E. Johnston, could alter Harney's loyalty to the Union. So, he continued to Washington to meet with his superior officer, General Scott.[182] In Harney's absence Lyon was given temporary command.[183]

The Camp Jackson Affair

On April 23, Confederate President Jefferson Davis responded to Governor Jackson's request for arms, agreeing to supply them. On April 24, U.S. Captain Montgomery reported a force of about 235 men with a battery of artillery, directed by the Arkansas governor, had taken possession of Fort Smith, the Arkansas military post near Missouri's border. U.S. Army Captain Sturgis and his command were forced to surrender and on their way to Kansas.[184] On May 4, Captain Langdon

---

181 *OR*, Series 1:670, L. Thomas to Lyon; Stevens, 75; Robert E. Shalhope, *Sterling Price: Portrait of a Southerner* (Columbia, MO: University of Missouri Press, 1971), 155.

182 Adams, 226; L.U. Reavis, *The Life and Military Services of General William Selby Harney* (St. Louis: Bryan, Brand and Company, 1878), 355; Parrish 25; McElroy, *The Struggle for Missouri*, 102, describes the incident as taking place during Harney's second recall.

183 Piston and Hatcher, 29–30, and Phillips, *Damned Yankee*, 200–203, suggest that Lyon achieved command by manipulating Blair's connections to the power structure in Washington. It is just as reasonable to conclude that Lyon was strongly recommended by Blair and selected by Lincoln and his war department because Lyon had proven his ability, "obsessive sense of duty," and determination to keep Missouri in the Union. Lyon was not known as a man who pandered to superiors.

184 *OR*, Series 1, Vol. 1:651, Report of Capt. Alexander Montgomery.

Easton reported that about fifty armed men carried off 102 carbines, 37 muskets, 9 pistols, 86 sabers and 34,0000 cartridges from the United States ordnance storehouse in Kansas City (Missouri).[185]

When General Frost and the governor mobilized the militia for instructional camps in early May, Frost established Camp Jackson in Lindell Grove which held several hundred state militia soldiers who were not far from the St. Louis Arsenal.[186] Captain Lyon was aggravated, understood the secession danger, and was no longer willing to remain on the defense while Jackson was covertly and actively on the offense. Lyon, acting as commander in Harney's absence, learned about the May 9 arrival of arms, sent by Jefferson Davis, into nearby Camp Jackson and was hell-bent on exposing the ruse and capturing the camp. Ulysses S. Grant, who was mustering U.S. recruits in nearby Belleville, Illinois, happened to be in St. Louis. Alarmed by finding the encampment at Camp Jackson and two opposing armies, Grant wrote to his wife, Julia, that he was worried about the danger of conflict and bloodshed in St. Louis. He later wrote about an encounter with a secessionist in the city (St. Louis) who told him: "Where I come from, if a man dares to say a word in favor of the Union, we hang him to a limb of the first tree we come to."[187]

Grant visited Frank Blair and Captain Lyon at the arsenal and expressed support for their purpose. On May 10, Lyon caught the secessionist recruited militia in their camp with the siege guns and arms for the purpose of taking over the arsenal. Among Lyon's troop commanders were Colonel Frank P. Blair, Lieutenant Thomas Sweeny, Colonel Franz Sigel, and Colonel Henry Boernstein. Lyon had calculated the timing of troop movements to coincide at different points until they nearly

---

[185] *OR*, Series 1, Vol. 1:652, Report of Capt. Langdon C. Easton.

[186] Snead, 152. Because of the 1858 act created by Frost and Jackson, Frost was allowed to encamp the state militia for six days wherever he pleased. He chose a spot overlooking the St. Louis Arsenal; Rombauer, 226.

[187] "Ulysses S. Grant's Experiences During the Camp Jackson Affair," Ulysses S. Grant National Historic Site. National Park Service. https://www.nps.gov/articles/000/ulysses-s-grant-s-experiences-during-the-camp-jackson-affair.htm

surrounded the camp. Rumors of marching troops spread quickly, and soon the streets were filled with "a living stream" of bewildered people, some with weapons. Secessionist Camp Commander Daniel Frost sent a dispatch explaining that the camp was legal and claimed that he held no hostility towards any federal property or plan to attack the Arsenal. Ignoring Frost's false denial, Lyon gave a summons demanding surrender with the promise that all would be treated kindly. Surrounded, Frost and his troops surrendered. There was no cheering or exclamation, and no bloodshed.

The procession of prisoners, mostly guarded by German troops, took time, allowing a violent street mob to gather. Lyon's troops led the prisoners he took toward the arsenal. The nearby hills were packed with onlookers. Many, including women and children, were on foot or on horseback, others were in carriages or buggies. A few secession supporters with wagons took rifles, shotguns, or other available weapons and attempted to aid the State Troops in the camp.[188] Lieutenant Colonel Robert Julius Rombauer was one of four Hungarian-American brothers who fought for the Union and was on site with the First Reserves troops under Colonel Almstedt. Rombauer described how St. Louis secessionists hated Lyon's German troops (who were strongly against slavery and who supported Lincoln) and were calling them derisive names. Hundreds of secessionists swarmed the streets, yelled "Black Dutch," and hurled stones and bricks.[189] Some in the crowd threatened with bottles, knives, hunting weapons, muskets, or pistols. Soldiers sustained the ethnic abuse for about an hour.

---

188 *The Last Political Writings*, 29–30. This description is attributed to the *St. Louis Republican*, St. Louis, May 10, 1861.

189 Rombauer 230, 231; Robert Julius Rombauer helped with plans for the Missouri Pacific Railroad and remained influential in St. Louis after the war. He became president of St. Louis Public Library and of the Board of Assessors, and was a member of Board of Education. findagrave.com/memorial/18217/Robert-julius-rombauer; Jordan, 240. Nativists and secessionists ridiculed Germans' religious and cultural practices and their sympathies with emancipation. Jordan notes how keepers of a regiment's history learned, even in Ohio, how much their German ancestors were disliked.

Rombauer reported that a few guns were pointed at Blair and Lyon. Some in the crowd started firing revolvers. One shot killed a Union soldier from Company F, Third Missouri. Another shot hit Captain Rufous Saxton. While the crowd was goading the gunman to shoot more, he was struck down by one of Lyon's soldiers with a bayonet. Because the procession stretched across many blocks, increasing numbers of onlookers pressed ever closer to the troops near the back of the long line. Some were curious, others were filled with rage: "Innocents were mixed with rowdies." The mob was assaulting from both sides near the rear of the column, where most of the onlookers densely pressed together. Captain Blandowski was shot in the leg, and as he was falling from his horse, he ordered the troops to return fire into the mob. As the soldiers returned fire above and towards the dense crowd, twenty-eight people were killed, including men, women, children, three prisoners, and, succumbing to his wound the next day, Captain Blandowski.[190]

Critics focus on Lyon's order to march the soldiers through the streets to the arsenal, but suggest few alternatives for holding the prisoners. The slow march through the streets with increasing crowds took time and made the troops and prisoners vulnerable to interference. For ardent supporters of secession and the militia who had been forced to surrender, it was a display of humiliation.[191] Lyon held the captured soldiers overnight at the arsenal and before releasing them, demanded that they pledge not to take up arms against the Union.[192]

Rombauer noted how following accounts varied, "according to the differing party positions and deficient information." He quoted a Confederate writer who described Camp Jackson as the shedding of

---

190 *OR*, Series 2, Vol. 1:107, Letters from J.B. Eads to Simon Cameron, Secretary of War, and from J. T. Sanderson, Chief Clerk, to the U.S. War Department May 11, 1861; Rombauer, 234–235; Adamson, 58–64; McElroy, *The Struggle for Missouri*, 78.
191 Phillips *Missouri's Confederate*, 254, quotes a citizen's reaction, "My blood boils in my veins when I think of the position of Missouri—held in the Union at the point of Dutchmen's bayonets—I feel enraged."
192 Adams, 231.

blood by Lyon's troops without real cause. Another asked why Gen. Frost put himself in a position to provoke an attack if he did not intend to fight?[193] Perhaps Governor Jackson planned the Camp Jackson debacle to prompt a military response, a provocation which he knew would incite an aggressive reaction.[194] Or, as one historian suggests, perhaps Lyon should not have taken defense of the arsenal so seriously, that it was a ridiculous mistake, a military blunder.[195] He concludes that Lyon had little need to be concerned because the lay of the surrounding land made it too unlikely, and most of the arsenal's guns had been removed. A reverse question asks why the secessionists continued to pursue their plan to attack the arsenal after learning from newspapers that the arms had been removed.[196] Did Frost and Price highly value the arsenal as a production facility and remain determined to take it to support secession even though a majority of the Union's existing arms had been removed? Should Lyon, who was in command of the arsenal, have patiently risked a bombardment with artillery sent from the Confederacy for the purpose of taking the arsenal?

Some critics suggest that Lyon's actions encouraged conditional Unionists, like Sterling Price, "off the fence" and into the secessionists' camp, but that was not the case. The attack on Ft. Sumter - the South's declaration of war - provoked citizens, North and South, to "jump off the

---

[193] Rombauer, 235–237.

[194] Phillips, *Missouri's Confederate*, 250–253. Although Camp Jackson is termed the "single most catalytic event," this source provides no first-hand accounts and describes how a "small fracas" during the prisoners' march propelled the mostly German Black Jaeger troops to fire on the innocent crowd. The author suggests that Jackson's efforts to arm Camp Jackson with help from the Confederacy and the following debacle was planned by the governor as a trap, knowing that if he kicked up hysteria it would work in his favor. Phillips calls it "Jackson's gambit." If so, then Governor Jackson is accountable for collateral damage and the resulting "massacre;" Hans Christian Adamson, *Rebellion in Missouri: 1861* (Philadelphia: Chilton Company, 1961). Adamson also refers to Jackson's "gambit."

[195] Parrish, 22, 241; Phillips, *Missouri's Confederate*, 252.

[196] Randy McGuire, "Solving the Mystery." The news that the guns were removed from the arsenal was reported in the *Daily Democrat*, April 27, 1861. Sterling Price and Daniel Frost had been supplied with weapons from the St. Louis arsenal during the Mexican War and the Missouri Militia's involvement in the border wars. Retrieved October 16, 2024.

fence." Sterling Price, like Jackson, greatly disliked Blair and Lyon for obstructing their goals and for being Republicans. He, too, had publicly supported Stephen Douglas during the National election and convinced the public that he was a conditional Unionist. He, too, claimed support for "armed neutrality" while using Lyon's actions to justify secession. If genuine, it was because Price believed the federal government would give in to Southern demands for the permanent extension of slavery. He had a long history of involvement with the Central Clique of the Democratic Party, and duplicity was an important part of their political strategy. The former governor hoped that Missouri would remain in the Union if slavery was guaranteed in the new territories, but he was at times passive, allowing his actions to be determined by others.[197]

As the Missouri governor, Price had appointed Claiborne Jackson as the state's first Commissioner of Banking. After his own election as governor, Jackson passed the position back to Sterling Price. By the time of Camp Jackson, Price was working with Jackson and Robert Barnes, the secessionist president of the parent branch of the Bank of the State of Missouri in St. Louis, to fund arms for the militia in order to seize the arsenal and take control of the city.[198] It is also unlikely that the governor would appoint him commander of the State Guard and send him to make the Harney-Price agreement if Price had only recently fallen "off the fence."

Lyon and Blair knew about Frost's "agreement" with Major Bell to cooperate in an attack on the arsenal, and his notes to the governor which suggested that he (Jackson) request arms from the South to enable an

---

197 Shalhope, 159, 135–136, 39. Price and Jackson shared a long history in Missouri Democratic politics. When Jackson was floor leader of the 1842 House of Representatives, Price's role was to convince legislators to tow the party line. Later Price became convinced that Republicans caused agitation, which threatened the Union. Price considered the Dred Scott decision a victory over Republican opposition to slavery.

198 Mark Geiger, "Missouri Banks and The Civil War: The End of a Pro-Southern Entrepreneurial Southern Elite" master's thesis, University of Missouri, Columbia, Missouri, 2000, 91, 93, 114n14. Letters between the governor and Commissioner Sterling Price dated May 9, 1861 (just before the Camp Jackson event) asked Price to soon send money (the $500,000.00 appropriated by the state in March) to Jefferson City or to the branch banks in Boonville, Lexington, and elsewhere in Little Dixie. Price was to "let no one know."

assault.[199] Rebels had taken arms from the Liberty arsenal and from the Kansas City, Missouri, ordnance department. Proof was in the letter from Governor Jackson to Jefferson Davis asking for arms from the Confederacy and in the arrival of those arms into Camp Jackson. The weapons, from the takeover by secessionists of the U.S. federal arsenal in Baton Rouge, included three thirty-two pounder cannon, twelve hundred rifles, and more.[200] Considering the central importance of the St. Louis Arsenal and knowing that "arsenal after arsenal and fort after fort" had been taken by southern secessionists, is it better to conclude that the Union should have simply dismissed threats of losing one of its most important arsenals, even if Lyon had taken steps to secure its arms?

Lyon had "stirred up a hornet's nest."[201] St. Louis citizens were howling from every perspective in the spectrum of opinions, igniting support for Jackson, while St. Louis Republicans believed they had just cause for righteous war. Lyon was there to protect the arsenal as his assigned duty and did so. Although the capture (and exposure) of Camp Jackson was an advantage for the Unionists by making clear the governor's lies and intentions, and Northern newspapers declared Lyon a Union hero, the governor and his followers strategically publicized the Camp Jackson affair as a massacre and Lyon as a murderer.[202]

Why was Camp Jackson an "epoch-making" incident?[203] Had the Union lost the arsenal and control of St. Louis, Governor Jackson could have acted for an ordinance of secession. Ulysses S. Grant wrote in his memoirs how he had little doubt that St. Louis and the arsenal would have gone into rebel hands if Lyon and Blair had allowed Camp Jackson

---

199 Phillips, *Damned Yankee*, 140.
200 D. E. Rule, "The 140-year Debate."
201 McPherson, *Battle Cry of Freedom*, 292.
202 See these websites for significant events in Missouri: "Civil War St. Louis Timeline,"www.civilwarstlouis.com/timeline/index.htm; "American Civil War in Missouri," The State Historical Society of Missouri. https://shsmo.org/guides/civil-war; "Civil War on the Western Border," Kansas City Public Library. https://civilwaronthewesternborder.org;
203 McElroy, *The Struggle for Missouri*, 87, 78, called Camp Jackson an "epoch-making incident, the right thing at the right time."

to stand.[204] Secessionist Basil Duke said they lost the war in Missouri because they lost the arsenal.[205]

Although Unionists were happy that Lyon had raided the "vipers' nest," even his superiors worried about his unpredictable rashness. Several powerful St. Louis men went to Washington to complain about Lyon's actions. Some had loyal friends or relatives who were in the militia camp. Others genuinely wanted to guarantee peace in the state. Historians may epitomize Camp Jackson as a great miscalculation which galvanized more Missourians into the secession camp. It certainly upped the level of hostilities, but the riveting agent was not the event. It was Jackson's spinning of it as a massacre while blaming the federal government. The governor cleverly deflected blame by making Lyon's actions the center of attention. He convinced many citizens that Lyon and the federals were fearful, coercive aggressors.[206]

Nathaniel Lyon was admired and despised, a pillar for Unionism who left behind a trail of enemies. Nevertheless, he was elected brigadier general by the Union volunteers in St. Louis and was approved by the U.S. War Department and the president on May 18, 1861.[207] Lyon had halted the growing aggressiveness of Missouri secessionists, but not for long. Governor Jackson turned to Plan C. After his failed Camp Jackson plot, the governor hurried to the statehouse in Jefferson City to call an emergency midnight session of the legislature and ask for the city's bells to ring.

---

204 Ulysses S. Grant's Experiences During the Camp Jackson Affair," Ulysses S. Grant National Historic Site. National Park Service. https://www.nps.gov/articles/000/ulysses-s-grant-s-experiences-during-the-camp-jackson-affair.htm

205 Peckham, 160; D. E. Rule, "The 140 year Debate."

206 Phillips, *Missouri's Confederate*, 252. Jackson had successfully convinced many citizens that the U.S. government were warmongers; *OR*, Series 1, Vol 1:671–672, Letter from U.S. Attorney General Edward Bates to Secretary of War Simon Cameron, April 27, 1861. "A great handle is made (and with wonderful success) of the false idea that the efforts of the administration are directed not to national defense but to subjugation of the South. All this does but impose upon us the more stringent necessity to make sure of St. Louis and Cairo. The fact is indisputable."

207 *OR*, Series 1, Vol. 3:4–5, May 11, 1861, Lyon's letter to Col. L. Thomas, Adj. General U.S. Army, describes details of Camp Jackson and explains his election as brig. general for the St. Louis volunteer brigade, which he is performing under authority of the president, and submitted to the (war) department for appropriate determination; Woodward, 257.

Jackson portrayed the Camp Jackson event as a brutal attack by Lyon's troops and claimed that Blair was leading three regiments of mercenaries coming to arrest them all (members of the state government) for treason. He begged men to stand by him. James Peckham (a first-hand observer as a Missouri legislator) described the "ludicrous" scene in Jefferson City as Jackson's supporters armed themselves with pistols and bowie knives.[208] The intimidated Assembly (including a secret night session) gave Jackson authority to place the state in an immediate state of defense. The long-debated Military Bill nearly completed the governor's plan. It was clearly in violation of duty as U.S. citizens, requiring only an oath to the state government. Every able-bodied man in Missouri was required to enlist into the state militia, and words contrary to the governor or legislature would result in the "heinous crime of treason to the state."[209] The governor appropriated millions of dollars from the state treasury for unconditional use. Jackson had gotten what he wanted: the power of a military dictator.[210] He knew that he needed more time and money to recruit and train secessionist troops (the militia had become the Missouri State Guard).[211] He quickly used sly political savvy to buy that time in the form of a truce.

The Price-Harney Agreement

After his recall and return to St. Louis, General Harney needed to pacify his uneasy Union army superiors and to calm the city after the Camp Jackson Affair. He threatened to declare martial law and to use the U.S.

---

208 Peckham, 165–172; Adamson, 75; Phillips, *Missouri's Confederate*, 253.

209 McElroy, *The Struggle for Missouri*, 89. The state legislators appropriated money from the state's charitable funds and schools and authorized millions in loans and bonds for the governor's nearly unrestricted use.

210 Peckham, 172, 176, 205; Phillips, *Missouri's Confederate*, 251, 258, explains that Jackson scripted Camp Jackson in order to trick the legislature into passing the Military Bill. Although the governor fought so hard and long to get the bill passed, there are few details to be found in the sources.

211 McElroy, *The Struggle for Missouri*, 89; Immediately after receiving news of Camp Jackson, the governor rushed into the General Assembly and told the rumor that three regiments of mercenaries were headed towards them.

Army to preserve peace, if necessary. In a proclamation he announced that no country in the world would be entitled to respect that would tolerate for a moment "such openly treasonous preparations (as the rebel intent of Camp Jackson)." He said that regardless of the unfortunate situation in the cotton states, "Missouri must share her destiny with the Union."[212] The St. Louis Safety Committee demanded that the federal government (and Harney) force the governor to return the arms taken from the Liberty arsenal and those from the Kansas City storehouse, and prevent further expansion of secessionist troops. This was Harney's "brilliant chance" to make a campaign against the growing strength of secessionists, but he failed to act on the moment which might have prevented the war.[213] Instead, he struck a truce with secessionists.

Governor Jackson called for a meeting between Price and Harney. On May 21, they announced the Price-Harney Agreement. General Price was entrusted to guarantee peace in the state but could not organize troops. Harney promised to prevent federal troops from advancing into the state, which meant that Lyon could not proceed without Harney's permission.[214] Did Harney naively believe Jackson's and Price's promises of peace and neutrality? There is considerable disagreement among historians about the intentions of the men involved in the St. Louis events. General Harney was described as having good "public course," but became a risk under the influence of his many secessionist friends when his judgment sometimes weakened.[215] Making a truce with the leader of the State Guard troops on their own terms was an insult to the Federals, and it gave Jackson more time to prepare for war as he ignored the order to not raise troops. Harney might have been convinced, but Blair and Lyon were not.

---

212 McElroy, *The Struggle for Missouri*, 85, 86; Adams, 235.
213 Rombauer, 242.
214 Adams, 235–236; Peckham, 245. In Harney's effort to maintain peace, he signed the Price-Harney Truce which obligated Price's Missouri State Guard to hold the state for the Union, with federal forces allowed only to control St. Louis, and not elsewhere in the state. Covert recruitment of secessionist troops continued while Union recruitment was thwarted.
215 Peckham, 198.

After securing the May 21 truce, Governor Jackson secretly sent Colton Green to Arkansas and Edward C. Cabell to Richmond to seek Confederate aid.[216] Blair received letters from across the state accusing Jackson and Price of breaking the truce by organizing military operations, communicating with Confederates, and mistreating unionists. General Harney took no action. He did not void the Truce or the Military Bill. President Lincoln and his Secretary of War asked the Adjutant General of the Army Lorenzo Thomas to remind General Harney of his foremost duties, which he did on May 27. Harney then repeatedly reminded General Price to maintain the agreement, while Price denied the reports as false rumors and said that he was maintaining the agreement. On May 29, Harney wrote to Washington with assurances that the agreement "will be carried out in good faith."[217]

Harney insisted that until the courts could decide on the constitutionality of the Military Bill, Lyon would be at the mercy of Jackson and his military.[218] Harney and the truce made Lyon powerless by forcing all Union troops to remain fettered in place. The truce pushed the limit of the federal government's trust in General Harney to keep Missouri in the Union.

Blair and Lyon had evidence enough to convince the federal government that Brigadier General William S. Harney had not adequately fulfilled his duty to enforce federal authority, nor done enough to protect Unionists around the state, or to stop secessionist activities. Two weeks earlier Frank Blair had received authority to deliver the ultimatum, if necessary, relieving Harney from duty. Blair recommended a reassignment for him, to avoid embarrassment.[219] Harney's superiors met again in Washington, D.C., and made the decision to spend no more time trying

---

216 Shalhope, 162.
217 Adams, 237–238. Harney's decision to trust Price was his "undoing." His army superiors believed it was his duty to stop the secessionists, not to negotiate on their terms. Yet, his biographer blames Harney's dismissal on the Blair family's political intrigue.
218 Rombauer, 242.
219 Adams, 237–238.

to determine Harney's intentions. It was not possible to know with certainty if he was or was not loyal to the Union. What they saw through the unknowable fog was that the Union could no longer risk the potential ominous consequences of his actions. The War Department, the president, and Blair, appreciating Harney's loyal service but concerned that he was a risk to the critical border state, relieved him. Brig. General Nathaniel Lyon was given command of the U.S. Army Department of the West.[220]

Two determining events, the failure to capture the arsenal (Camp Jackson) and the news of General Harney's dismissal, prompted Governor Jackson's request for the Planters' House Meeting. He claimed that it was an attempt at peace. His intentions were perhaps real, but the request was more likely another ploy to gain time and improved opportunity.

---

220 Adams, 237, 238; Parrish, *Turbulent Partnership*, 25–31; Reavis, 372–373; Piston and Hatcher, 41; Rombauer 246, 252; Peckham, 211–213, 222–227.

CHAPTER FOUR
CLAIBORNE FOX JACKSON

It has been my earnest endeavor under all these embarrassing circumstances to maintain the peace of the State and to avert, if possible, from our borders the desolating effects of a civil war.
—Claiborne Jackson, "Proclamation" June 12, 1861 (Appendix D)

Claiborne Jackson's biographer explains the strong influences on Jackson from his Southern identity, long political involvement, and the culture of power held by the slave owners of Boon's Lick, the area that held most of Missouri's slave-owning property owners. This Missouri River belt region is also called "Little Dixie" because the people felt closely aligned to the southern cause.[221] Claiborne was born in Kentucky in 1806 to slave-owning tobacco planters. After his brothers had left home, he helped his father in the fields and thereafter, though tall, strong, and ambitious, he never wanted to dirty his own hands with soil again.[222] In 1826, Claiborne

---

221 Phillips, 4, 30, 80, 81.
222 Phillips, *Missouri's Confederate*, 54.

followed his older brothers who had moved to Missouri. He became a merchant in the booming town of Franklin, in Howard County central to Missouri's Boon's Lick region.

People migrating from the South came to Missouri to pursue opportunity and economic independence. The white population in Boon's Lick counties contributed about sixteen percent of the state's population. It was, at the time, the state's fastest growing area with most of the state's slaveholding property owners.[223] The men in that part of the state called themselves farmers because, unlike southern planters, they grew a wider variety of crops. But these slaveowners, unlike many common farmers and homesteaders, did little of their own farm labor.[224] For these Missouri farmers slavery was no evil but a pragmatic necessity. For Boon's Lick residents, progress depended on freedom from interference and government support of slaveholding.

A "lifelong ligature" allowed Jackson to devote his time to the politics of a Southern Rights Democrat. When in 1831, 1833, and 1838, Jackson married in turn three daughters of the wealthy and well-respected Dr. John S. Sappington, his political and financial position was quickly secured. The first, Mary Sappington Jackson died of the ague. Louisa died in an accident, and before marrying Claiborne, their sister Eliza's marriage was annulled following a scandal. Jackson was elected to the Missouri State House of Representatives in 1836 and in 1842, reelected in 1846 and again in 1852.[225] There were men with extreme antagonistic ideologies in the state with no overwhelming wave of opinion, and Claiborne Fox Jackson was deeply vying to sway the tide.

Driven by the desire for wealth, status, and power, he became a player in the unofficial organization involved with policy and nomination decisions for the state's controlling Democratic party, the "Central Clique,"

---

223 Phillips, 24
224 Phillips, 38, 39, 41.
225 Phillips, 69–91.

and Jackson became their leader.[226] Although an able politician, he was never considered eloquent or of more than moderate abilities.[227] He thrived in "backroom style of governance" and crossed into dirty politics in 1840 when he published an editorial falsely accusing the Whig gubernatorial candidate of election fraud. The two parties dodged a challenge to duel.[228] Although Jackson never admitted guilt, he proved that he would do whatever was needed for public image and for party politics.

The "Little Dixie squirearchy" in Boon's Lick held a disproportionate level of political, economic, and social power, and Jackson's connections taught him lasting strategies for what was to come.[229] Jackson learned the lessons which would matter most to him: the accretion and disposal of public monies and importance of the "Clique" (secret power politics). Jackson tended to ignore certain issues, even those with potential benefits, selecting those that were sure bets to benefit Boon's Lick slaveholders. He understood how to use divisiveness as a political tool, pitting Boon's Lick landowners against elitist "business Democrats" while encouraging locals to view St. Louis as a threat to their well-being.[230]

What happened in Kansas in the 1850s did not stay in Kansas.

As Iowans and Northern citizens became increasingly enraged over the 1854 Kansas-Nebraska Act, Missourians were equally horrified to learn that they were not alone in seeking opportunity in the new territorial

---

226 Phillips, 81–82; Adams, 218; Christopher Phillips, "Claiborne Fox Jackson," *Civil War on the Western Border*, https://civilwaronthewesternborder.org. In Missouri state politics, the "Central Clique" were politicians mostly from the central Missouri river belt region and other powerful persons who instructed Missouri U.S. senators and representatives to vote for slavery and its extension. Their covert actions, often in guise of moderates, were staunchly in support of Southern rights.

227 Phillips, *Missouri's Confederate*, 82.

228 "Historic Missourians: Claiborne Fox Jackson," State Historical Society of Missouri. https://historicmissourians.shsmo.org/claiborne-fox-jackson; Phillips, *Missouri's Confederate*, 94–98.

229 Geiger, "Missouri Banks and The Civil War," 1,4.

230 Phillips, *Missouri's Confederate*, 80.

land, as if the 1854 Act had been created to benefit slaveholders. They viewed Kansas as their opportunity to expand "democratic" promise, as they understood it, and to "triumph over a...thoroughly inferior East."[231] Kansas was their neighbor and their *right*.

Missourians, like Claiborne Jackson who were supporters of U. S. Senator David Rice Atchinson, pledged to "extend the institutions of Missouri (slavery) over the territory (Kansas) at whatever sacrifice of blood and treasure."[232] Soon after Daniel Frost was elected to the Missouri Senate (1854), he helped enact a law for organizing state militia and led a brigade to Missouri's southwest border to suppress an expected invasion by angry Jayhawkers.[233] As a state senator, Claiborne Jackson was a leader of Missouri Border Ruffians who crossed the border into eastern Kansas to vote in a (phony) election of a pro-slavery Territorial Legislature.[234] He wrote in an 1855 letter, "If this is to become 'free-nigger' territory, Missouri must become so too, for we can hardly keep our negroes here now." They believed that Boston abolitionists would come steal their slaves. State's rights radicals abhorred "hessian mercenaries" who were moving into Kansas, sent by Eastern Emigrant Aid Societies "for the horrendous purpose of doing the work of others."[235] The depth of espoused hatred towards non-Southern people is remarkable.

---

231 Phillips, *Missouri's Confederate*, 197.
232 Potter, 200.
233 "Frost Family," ArchivesSpace Public Interface. https://archives.slu.edu/agents/people/341; "Daniel Marsh Frost (1823—1900)." Missouri Encyclopedia. https://missouriencyclopedia.org/people/frost-daniel-marsh. This act later culminated in the establishment of Camp Jackson where Frost served as brigadier general for the camp and planned an attack on the arsenal.
234 Adamson, 7–8; "Missouri-Kansas Border War." Missouri Encyclopedia https://missouriencyclopedia.org/events/missouri-kansas-border-war; Jason Roe, "The Contested Election of 1855," Civil War on the Western Border, https://civilwaronthewesternborder.org/blog/contested-election-1855. Most settlers in Kansas were from Illinois, Indiana, and Ohio. There were also radical abolitionists from New England. By law, voters had to be inhabitants of the new territory. Jackson, with U.S. Senator David Rice Atchison, led Missourians on March 29, 1855, to fraudulently vote for a pro-slavery territorial legislature in Kansas. Atchison is quoted as saying: "We will be compelled to shoot, burn, and hang."
235 Phillips, Missouri's Confederate, 199, 201, 204. Men on opposing sides fought in the guerilla wars, including many who held no convictions.

Senator Atchison, in a note to Jefferson Davis admitted that he was rabid and vicious, urging Missouri settlers in Kansas to hang all abolitionists without trial.[236] It seems that many Missourians were unaware of how neighboring Iowa was being settled by immigrants and migrating farmers from Ohio, Illinois, Indiana, eastern and Southern states, who were willing to do their own farm work. The secessionist-minded Missourians hated Germans for not supporting slavery and their politics, but one Missourian who settled in Kansas was equally furious about other Americans who wanted to live there without slavery. He called Kansas "the unwilling receptacle of the filth, scum, and offscourings of the East and Europe."[237] They were terrified that Kansas might become a non-slaveholding state. Although abolition societies sent people to Kansas to settle it as a free state, Missourians used secret societies and were first to openly use force in Kansas.[238] Motivated by fear and ambition, and with leaders like Jackson and Atchison, thousands of Missourians crossed the border to vote illegally, fight, or otherwise claim Kansas as theirs.

Despite the fake votes by pro-slavery Missourians, armed guerilla violence, attempts at a state dictatorship which made speaking against slavery a crime, and steady interference, a diverse group of citizens voted for a Kansas constitution without slavery.[239] Kansas was admitted to the Union as a free state on January 29, 1861, but the violence and intense hatred remained long after.

First Commissioner of Missouri Banking

Hostile political debate in Missouri had trickled into divisions between chartered banks and savings banks. Those who supported chartered

---

236 Shalhope, 110

237 Phillips, *Missouri's Confederate*, 198; Brooksher, 10; Potter, 200. Missourians committed to Senator Atchison (like Claiborne Jackson) pledged to "extend the institutions of Missouri (slavery) over the territory at whatever sacrifice of blood and treasure." Atchison, Jackson, and their followers saw it as defending their homeland against Yankee mercenaries. However they rationalized it, they tried to steal the election, and the Kansas territorial Governor Reeder let it stand.

238 McPherson, *Battle Cry of Freedom*, 290; Potter, 200.

239 Ward, *The Civil War*, 21. 5,000 proslavery Missourians seized polling places and installed a legislature.

banks often referred to the others as Austrian or Dutch, meaning abolitionists or free-soil supporters. It was also a time of little banking regulation and widespread money devaluation. In 1857, Claiborne Jackson helped craft a bill that created a state Commissioner of Missouri Banking. The Democrat-controlled Missouri General Assembly and Governor Sterling Price appointed him as its first Commissioner, with a salary of $5,000 a year.[240] Jackson then worked closely with many banking officers, elites who strongly supported the Southern cause. He soon controlled the banking resources in much of the state.[241] Jackson helped create a law which allowed for the circulation of convertible currencies. Sponsors of the bill warned the General Assembly that much depended on trustworthiness. In 1858, Jackson controlled the bank records and evidence, the General Assembly made it possible for him to use those records for punitive audits of savings banks, which he did.[242]

When Jackson resigned in the summer of 1860 to run for governor, the office went to former Governor Sterling Price who replaced him as the state's Commissioner of Banking. Later, Jackson and Price worked closely with secessionist-leaning bankers, mostly outside St. Louis, to subvert the state's banking system and support their plans for taking Missouri out of the Union. The governor and Price, with a group of senior politicians and bankers, diverted half a million dollars from banks and the state treasury to use for secession efforts. Bankers gave thousands of unsecured loans, channeled through state branch banks, to key pro-Confederate citizens who supplied local military units. If, as they expected, secession was successful, Missouri's new Confederate

---

240 Phillips, *Missouri's Confederate*, 220.
241 Mark W. Geiger, "Indebtedness and the Origins of Guerilla Violence in Civil War Missouri," *The Journal of Southern History*, 75, no. 1 (February 2009) 3–5, 10, 12. https://www.academia.edu/790703/Indebtedness_and_the_Origins_of_Guerrilla_Violence_in_Civil_War_Missouri The fraud against bank customers and investors led to massive defaults beginning in October 1861, with wealthy Confederate sympathizers liable for the bank debts; See also Mark W. Geiger, *Financial Fraud and Guerilla Violence in the Civil War 1861–1865* (New Haven: Yale University Press, 2010).
242 Geiger, 18, 39

government would repay the banks through bond sales. But Jackson's government, after abandoning its position in the state capital after the Planters' House Conference, became a government in exile and lost their war. Unfortunately for many landowners who supported the scheme, it led to widespread bankruptcies across Missouri. The collapse of the rebellion took down many landowners, wealthy planters, and bankers.[243] The banking elites and the Missouri secessionists who had supported Governor Jackson were destroyed by their politics and the war. It is unlikely that Missourians would have attributed the devastating consequences to the fraud committed by Jackson and Price, but likely blamed those who had to act on the legalities of defaulted promissory notes.

The Great Pretender

When Jackson ran for governor in 1860, he owned forty-seven bondspeople (slaves) and twelve hundred acres of land. In April, he was the state chairman of a party which strongly supported the platform that slavery could not be excluded from territories either by Congress or by territorial legislatures. Jackson was one of "the state's most dogmatic proslavery politicians" while some citizens were also taking extreme proslavery stances. Jackson's closest competitor in the campaign for governor was Sample Orr, a farmer from Greene County who advocated compromise. Jackson "haughtily" ignored Orr's challenges to debate.[244] Claiborne Jackson had made enemies, even in his own party, who, for example, said he had sold out to bank influence until he had made a fortune, while discounting the value of money for others. However, in the tide of 1860 politics, Jackson developed a brilliant strategy for winning the governorship. Jackson, a "shrewd judge" of popular mood, unified many of the divided Democrats by claiming neutrality. Although the *Jefferson Inquirer* called his speeches "glittering generalities," many vot-

---

243 Geiger, "Missouri Banks and The Civil War," 91, 93, n.14.
244 Parrish, 4.

ers believed his false claims. His biographer characterized the moment: "Almost with a wink and a nod, Claib Jackson managed to be everything to nearly everybody."[245]

Although Orr was a tenacious campaigner, he lost the August 6 election to Jackson, who won 47 percent of the popular votes. Orr, who won 42 percent of the votes, warned that if Jackson was elected: "you must prepare to withdraw from the Union, shoulder your muskets, resist the federal government, and march to victory over your brothers and friends in your sister states."[246] Three months after his win, Jackson had to face Lincoln's Presidential election. The national election did not reflect the will of the people of Missouri or of Southerners. Support for Lincoln in the South was very unlikely even if his name had appeared on ballots in the nine states where it did not.[247] Neither Jackson nor the South willingly accepted the results of the American democratic election when it did not go their way. Lincoln's election was a monumental threat for politicians like Jackson because they feared seismic change for the South.

Secession Momentum

By 1860 the South was ready to secede and had established successful tactical schemes for making it happen: deception, obstruction, covert actions, misleading news, and takeovers of federal arsenals and arms.[248] Jackson skillfully used these in his determination to become governor and take the neutral state of Missouri into the Confederacy. One important strategy was keeping key people in important government and military offices to manipulate power and resources and to hinder Union

---

245 Phillips, *Missouri's Confederate,* 80, 217, 229.
246 Ibid, 230–231.
247 Harold Holzer, "Election Day 1860" *Smithsonian Magazine,* November 2008. https://www.smithsonianmag.com/history/election-day-1860-842666751/
248 Potter, 389, 392–395.

responses.[249] This was a pervasive and effective model for obstructing Northern efforts. It would have been a difficult time for those in the federal government to know whom to trust, with people in key offices scheming behind the scenes to enable the Confederate cause.

Some Southern leaders incited state delegates into voting for secession by sending telegrams just before a convention with threatening falsehoods about northern brutalities, using fear as a technique to rally support.[250] Perhaps the greatest tactic was use of the term *coercion*, creating fear of being forced to take a position not of one's own free choice.[251] As president, Lincoln promised to maintain slavery as it existed according to the Missouri Compromise if the South would remain in the Union. But the South insisted that if the North did not agree to their demands for the extension of slavery, they would secede. And if the North should use coercion against seceded states, it would cause the war. Few Missourians seem to have understood this as a paradox. They were overwhelmingly against federal coercion of seceded states. Yet it was the federal government's only remaining option to reunify the United States, unless it agreed to Southern demands for the permanent protection and expansion of slavery. President Lincoln did not concede to the blackmail.

Governor of Missouri

By the mid-nineteenth century, immigration, territorial and agricultural expansion, industrialization, and the demand for labor were transform-

---

249 Rombauer, 163. Senator Yulee of Florida wrote that "by remaining in our (Congressional and cabinet officers') places until March 4…we can keep Mr. Buchanan's hands tied and disable the Republicans."

250 Rombauer, 162, quoting Colonel T. T. Gantt, a States' Rights Democrat speaking at the Missouri State Convention, who proudly told about a telegram falsely claiming that the federal government had sent an army to Charleston, which reported that "old men, helpless children and women were being slaughtered by the hundreds." It's unknown how often this strategy was used across the South to incite citizens to vote for secession.

251 Snead, 197; Phillips, *Missouri's Confederate,* 252. After Camp Jackson, many people joined the cause of States' rights when secessionist newspapers represented the Federal government as the coercive power.

ing the American economy and population.[252] Boon's Lick was no longer the fastest growing part of the state in a rapidly changing Missouri. By 1860, railroads, increasing interstate trade, and immigration had dramatically changed Missouri's demographics. St. Louis had become one of the fastest growing cities in the U.S. Many people in the state were increasingly national rather than regional in their outlook. The majority of Missouri citizens did not support secession, as shown by the state's voting in the 1860 state and presidential elections.[253] Appealing to the majority, Jackson successfully created his campaign with a false image of a governor committed to armed neutrality and peace.[254]

After his election, in his inaugural speech January 3, 1861, Claiborne Jackson revealed his true intent, "Missouri...will best consult her own interests...by a timely declaration of her determination to stand by her sister slave-holding states."[255] He didn't tell the people of Missouri that he was about to do everything possible to make that happen. He shortly called for a convention that would establish the state's relationship with the Union, expecting the elected delegates to vote for secession. However, Missourians overwhelming elected delegates who voted to remain in the Union. Jackson continued to do things in his own "backroom" style of power politics.[256] He had an effective network of newspapers, politicians,

---

252 McPherson, *Battle Cry for Freedom*, 6–9; Cutrer, 24–25. The central valley was losing its influence to the more industrialized counties. The fastest population growth was near St. Louis. This weakening power made alignment with the south even more important for Missouri secessionists.

253 Parrish, *Turbulent Partnership*, 5–7. Results of the national election in Missouri showed a clear trend of voting for conservatives or moderates (centrists) who were also the majority of those elected for state offices; Phillips, *Missouri's Confederate*, 183, 232; Piston and Hatcher, 91. Missouri held the smallest percentage of slaves other than Delaware. The percentage of slave-holders represented just 2.3 percent of the free population of Missouri. But the importance of slave property was part of the consciousness and wealth of many people in Boon's Lick and many believed it was threatened.

254 Phillips, *Missouri's Confederate*, 243, 248; Christopher Phillips, "Jackson, Claiborne Fox," *Civil War on the Western Border.* https://civilwaronthewesternborder.org/encyclopedia/jackson-claiborn-fox. Accessed March 21, 2022; "Claiborne Fox Jackson," *Historic Missourians.* https://historicmissourians.shsmo.org/claiborne-fox-jackson/.

255 Phillips, *Missouri's Confederate*, 235.

256 Cutrer, 27.

and people in powerful positions who worked in concert to achieve his secessionist goals. Jackson had learned from seceded states that fake news and fear were useful for embedding the notion that "northern aggression" would disrupt the Union, thereby blaming the North for the war which the secessionists were already planning.

Jackson exploited the potential of war by portraying citizens as threatened potential victims and himself as defender of the state.[257] Jackson's response to Lincoln's request for troops following the assault on Fort Sumter was intended to inflame the emotions of people, calling the president's request "inhumane, diabolical and revolutionary."[258] He exclaimed the merits of constitutional rights and legality while ignoring and trying to overthrow those which interfered with his intentions. Jackson quickly moved to push Missouri towards secession, taking control of the St. Louis Police Force and mobilizing pro-southern state militia.[259] He understood the importance of gaining support from the Missouri General Assembly to claim legality, even if he had to use the power "Clique" and secrecy. For all parties, there was little concern for intent of the law for a country under siege from within.

The governor was surprised by General Harney's May 14 Proclamation which supported Lyon's actions at Camp Jackson and expressed loyalty to the Union. Quickly, Jackson maneuvered Harney by "duping" him into the Harney-Price Truce. Jackson had no intention of honoring the agreement.[260] After Harney's dismissal, the governor and Sterling Price immediately began preparing for war. Price issued secret orders to the Brigadiers of the various state military districts to organize troops and prepare state flags. Jackson ordered military and state workshops moved to Boonville, which was close to his secessionist base of support. It was

---

257 McElroy, *The Struggle for Missouri*, 87–88; See also Ware's (107–109) and Burmeister's (06-20-1861) diary entries dealing with effects of secessionists' propaganda in northern Missouri newspapers.
258 Piston and Hatcher, 27.
259 McPherson, *Battle Cry of Freedom*, 290.
260 Phillips, *Damned Yankee*, 205.

the location of an important branch bank which held financial support for secession and was a good location for controlling Missouri River traffic in a battle.[261]

The Planters' House Showdown

Sparks of war had blown across Missouri well before the Planters' House Hotel Meeting. Governor Jackson had successfully bullied his constituents, the Missouri government, and the federal government into a paralysis of "neutrality" while stalling for time. Lyon understood this.[262] Jackson needed more time to ready for war, but a truce would have to be made with Francis Blair and General Lyon, the new commander of the U.S. Army of the West. [263] Jackson's supporters called for a conference with Lyon and Blair on June 11, 1861, at the Planter's House Hotel in St. Louis. [See Appendix C, Timeline of events preceding the June 11 Meeting.]

It is important to know details of the June 11 meeting, as readers are likely to see the oft-repeated version of "Lyon's declaration of war" published early the next day, June 12, by the editor of the secessionist *St. Louis Bulletin*, Thomas L. Snead, and reproduced in his book twenty-one years after the end of the war. Snead was at the meeting as Governor Jackson's secretary.[264] According to his account, after meeting for four or five hours, Lyon said in his slow, deliberate style:

> Rather than concede to Missouri the right to demand that my government shall not enlist troops within her limits, or bring troops into the state whenever it pleases, or move its troops at its own will into, out of, or through the State... rather than concede to Missouri for one single instant the right to dictate to my government...I would [rising and

---
261 Rombauer, 260–261; Geiger, "Missouri Banks", 91–93.
262 Rombauer, 261.
263 Shalhope, 169. Jackson was getting no troops from Jefferson Davis who did not trust Jackson because of his "devious stall" for time and other actions.
264 Phillips, *Missouri's Confederate*, 239; Piston and Hatcher, 147.

pointing] see you, and you and you, and every man, woman and child in the state dead and buried.

Then, according to Snead, Lyon turned to the governor and said: "*This means war.*" ²⁶⁵

This is the commonly reproduced version with much redacted from the long discussion.²⁶⁶ It is not a complete surprise to read such violent rhetoric, knowing that Lyon was frustrated and furious. He had used very similar language in his letters from Kansas. As early as 1855 he

---

265 Snead, 199–200. Snead did not give a full account of the long discussion and wrote that Lyon proclaimed war. Snead later served as General Price's adjutant general and chief of ordnance and became a member of the Confederate Congress.

266 Examples of sources which rely on Snead's account, in order of publication date and ending with websites: Hans Christian Adamson, *Rebellion in Missouri: 1861* (Philadelphia: Chilton Company, 1961), 113; William E. Parrish, *Turbulent Partnership: Missouri and the Union 1861–1865* (Columbia: University of Missouri Press, 1963), 51; Robert E. Shalhope, *Sterling Price: Portrait of a Southerner* (Columbia: University of Missouri Press, 1971), 165; James M. McPherson, *Battle Cry of Freedom: The Civil War Era* (New York: Oxford University Press, 1988), 292; Christopher Phillips, *Damned Yankee: The Life of General Nathaniel Lyon* (Baton Rouge: Louisiana State University Press, 1990), 214; Edwin C. Bearss, *The Battle of Wilson's Creek* (Cassville: Litho Printers and Bindery, 1992), viii; William Riley Brooksher, *Bloody Hill: The Civil War Battle of Wilson's Creek* (Washington: Brassey's, 1995), 80. The reference is attributed to McElroy who wrote, "Col. Snead has published this account" but ignores Conant's account from the same page. The author also quotes Snead's version for the title of chapter VI, "This Means War"; William G. Piston and Richard W. Hatcher, *Wilson's Creek: The Second Battle of the Civil War and the Men Who Fought It* (Chapel Hill: University of North Carolina Press, 2000), 42; Christopher Phillips, *Missouri's Confederate: Claiborne Fox Jackson and the Creation of Southern Identity in the Border West* (Columbia: University of Missouri Press, 2000), 257. This includes a reference to Peckham, in whose book there is no such declaration of war. Peckham's version (247– 248) is Conant's version; Jeffrey L. Patrick, *Campaign for Wilson's Creek* (Abilene: State House Press, 2018), 13-14, 50-51. The chapter titled "This Means War" 49, is Snead's quote; Thomas W. Cutrer, *Theatre of a Separate War: The Civil War West of the Mississippi River 1861-1865* (Chapel Hill: The University of North Carolina Press, 2017), 33; "The Battle of Wilson's Creek: The Camp Jackson Affair," *National Park Service*, nphistory.com/publication/civil_war_series/26/sec2.htm; "Planters House Hotel Meeting," *Civil War on the Western Border*, https:/civilwaronthewesternborder.org/timeline/planters-house-hotel-meeting; Kristen M. Trout, "Fallen Leaders: Brigadier General Nathaniel Lyon," *Emerging Civil War*, https://emergingcivilwar.com/2021/08/10/fallen-leaders-brigadier-general-nathaniel-lyon/; "Major Horace A. Conant and the Planter's House Hotel Meeting," *Missouri's Civil War Blog*, https://mocivilwarblog.wordpress.com/tag/horace-conant/. Oddly, this blog gives Snead's account of the meeting and not Conant's; An exception is www.civilwarstlouis, the site hosted by D. H. Rule and G. E. Rule since January 25, 2001, "to share less explored civil war research." This website provides Snead's and McElroy's accounts in "Meeting at the Planters' House," stating that McElroy gives "one of the most complete and detailed descriptions of the meeting to be found."

wrote how their (rebels) aggression would not be checked until they were taught a lesson in fire and blood. Just before leaving for St. Louis, he wrote, "I would rather see the country lighted up with flames...than that the great rights and hopes of the human race should expire before the arrogance of the secessionists."[267] Lyon was radical about preserving the Union and he was not naive. He was aggressively enlisting and training loyal troops and was well-informed about Jackson's actions.

It remains useful to know important details of the five-hour stalemate not found in Snead's account. Major Horace Conant, who attended the meeting as the secretary for Lyon and Blair, wrote his report of the meeting which appeared June 13 in *The Missouri Democrat*. Peckham's (1866), McElroy's (1909), and Rombauer's (1909) books include both Snead's and Conant's accounts.[268] Conant reported that after several hours of discussion, Sterling Price described at length how he had carried out the understanding (the May truce with Harney), having not violated it "one iota." Lyon asked how that could be, since General Harney had proclaimed the Military Bill as unconstitutional and treasonable. He produced a copy of the memorandum sent by Harney and read to Price on May 21, stating that Harney viewed Price's armed troops as antagonistic to the U.S., calculated to precipitate crises and should be suspended. General Harney also objected to the requirement that any troops not organized by the state's provisions were to be disarmed by the state, which meant the possibility of the state taking his own federal government-issued firearms.

Confronted by the evidence, Price was thrown into confusion. He reddened, saying he did not recall any such thing. He could only repeat his demand that no Union troops pass through the state or be stationed there, as it would occasion civil war. Missouri would remain neutral. Governor Jackson interjected rarely and in "parrot-like" reiterations that

---

267 Rombauer, 151, 152, letter dated January 27, 1861; See Appendix B for selections from Lyon's letters.
268 Peckham, 247–248; McElroy, *The Struggle for Missouri*, 110–113.

"U.S. troops must leave the state and not enter it. I will then disband."[269]

General Lyon gave the reasons the U.S. troops could not and would not leave the state. Lyon explained that he had no authority to overturn the rights of the federal government and said it was the duty of Union government to protect citizens, the civil process, and federal institutions. Jackson's demands would leave the state vulnerable to invasion or insurrection. Governor Jackson then asked to delay the discussion by correspondence. Lyon rejected postponement and instead asked that all participants commit their views in writing at that moment, to be published and read by the citizens. The governor and Price refused to reveal their expressed views for the press.

It was a stalemate. Lyon concluded that haggling with secessionists was an endless cycle of concession, and said:

> Governor Jackson, no man in the state has been more ardently desirous of preserving peace than myself. Heretofore Missouri has only felt the fostering care of the Federal Government…Now, however, from the failure on the part of the Chief Executive to comply with constitutional requirements, I fear she will be made to feel its power. Better sir, far better, that the blood of every man, woman and child of the State should flow than that she should successfully defy the Federal Government.[270]

Lyon made no declaration of war but used threatening words to

---

[269] Peckham, 243–247. The memo had been read to Price on May 21; McElroy, *The Struggle for Missouri*, 112. The young Union soldier who spent 15 months in Confederate prison camps observed from people in the South, their "emphatic reiteration of bald statements." John McElroy 1879, *Andersonville: A Story of Rebel Military Prisons* (Toledo: D.R. Locke, 1879); Shalhope, 164, suggests that General Price was genuinely hoping for reconciliation while Jackson was covertly stalling for time, and Lyon was too shrewd to be tricked.

[270] Peckham, 248; McElroy, *The Struggle for Missouri*, 115. Major Horace A. Conant served as Lyon's aide-de-camp at the meeting. Conant's account was published in the *Missouri Democrat* on June 13, 1861. McElroy includes both Conant's and Snead's accounts; "Meeting at the Planter's House" https://www.civilwarstlouis.com/articles/meeting-at-the-planters-house. The website presents McElroy' balanced reports, but cautions readers about his repeated use of "white trash" for Missourians. Note, however, that McElroy later in the text explains that he is referring to those "impatient" with laws who fought as bushwhackers but who would not enlist in the Missouri State Guard, which was comprised of "very excellent material" (96); See also Peckham, 243.

remind Jackson that his failure to comply with constitutional requirements and federal law would lead him to feel the full force of the power of the United States.

Perhaps, as Snead later wrote, "(Lyon) handled it in the soldierly way to which he had been bred, using the sword to cut the knots that he could not untie."²⁷¹ If Snead was correct, then Lyon unofficially declared war during the meeting, but there are key points ignored by Snead which remain neglected by historians who rely on his account.²⁷² Fuller context of the conversation casts different conclusions about the failed Planters' House Meeting.²⁷³ If Conant was correct, then Lyon used threatening language and intimated war *should* the governor *successfully* dictate power over the federal government. Important terms are missing from Snead's version. In this case, The Planter's House Meeting was another attempted "sham," and Governor Jackson proclaimed war with his long-winded declaration, which was ready for publication early the next morning, June 12.²⁷⁴ [See Appendix D]

Governor Jackson Declares War

While rushing back to Jefferson City about 2:00 a.m. and before hurriedly evacuating state government records and finances, the governor asked Thomas. L. Snead to prepare his version of the meeting and proclama-

---

271 Snead, 199.

272 Parrish, 31, 211n38. This author supports Snead's account because it "has been accepted by a majority of historians," but does not say which historians commonly accepted it, or why. He does provide a footnote informing readers that Major Conant quotes Lyon in a "slightly different way."

273 Snead failed to mention how Lyon confronted Price with the very memo delivered from Harney to Price on May 21, accompanied by a witness. Price denied by saying that he didn't remember. Some historians fail to mention that Lyon suggested writing down their views for immediate publication, which Jackson refused. Their simultaneous personal statements printed verbatim could not have easily been misconstrued. Brig. General Lyon, Commander of the U.S. Army's Department of the West, stated clearly the position of the federal government which had authority over a union state and was not willing to submit to secessionist demands to leave no troops in Missouri. The United States could not abdicate its duties to Union citizens.

274 Piston and Hatcher, 42; See Snead, 201, "Governor's Proclamation, June 12"; Peckham, 249–252; McElroy, *The Struggle for Missouri*, 118.

tion, in which Jackson openly revealed his plans to coerce Missouri into the Confederacy with the help of Confederate troops. By daybreak it was already widely distributed in the press.[275] It is possible that Jackson planned ahead for this opportunity to be the first to deliver his rendition of the meeting as soon as they left the Planters' House Meeting. His biographer admits that Jackson's Proclamation was "disingenuous," intended to convince citizens that the federal government was the aggressor.[276] It read in part, "unparalleled outrages have been inflicted on...liberties of its people by wicked and unprincipled men, professing to act under authority of the United States Government...unoffending and defenseless men, women, and children ruthlessly shot down and killed."[277] This was in keeping with the governor's portrayal of "Lyon the murderer" after the Camp Jackson event.[278] It was how Fire-Eating extremists, like Jackson, used misleading rhetoric to manipulate opinions.

Lyon had ordered safe passage for Jackson's and Price's return to Jefferson City and had no troops awaiting or following them. The day after the Planters' House meeting, Lyon read Snead's newspaper account with the governor's declaration of war and claims that Jackson had agreed to all of Lyon's humiliating requests. He learned that Jackson and Price ordered the burning of railroad bridges and telegraph lines after Lyon had ordered the promise of safety from arrest.[279] Lyon explained to his superiors the immediate threats to the fragile Union state. Then he acted

---

275 Phillips, *Missouri's Confederate*, 258, 260; Snead 201. State officers had packed documents for a quick evacuation.

276 Phillips, *Missouri's Confederate*, 258.

277 Peckham, 249–252. Peckham reproduced the Governor's lengthy Proclamation as it appeared in newspapers across the state. It included inflammatory phrases such as "armed bands of lawless invaders" and "they intend to exert their whole power to subjugate you... the military despotism which has usurped the powers of the federal government;" See Appendix D for Jackson's June 12 Proclamation.

278 Phillips, *Missouri's Confederate*, 256.

279 Peckham quoting from Lyon's letter sent before the June 11 Conference, 244, "They shall be free from molestation or arrest on account of any charges pending against them on the part of the United States;" Phillips *Missouri's Confederate*, 255, 253. "No federal troops moved from St. Louis toward Jefferson City." Jackson ordered the State Guard to, if necessary, burn the railroad bridges over the Gasconade and Osage Rivers in anticipation of a federal advance.

swiftly and decisively, making his actions as clear as Ozark streams. Aware and worried about the governor's earlier requests for assistance from Confederate troops in Arkansas, Lyon had made a plan to send troops to southwest Missouri in the event of an outright secessionist rebellion. He had not yet acted on those plans but did so after Jackson's Proclamation. Lyon had command over St. Louis, ordered the First and Second Infantries from Iowa into Missouri to control the state's northern railroads, and on June 13 left to fight the enemy. Lyon didn't need to repair the burned railroad bridges; he went after Jackson and Price on the Missouri River.

In May, before the Planters' House Meeting, Lieutenant Governor Reynolds and Jackson's secret emissary, Edward C. Cabell, made trips to Richmond asking for assistance. Jefferson Davis had agreed to send Confederate arms to the governor for a Camp Jackson assault on the arsenal, but he did not agree to send the troops requested by Jackson because the state had not voted for secession.[280] In early June, Jackson sent Captain Colton Greene to Confederate General Benjamin McCulloch with an urgent request that he advance from Arkansas into Missouri.[281] Soon after Harney's removal from office, Jackson had ordered state military commanders and arms moved to Boonville. Boonville had the advantage of being in central Boon's Lick where Jackson could be supported. His appointed General John B. Clark was already there when the governor arrived.[282] Governor Jackson's flight to Boonville was preplanned, not forced.

After removing state currency and records on June 12, the governor and state officials immediately abandoned their offices. There were no Union troops in Jefferson City, nor were there any Union troops yet

---

280 Phillips, *Missouri's Confederate*, 255 n.18, 264.
281 Snead, 230. Greene arrived June 13.
282 Phillips, *Missouri's Confederate*, 260; Snead, 201; James Denny and John Bradbury, *The Civil War's First Blood: Missouri, 1854–1861* (Boonville: Missouri Life, Inc., 2007), 29. Boonville had the advantage of being in central Boon's lick where Jackson could be supported. Brooksher, 81, 82. Jackson and Price were "expecting Lyon to be in hot pursuit." Jackson's Proclamation "removed any chance of avoiding armed conflict."

on their way. Governor Claiborne Jackson and General Sterling Price quickly fled upriver on the *White Cloud*, arriving in Boonville June 13, the day Lyon left St. Louis. They were not forced into exile. Given Jackson's plans and actions, it is hard to justify the claim that "Nathaniel Lyon was responsible for driving Governor Claiborne Fox Jackson and his followers into exile. Thereby he brought civil war to Missouri."[283]

Lyon's boats arrived at the deserted capitol in Jefferson City June 15, then left for Boonville where the governor and his troops were waiting for him. They skirmished on June 17. The governor watched the fighting from a distant hill. Price, struck by dysentery, left for Lexington, a rallying point for rebel troops and the location of another important state branch bank. Counting on their Confederate alliance, Jackson and Price and many of the state's elected officeholders rode southwest to organize volunteers and meet with Confederate officials in Arkansas.[284] The Missouri capitol and state government had been abandoned and lacked executives to supervise state operations.

By late July, citizens who were loyal to the Union continued to predominate in Missouri. The state convention of elected delegates which the governor had earlier called in hopes they would vote on secession, had agreed to reconvene in case of an emergency. Although "scarcely legitimate," the provisional government was comprised of the delegates fairly elected from Missouri senatorial districts, and was the immediately available group which represented the people of Missouri.[285] The delegates deposed Governor Jackson, appointed themselves the provisional government with a new governor, nullified the militia law, and called for an official statewide election to be held later.

---

283 Parrish, 16.
284 Snead, 216.
285 Parrish, *Turbulent Partnership*, 33. A majority of citizens wanted to remain neutral. Secession extremists, like Jackson, Reynolds, and Price, were a minority. To Jackson's dismay, the convention delegates met as the only state-wide duly elected persons who could quickly fill the necessary offices of the state government after their (self-imposed) exile.

Lyon's official declaration was a response to the governor's Proclamation and was not ready for publication until June 18, written after skirmishing with Jackson's troops at Boonville. He addressed the many false accusations made in Jackson's Proclamation and gave a promise of safety for citizens and prisoners who would not oppose the federal government.[286] [Appendix E]

The small, red-headed Union General and the tall, wealthy, and powerful secessionist governor had dumped fuel on Missouri tinder. Claiborne Jackson was an able and experienced politician. He was adept at strategies and action plans, able to make decisions and employ resources. He relied on other "Fire-Eaters" whose unrestrictive make-up, like his own, made them appear stronger in numbers than they were. Jackson successfully used legislative acts, a secret power clique, bank financing, state and private monies to support his mission to secede. He was assisted by ex-Governor Sterling Price who, in his role as Banking Commissioner of Missouri, helped finance Jackson's plans. Jackson and Price skillfully pursued their personal ambitions and goals even though a minority of Missourians favored secession. [287] Jackson was the only governor to declare secession without legal authority from a state delegation.

After the Battle of Wilson's Creek, Jackson and General Price did not give up fighting for their cause until they were defeated at the Battle of Pea Ridge, Arkansas (March 7, 1862). Then, with a group of other wealthy Missouri secessionists in Little Rock, Arkansas, Jackson continued to recruit Confederate troops and campaign for financial support. The governor in exile also travelled to Richmond to meet with Jefferson Davis and ask for support and recognition of Missouri as a Confederate state. Although Jackson and a few loyal supporters on November 28, 1861, proclaimed that Missouri was a Confederate State, it was never officially recognized by the Confederacy or the Union because secession-

---

286 Peckham, 274–275.
287 Potter, 105. A majority of southerners believed disunion was disloyal.

ists did not control the state.[288] Governor Jackson's story demonstrates how he attempted to lead Missouri into secession by "minority coercion." His actions earned him "lasting acclaim or scorn–for his brief, yet show-stopping performance."[289] Claiborne Fox Jackson died December 7, 1862, of pneumonia related to cancer and tuberculosis.[290]

On June 13, 1861, the First Iowa Infantry left its Keokuk training camp and loaded onto a steamboat headed for Hannibal, Missouri. The Iowa soldiers knew little about the remarkable events which had taken place in St. Louis, but were united in having an enemy to target: Governor Claiborne Jackson. The boys were anxious to learn about Nathaniel Lyon, the Brigadier General who had ordered them into Missouri, and they readied for battles that might be ahead.

---

[288] "Claiborne Jackson, 1861", Office of Governor, Record Group 3.15, Missouri State Archives, Jefferson City. Retrieved online 8/25/2021.
[289] Phillips, *Missouri's Confederate*, ix. Jackson was the "focal point for a movement for secession in the neutral state before a federal sortie exiled him from office."
[290] Phillips, *Missouri's Confederate*, 272–273.

PART III

THE FIRST IOWA INFANTRY IN LYON'S MISSOURI CAMPAIGN

CHAPTER FIVE
JUNE 14 TO JULY 3, 1861

Missouri, Land of Misery and Long Miles
—Reminiscences of The Thirteenth Regiment Illinois
Volunteer Infantry

When the First Iowa soldiers entered the war, they fought in a fiercely divided Union slave state, the source of much strife and buzz in the summer of 1861. The soldiers had little awareness of the events which had preceded General Lyon's orders for them to come to Missouri, nor were they prepared to meet the fierce secessionist anger awaiting them. Believing they were there to guard Missouri railroads, but after learning about Governor Jackson's Proclamation, Frank Wilkie warned people back home that it would likely throw Missouri into civil war.[291]

General Lyon, from his camp near Boonville, received news that Colonel Samuel Curtis and the Second Iowa Infantry had arrived in St. Joseph and were stationed along the railroad line where rebels in northwest Missouri were bushwhacking. Lyon sent a telegram from Hermann, Missouri, to Colonel Harding, his appointed adjutant general,

---
291 Banasik (Wilkie), 63.

requesting Colonel Bates at Keokuk to come to Hannibal, then down the North Missouri Railroad to Renick, where he would find a party of secessionists at Arrow Rock.[292] But Bates and the First Iowa Infantry had already landed in Hannibal, expecting to guard railroads.

Eugene Ware details their arrival in Missouri, June 14. They reached Hannibal in the dark of the night, "a straggling, struggling, western, wooden Missouri town," and stood on the street waiting for orders. Nobody seemed to know what they were doing. The officers were gone, and the soldiers had to take care of themselves. Eugene writes that the "mudsills" slept on the street with no supper. He knew that the South Carolina Senator Hammond's term was meant as an insult to laborers, but the northern working men proudly adopted the name knowing that mud-sills, the lowest timbers of a mill's foundation, were usually made of black walnut that could resist the actions of mud and water.[293]

Railroad Guard Duty

Six companies, A, B, D, E, F, G, of the First Infantry were sent over the Hannibal and St. Joseph line to take possession of bridges, capture the most unbridled secessionists, and protect the Union supporters and Macon City, an important junction of the two largest railways in Missouri. [294] Secessionists had burned bridges, torn up tracks south of Renick, and taken command of one of the engines needed to proceed.[295]

---

292 James Peckham, 255–256; In July, Price issued orders for the destruction of the North Missouri RR and nearly succeeded, destroying 100 miles of bridges, damaging stations, cars, and engines, and burning fuel supplies. "About the Wabash Railroad," *Wabash Railroad Historical Society*, http://www.wabashrhs.org/p/wabash-railroad.html.

293 Ware, 33, 107. In 1858, South Carolina Senator James. H. Hammond called working people "mudsills," meaning that the North had become a manufacturing community where progress depended on its skilled laborers which were like the lowest timbers of a mill's foundation.

294 Banasik (Wilkie), 64n109. The town was at the junction of the North Missouri Railroad and the St. Joseph and Hannibal Railroad; En.wikipedia.org/wiki/Macon_Missouri. The post office there was named Macon City in 1856. The name was changed to Macon in May 1898.

295 Banasik (Wilkie), 63, 69.

A second engine had been crippled, but was repaired by Corporal Bill Company E.[296]

Palmyra, with its one-hundred foot long South River Bridge, was another hotbed of secession. Burmeister's Company K was ordered to protect the bridge which was about thirteen miles from Hannibal. After they arrived, strangers thronged through their camp and told them to expect an attack. That night George meditated deeply about what strange changes come into a person's life.[297] Eugene said his company loaded onto livestock cars for Macon City, where they heard about five hundred enemy infantry and two hundred cavalry were camped nearby. They soon learned that every rumored estimate of nearby enemy involved about five hundred infantry and two hundred cavalry.[298] The boys didn't know if such information was rumor, misinformation used to deter them, or truth. They also learned that citizens believed the rebels who told them that Union soldiers would burn and demolish everything.[299] There was a steady stream of horsemen riding south. Southern sympathizers dominated northern Missouri sentiment and they were "bloodthirsty." Every train car was fired into, and bridges, like open train cars, became shooting targets for the secesh. Every afternoon soldiers were sent out in squads to guard bridges overnight. Every night shots were fired at the bridge guards.[300] For the first time the Iowa soldiers felt surrounded by danger and would share the unspoken sensation of fear throughout their remaining time in Missouri.

Both Burmeister and Ware described soldiers giving speeches as they traveled through Missouri. Orators emerged from the regiment and would take any opportunity to give a "red-hot, spread-eagle Union speech." "We were both missionaries and musketeers...When we captured a man, we

---

296 Ware, 119. William J. Fuller was Third Corporal in Burlington Company E.
297 Burmeister, 06-15 to 06-16-1861.
298 Ware, 108, 121.
299 Burmeister, 06-18-1861.
300 Ware, 119, 123.

nearly talked him to death."[301] It isn't clear whether troops were ordered to counter Jackson's propaganda, or whether the soldiers just took on the task of patriotic conversion. Giving and hearing the speeches would have reinforced their own principles of duty and loyalty to the Union. Ware seemed proud of their oratorical abilities: "It was musketry and discussion, cold lead and controversy."[302] The maturing boys shared hatred of the enemy. Even mutual frustrations were unifying forces.

Early in the war, the Lincoln administration was fearful of angering those Union supporters who were slave holders. At this time, the summer of 1861, President Lincoln and most Northerners were willing to let slavery continue in the southern states but were strongly against its extension. In spite of constant pressure by radical abolitionists to free slaves and punish secessionists, there was no emancipation policy and no intent, yet, to free the slaves.[303] Lyon ordered his troops not to steal property or shelter slaves. Burmeister explained, "Our regiment does not give them (negroes who want to join the camp) any inducement else hundreds would willingly join us, but such a policy would be our injury."[304] The Iowans also knew well the hated Fugitive Slave Act. They also had to turn away many Unionists who feared for their lives and wanted safety in Union camps. The Iowa soldiers were often confused about the many army regulations and the hostile environment which surrounded them. If the thoughts and actions of individuals are situated in particular, fathomable contexts, then the ambiguous, uncertain rumor buzz in Missouri influenced the soldiers' comprehension of why, what,

---

301 Ware, 107–109, 119.
302 Ware, 108.
303 Walter Barlow Stevens, 10(2); "On This Day," National Constitution Center , https://constituioncenter.org/blog/on-this-day-lincolns-emancipation-proclamation-changes-history/. Laws at the time were unclear about what could or should be done with slaves of disloyal citizens in loyal states, until later the following year, September 22, 1862, when Lincoln announced a plan for emancipation unless the South rejoined the Union. He followed with the Emancipation Proclamation on January 1, 1863.
304 Burmeister, 06-20-1861.

and where, with potential disorder.[305]

Meanwhile, the Iowa soldiers heard rumors (often false) about Lyon's actions in Missouri and were excited to join him: "Every ten minutes there is some story going round about a battle or an army of rebels...and it is impossible to find out the truth about anything."[306] The Iowa soldiers despised Missouri secessionists and were determined to keep their neighboring state in the Union. George showed surprise at the reciprocal anger of Missouri secessionists, unaware perhaps that most of the state's slaves were being used to develop and plant new tillable land in northern Missouri, where many Missourians were loyal to Governor Jackson. They saw groups of recruits on horseback, going to join General Price.[307] Local secessionists were determined to maintain their right to own slaves and falsely believed that the Union soldiers were there to free the slaves. They were hostile. Jacob Ritner described how locals thought they were there to steal everything, free the Negroes, and ravish the women: "And they had always heard in advance that we had done so at the last town." The Macon City newspaper, *The Missouri Register,* was "bombastic" and inflamed hatred toward Union supporters claiming that any Yankee's blood would flow if he came onto Missouri soil.[308] Eugene characterized the Missouri "Fire eaters" as great rebel-and-rabble rousers who were "windy, bitter, and extreme," and of no military use. The Iowa soldiers were threatened and afraid, jeered and hissed at, and sometimes shot at, by people who didn't want them around.

---

305 See Gary Alan Fine, "The Sociology of the Local", 355–376.
306 Larimer, 47.
307 Ware, 122.
308 Ware, 115, 116; Larimer, 35; Banasik (Wilkie), 67,72. Wilkie reported on the propaganda: they said that we came here to "steal their niggers [derogatory term used by racists for Black Americans], hang the men, and ravish the women...[break up] all the stores and private houses...The mightiest blow secession could receive in this state, would be simply to disabuse the minds of the masses."

"The Happy Land of Canaan"

Perhaps to buffer fear, the soldiers of the First liked to sing. While in Macon, the boys learned a tune from a Dubuque soldier, the "tempestuously musical" so-called French Jo. In his version, "The Happy Land of Canaan" was a folk lore ballad about the late abolitionist John Brown. Jo woke up everybody and taught them the song. The metre was broken and awkward, but it was catchy and easy for the boys to add new verses. "From that night it became our regimental song, and we sang it on long and weary marches and when the stars were shining and when the enemy was in view."[309]

>Oh, the Iowa First, are the boys that dare the worst;
>And on the rebels they are slowly gaining.
>If they'll fight instead of run,
>We will show them lots of fun:
>And they'll never see the Happy Land of Canaan.
>
>We love our country wide, And its banner is our pride-
>We pledge our lives and fortunes to sustain 'em.
>If we perish in the cause
>Of the Union and its laws,
>We are sure to reach the Happy Land of Canaan.
>
>Chorus
>O-ho. O-ho. O-ho.
>A-ha. A-ha. A-ha.
>The time of retribution am a-coming;
>For with bayonet and shell

---

[309] Ware, 113–114; Ben Gray Lumpkin, "'The Happy Land of Canaan': An Unpublished Civil War Song." *Civil War History*, 11:1, 1965, 44. Published versions of the song were common during the late 1850's. It was composed and sung in many variations and was adapted by soldiers to fit Civil War situations; Banasik (Wilkie), 375. The First Iowa soldiers created many new verses. The editor includes various verses, 375–376.

We will give the rebels hell:

And they'll never see the Happy Land of Canaan.[310]

The troops were constantly expecting attacks from the surrounding secessionists. They never knew what to expect from the many strangers who came through camp or from the towns they entered. Rumors were abundant, some frightening, some inspiring. Soldiers were often unsure of their immediate purpose.

George summed up the regiment's time in Missouri, describing how they immediately encountered hostile reactions to their presence. Propaganda had informed Missourians that union soldiers would do them harm by burning, looting, and stealing. Missouri citizens who were Union supporters had been harassed and threatened by secessionists.[311] On June 18, the First Iowa regiment took the train from Macon south to Renick.[312] As William Branson put it, we "left for we know not where on the Northern Missouri RR."[313]

Meanwhile, General Lyon had followed Jackson to Boonville and won a small battle there on June 17, before going into camp. General Price and Governor Jackson rode south.[314] On June 18, Lyon received word from the War Department that Missouri had been placed under the jurisdiction of the Army's Department of Ohio. Lyon promptly acknowledged the command of Brigadier General George B. McClellan.[315] However, McClellan, who was focused on battle conditions in the East and knew little about Missouri, informed Lyon, "Carry out such views in Missouri

---

[310] Ware, 199–200; Piston and Hatcher, 51. Some of the verses were racist, but it isn't clear that those verses were attributed to the First Iowa or to some other regiment that was singing "Land of Canaan."

[311] Burmeister, 06-13 to 06-18-1861.

[312] Banasik (Wilkie), 74.

[313] William Branson Diary, 06-18-1861, William was from West Liberty, enlisted with Muscatine Company C. *Roster and Record*, 1:15.

[314] Piston and Hatcher, 78; The battle was a skirmish where Lyon's 1700 troops easily routed 450 Missouri State Guard. Scott et. al., The estimated numbers of soldiers on each side vary widely.; See also Mark Hudziak, "The Battle of Boonville, Missouri, June 17, 1861," *The Iron Brigader*. https://ironbrigader.com/2018/10/26/the-battle-of-boonville-missouri-june-17-1861/ Retrieved 5/16/2020.

[315] Peckham, 279.

as seem most advantageous, very much as if you were in charge of a separate department."[316]

On June 18, Lyon ordered Colonel Bates and the First Iowa Infantry to leave railroad guard duty at Macon City and join his troops in Boonville. Bates responded, but his message to Lyon never arrived. When two Iowa soldiers with short-clipped hair were foraging in the woods and found some still-wet laundry, "Big Baldy" and "Little Baldy" found several dispatches sent by Colonel Bates in response to Lyon's orders. Bates's messenger had probably been killed.[317] Bates no longer wondered why Lyon had sent no confirmation. General Lyon expressed great concern in a June 18 letter to Col. Harding at the St. Louis Arsenal. He hoped that Iowa troops were in the area, but had not heard from them and added, "My suspense is now painful." He also noted regret that his proclamation had not been published promptly so that he could have distributed it in the region.[318]

On June 19, ten companies of the First Iowa Infantry began the first of the long, hot marches on few rations that would become trademarks of their Civil War experiences in Missouri. Their uniforms were already ragged.[319] Eugene drew a map of their route for his memoir. They were happy not to be stuck guarding the railroads for the rest of the summer; they would instead be with Lyon, the scrapper.

George heard rumors that Lyon's troops routed four thousand State Guard troops in the Boonville battle and captured cannons, steamboats, and provisions. Eugene overheard camp talk about Boonville where Lyon's men charged and fought, fired, and loaded, lying on the ground. He was excited to hear about fighting on the ground, because that was

---

[316] Phillips, *Damned Yankee*, 224; Peckham, 265.
[317] Ware, 124. Eugene described the boys as looking much alike with very short, scissor-cropped hair.
[318] *OR*, Serial 3:385, X. Peckham, 276. In a June 18, 1861, letter to Col. Harding at the St. Louis Arsenal, Lyon noted how the local people had been told that the Union soldiers would do them great violence and harm.
[319] Ware, 117.

JUNE 14 TO JULY 3, 1861

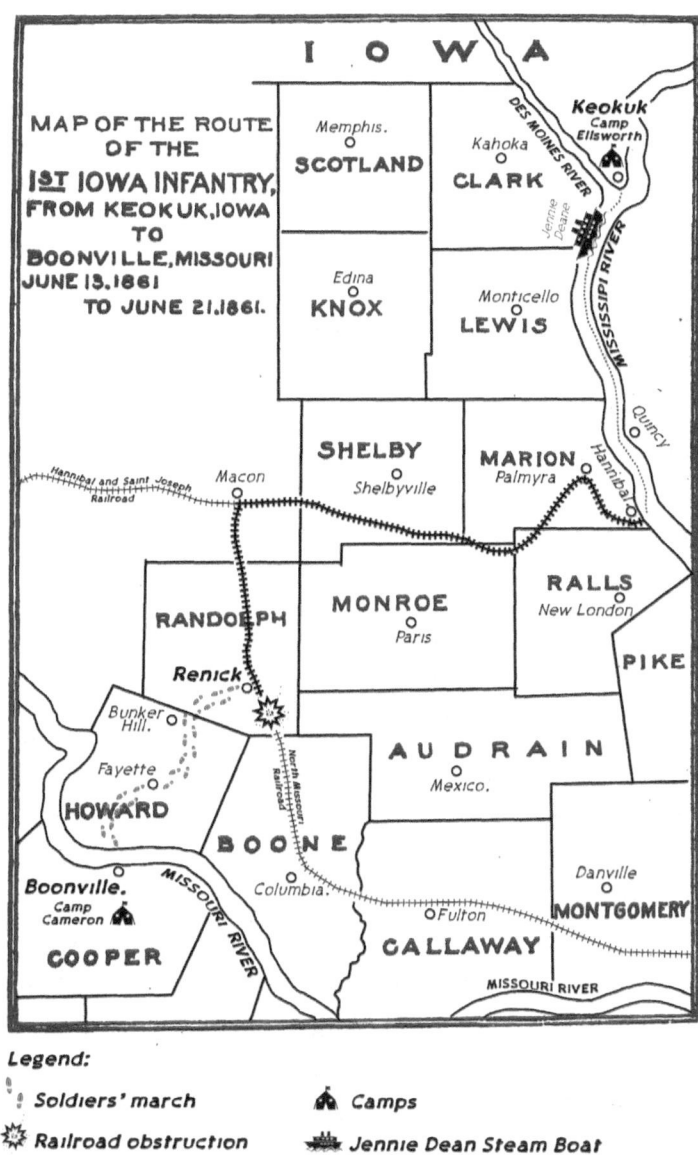

Map of the Route of the 1st Iowa Infantry from Keokuk, Iowa to Boonville, Missouri June 13, 1861, to June 21, 1861. Eugene Ware, *The Lyon Campaign in Missouri: Being a History of the First Iowa Infantry, 1861*. 1907. (Iowa City: Camp Pope Bookshop, 1991). Icons and Legends added by Shila de Morais, 2021.

Company E's strong suit. "We had worn out our uniforms at it, rolling on the ground...But we also heard that Lyon was trapped. The rebels said we could not reach him without a fight." [320] Other (false) gossip told how Lyon had lost the battle and returned to St. Louis.

George describes how the First Iowa regiment left Renick on foot, wading through creeks, sleeping on roads or sometimes under bushes in beds of water. Food supplies were empty. Some soldiers complained, but they were anxious to face the enemy.

> Very early this morning our regt. pursued its march toward Boonville, our company acted as rear guard in the forenoon...[I] stood guard in place of one of my comrades, who was unable to stand as sentinel. The negroes are in our favor, and ridicule their masters exceedingly, on account of their cowardice.[321]

George comments on the lushness of the surrounding vegetation and grain crops ready for the reaper, while the men had scarcely enough food to eat.

Eugene had rear guard duty on the fourteen-mile march from Renick to Bunker Hill, which made him vulnerable. It was the most dangerous place when marching. As he arrived at camp, "There was never a more exhausted mudsill."[322] Jacob Ritner wrote to Emeline, "We passed only one stream of running water on the route, and slept in the open air with our arms and clothes all on, as it was reported...that the rebels were gathering to meet us."[323] On June 20 soldiers in the First were called out at 2 am to resume their march. Although surrounded by double their numbers, the enemy was poorly organized and could not get an advantage. After several more hours of marching the Iowa soldiers heard a loud cheer from the advance guard announcing they had reached the Missouri River.[324]

---

320 Ware, 123–124.
321 Burmeister, 06-20-1861.
322 Ware, 125.
323 Larimer, 35.
324 Banasik (Wilkie), 85.

JUNE 14 TO JULY 3, 1861

Through the Spotting Glass General Lyon meets the First Iowa, and they meet him

Eugene described how they could see tents across the river when a ferry-boat came. There were two men alone watching the boat cross over:

> One had blue army pants, a linen coat and a black felt hat; it was Lyon. The other was dressed in citizen's clothes with an army cap [Frank P. Blair]...he watched us and turned up his face ever and anon to talk with Lyon, who was gazing at us through a field-glass.[325]

Colonel Bates and the First Iowa had marched fifty-eight miles in less than two and a half days. They landed on the other side of the Missouri River on June 21.

> Lyon looked us over and we went onboard of a big steamboat, as a temporary camp-ground...At night a strange rumor went around...that Lyon had "cussed" our colonel black and blue [for having] marched raw troops like that.[326]

Boonville was where Nathaniel Lyon first measured up the First Iowa soldiers, and they him. He ordered the regiment to stay on steamboats for three days before they went into Camp Cameron on June 24. If it's true that Lyon cursed Colonel Bates for marching the First too hard as reported by Ware, we can conclude two things. Lyon was shocked at what he saw through his field glass that day from the banks of the Missouri River. Nevertheless, he stored a piece of information that he soon used: these Iowa troops could march hard and fast for a very long distance.

From the soldiers' point of view, Lyon didn't look much like what they expected from a West Point graduate, a seasoned Army officer, or the hero of Camp Jackson and Boonville. They had heard he was aggressive,

---

325 Ware, 127–128; According to Ingersoll (22), Lyon put the First Iowa on steamers in case he needed to call them up for a fight at a moment's notice.
326 Ware, 128–129.

but saw that he was small and didn't wear a uniform. It's unclear what more the boys actually knew about Lyon. They might not have known that he was quick-tempered and rash, had rigid notions of right and wrong, or that his temper and tendency to employ harsh punishment for ill-behaved soldiers had caused trouble with his superior officers more than once.[327] Wilkie described his first impressions: [Lyon's eyes] "look as if something is constantly going wrong or different from his wishes." Lyon smiled little or not at all and asked questions in a harsh voice. "You think he is preparing to find serious fault." [328]

When Eugene and George joined Lyon's troops, they were part of a bigger unit, a brigade (commonly four regiments commanded by a brigadier general). Brig. General Lyon's brigade included the First Missouri Infantry under Colonel Blair; Second Missouri Infantry under Colonel Henry Boernstein; James Totten's Battery, 2nd U.S. Artillery; and Company B, the Second U.S. Infantry Regulars who had gone with Captain Lyon to St. Louis from Fort Riley, Kansas. There were also two hundred Regular Army recruits, and the First Iowa Infantry under Colonel John F. Bates. General Lyon sent a report to McClellan, his new commander, about Jackson's Proclamation and their engagement at Boonville, adding "The rumor which has been so long prevalent in regard to the contemplated movement from Arkansas under Ben. McCulloch... is no longer to be doubted."[329]

Eugene Ware shared his experiences on the steamboat: "At night... bushwhacking secesh wanted to try their rifles from long range on the (eleven) brilliantly lighted steamboats."[330] The boys were not allowed off the boat so spent their time washing and mending, writing letters, and mastering poker. Eugene described several of the boys with endearing details. Henry O'Connor of Muscatine Company A, forty years old and

---

327 Phillips, *Damned Yankee*, 37–39.
328 Banasik (Wilkie), 99.
329 *OR* Serial 3:11 X. Lyon, from Camp Cameron to McClellan, June 22, 1861.
330 Ware, 130.

an experienced politician, was their best speaker. "He was like an old flintlock—he required 'priming' before he would to go off."[331] Bill Heustis was a twenty-year-old "veal" enlistee, living in Des Moines County but born in Virginia.[332] He was the wit: "tall, lean...and good-natured as a colt...He talked little but when he spoke he said something."[333] Charley Stypes was a twenty-three-year-old German-born boy from Des Moines County.[334] "He could play accordion for forty-eight hours...he could play an accompaniment, a mocking-bird, a steamboat whistle, or a roll of thunder." William F. Brandebury, twenty-six, born in Pennsylvania, was the "boss" ballad-singer of the regiment. Fletch had a beautiful voice and learned every song that was sung. He sang ballads like "Old Black Jo," "Camptown Races," and "Ellen Baye." "We listened with rapture."[335] Not all nicknamed comrades were beloved. The soldiers called Joseph O. Shannon, first corporal of Company E, "Corporal Churubusco" because he bragged much about the Mexican War. Their time together convinced Eugene that the corporal was a better braggart than soldier.

The steamboats could be run up and down the Missouri River during the day. The three days together in close quarters on the boats and after, in Camp Cameron, was an important time for building company community. After three days on the boat, soldiers in the First Iowa infantry left for shore to pitch tents with Lyon's other troops.[336] The officers were busy buying and fencing-in mules. Breaking them in entertained the soldiers, it was like a big circus:

> Here we learned an interesting fact in the natural history of the Missouri Army mule...the mule wanted to bray at precisely twelve o'clock at night...At our regimental headquarters was a covered farm wagon with a team of

---

[331] Ware, 109.
[332] *Roster and Records*, 1:12–88, Company E.
[333] Ware, 116.
[334] *Roster and Records*, 1:12–88, Company E.
[335] Ware, 106, 131.
[336] Ware, 131.

strong Missouri mules. At midnight one of them in the dark silence would send off a loud, self-conceited, egotistical bray. It would be taken up here and there until the camp was in a perfect uproar…How they could come so near guessing midnight was a puzzle to us.[337]

Wilkie described the general for Iowans back home, noting how Lyon gave the impression that he didn't like them:

He is…some five feet eight inches in height, and weighs perhaps one hundred forty to one hundred and fifty pounds… His eyes are his most remarkable feature, either blue or gray, at times perhaps both. A sort of stormy expression…dwells constantly in them…[He] is a strict disciplinarian, has the full confidence of his men, among whom, or at least among the Regulars, he is known as "Daddy…" I don't think he has anything like physical fear.[338]

As soon as they arrived in camp at Boonville, George went to town and hired a Swiss woman to bake pies to share with his friends. He wrote about food, living conditions, and Lyon. Their rations consisted of water, crackers, bacon and coffee. George took a bath in the "big muddy" and came out pretty yellow. The atmosphere on the boat was so foul that George welcomed the fresh air as they went into camp. A few companies returned from trying to find Jackson, but nobody knew where he was. "[My objection to] Lyon is that he entirely too lenient to…secessionist prisoners, one of which…boldly declared his rebels principles before the Gen told him to go home and mind his business as a loyal citizen of the U.S."[339]

The Regulars (soldiers in the permanent U.S. military forces) from St. Louis were finely outfitted with striking U.S. uniforms and sparkling

---

337 Ware, 132–133.
338 Banasik (Wilkie), 99.
339 Burmeister, 06-22 to 06-25-1861; Banasik (Wilkie), 70–72. Wilkie confirms Lyon's "soft" treatment of secessionist prisoners.

rifles. The Iowa soldiers now felt embarrassed by their mismatched shabby outfits and outdated flintlock muskets. Wilkie, too, expressed shame in his June 22 report.[340] He described the Iowans as looking like an army of scarecrows: "You ought to see crows, buzzards, rabbits, and, everything else with legs and wings 'get up and git' the very instant an Iowa man comes in sight." [341] Soldiers in the First Iowa thought that the Regular soldiers were fed better than the volunteers. Ware and Wilkie mentioned hearing camp jokes made about the scruffy First Iowa volunteers. The jokes caused friction.

The regiments mostly kept to themselves and had doubts about the others. Eugene wrote how the Iowa regiment boys were all about alike:

> They did not want to go home without a fight. There became the greatest fraternity among them. We did not associate much with the other soldiers...The latter had come from St. Louis, the source of supply...Where we beat them was on drill and fiber.[342]

He commented on drilling, Lyon's need for transportation, outdated muskets, and getting paid. Eugene says they drilled in the mornings and skirmish-drilled in the afternoons, while carrying their canteens and haversacks. All the other troops and even the quartermaster were also drilling.

Lyon was working as hard and fast as possible to organize a transportation train, while it seemed that the secessionists were impressing wagons and mules from willing people.[343] The government wagons were big and heavy, drawn by six mules each. They were hitched up and hauled around for practice. On June 26, the soldiers' cartridge boxes were inspected, and each soldier was supplied with forty rounds. "The

---

340 Banasik (Wilkie), 85.
341 Banasik (Wilkie), 113.
342 Ware, 157.
343 Ware, 133–134.

(musket) ball was somewhat errant in flight, but if it hit a man at the distance of a mile it paralyzed him. The shooter had time to recover from the 'kick' by the time he had got the gun reloaded."

On the same day the regiment was paid by Capt. Chambers for its State service prior to being mustered in. Ware received $9.15. "My government ought to have furnished it, but my government was having a mighty tough time of it just then...The rebels had got the first and best of everything."[344] They received their delayed state pay while in Boonville, but it seems that neither George or Eugene had any information about how the money had arrived. It was quite a heroic feat accomplished by two bankers, Ezekial Clark from Iowa City and Hiram Price from Davenport. Ware simply noted that he bought a new overshirt, and Burmeister recorded, "The 1st Regt...received their money for state services, I received seven dollars, this cheers us up."[345] The pay was valuable to Eugene and George, allowing them to buy a few things to wear or eat. Late that night the camp was "boiling over" with jokes, music, and dancing.[346] Information about how the money got to them would not have been readily available to the troops unless Hiram Price, who personally handed the money over to Colonel Bates, had stayed around to tell the story to the officers or soldiers. But it's likely that Mr. Price wanted out of there as quickly as possible. His partner had earlier left for New York, leaving him alone to find his way safely back to Iowa through rebel territory.[347]

Eugene was proud that the Regulars had noticed their skirmish drill, said to be the best of any of the troops. When the boys from Company E came in from drill on June 29, the Regulars cheered, and the town citizens asked them to give an exhibition drill. After their drill ended, their captain was drunk. The boys in Company E were not happy. They disrespected Captain

---

344 Ware 135–137.
345 Burmeister, 06-26-1861.
346 Banasik (Wilkie), 95.
347 Hiram Price, "Paying the First Iowa," *Palimpsest* 3 (February 1922): 63; Lyftogt, 187, 188.

Streaper's drinking and negligence. He seemed to have "no devotion to his task." They had earlier, while still on the boat, signed a petition asking him to resign. When he learned about the petition, Captain Streaper had threatened the soldiers and dismissed the two corporals who had signed it. Eugene said they felt disgraced and decided it was finally time to act.

They took their complaints to several officers, who said they could do nothing. The soldiers related the facts to the colonel, but he was not interested, then went to the lieutenant-colonel, who said he was not in command of the regiment. The major agreed that although the captain was a damned fool, a major could do nothing. They went to the adjutant, who told them to put it in writing and to file the charges. A superior officer, maybe Lyon, trusted, or verified, their suspicions. Without hearing how it had happened, the captain was dismissed. Suddenly First Lieutenant Abercrombie became a commander, and the corporals were restored.[348]

Eugene said they had also identified peer leaders from within their companies, "Every company had men who were brighter and abler than all their officers...They were the ones who made up the mind of the company and gave it its excellence."[349] Ware's Company E refused to accept the poor leadership of their captain and they had misgivings about Lyon. The troops had been in Boonville for more than a week.

While waiting around, the soldiers heard from a St. Louis German soldier details about Camp Jackson. The rebels had gotten muskets, a thousand of the best cannon and camp equipment. They heard that the secessionist plot would have been successful if it had not been for Lyon, his officers, and their men.[350] On July 1 Ware noted that they also had more factual details of Lyon's skirmish at Boonville because it was published in local newspapers. Were they just then learning about Camp Jackson? Truth or rumor, it gave the soldiers respect for Lyon and the officers who

---

[348] Ware, 129, 144, 145. (The records show the captain of Company E was absent under arrest in Keokuk since July 1, 1861.)
[349] Ware, 141.
[350] Ware, 153

had been in St. Louis and were now leading the troops beside them.

After hearing about the Camp Jackson Affair and the battle at Boonville, the soldiers trusted that Lyon knew what he was doing. They respected how Lyon and his troops had secured the northern Missouri railroads and the Missouri river for the Union cause. They knew Lyon wanted to catch the rebels in a fight, and they wanted the same. Although the boys were more intimately connected with other men in their companies and regiment through daily activities and common interests such as prayer meetings or playing cards, by the end of time in camp at Boonville, Nathaniel Lyon also became part of their collective identity. Despite not always liking him, the troops belonged with the general who represented their pro-Union, anti-secessionist goals. If he would fight, they could fight and bring honor to their local communities and to their companies.[351]

"The Motley Crew"

The First Iowa boys daily encountered the other soldiers in Lyon's Regular Army companies and those in the First Missouri. Both Burmeister and Ware commented on how different their boys looked in comparison to the other troops. In the First Iowa no two companies were uniformed alike, some with jackets, some without, some with long-tailed coats of different shapes and colors. All the outfits were in bad condition by this time: "It was a motley crew...The Iowa regiment boys were all about alike: they were ragged and saucy and their ninety days were up in July (a misunderstanding.)"[352] Wilkie wrote that the boys were "ragged and dirty and woe begone." He felt ashamed of the Iowa boys.[353] Despite what they lacked, the First Iowa Infantry soldiers had confidence in their abilities,

---

[351] In the Civil War, primary groups may have started as bands of close-knit friends, but camaraderie was fluid, stretching to include others in the company and regiment, and sometimes to officers. Although primary groups would have expanded or contracted depending on the circumstances, companions from within a soldier's company remained members of his primary group.

[352] Ware, 156–157; See Chapter 7 for more about the misunderstanding.

[353] Banasik (Wilkie), 85.

drill, and endurance. Pride made up the bulk of what little they had.

General Lyon recognized that Springfield was the key to southwest Missouri and the point where Jackson's and Price's troops would join Confederate troops coming up through Arkansas. He understood if that happened, the combined secessionist forces would be formidable. Springfield, a prosperous community with several banks, was an important center of converging public roads, located 120 miles from the Pacific Railroad terminus at Rolla. It was primarily Unionist but also had a strong secessionist element, and slaves could be purchased there.[354] After abandoning the state offices, the governor and General Price planned to rendezvous with Confederate troops led by General Ben McCulloch and hoped he would help them coerce Missouri into the Confederacy. Lyon hoped to catch the governor of Missouri and General Price in a trap before they could join McCulloch's troops, but they had a head start and were moving fast.[355]

Before leaving St. Louis, Lyon ordered General Thomas W. Sweeny's and Colonel Franz Sigel's Third Missouri Volunteers, seven companies of the Fifth Missouri under Colonel Charles Salomon, and two batteries of artillery to leave for southwest Missouri to keep Jackson's and Price's troops from uniting with the Confederates.[356] Lyon ordered General Sweeny to build a supply depot at Rolla and to keep guard there, in hopes of providing wagons and supplies for Lyon's troops when they arrived in Springfield. Sweeny sent Sigel's column ahead and remained in St. Louis to organize supplies. Sigel was able to move quickly with the advantage of rail-road transportation to Rolla. When he arrived on June 23, Sigel had to deal with poor transportation, bad roads, and no cavalry

---

354 Piston and Hatcher, 79–81.
355 Piston and Hatcher, 45.
356 Snead,166; Piston and Hatcher, 76. Captain Thomas W. Sweeny of the Second U.S. Infantry was selected brigadier general of five regiments of Home Guard, although his rank at that time was never officially recognized; Randy R. McGuire, "Solving the Mystery of the Arsenal Guns, part 2. Events of Early 1861 Affect the St. Louis Arsenal." www.civilwarstlouis.com/arsenal. Retrieved 1/10/2021. Sweeny relieved Lieutenant Robinson and took command of his troops to protect the arsenal. Sweeny was one of the few Regular Army officers to participate in the Camp Jackson Affair and became Lyon's loyal ally.

for reconnaissance for the 120-mile march from Rolla to Springfield and an expected battle.[357] Sweeny arrived July 1 and learned that none of the ordered transportation and few of the supplies had arrived.[358]

Lyon also ordered Major Samuel D. Sturgis from Fort Leavenworth, Kansas, with two Kansas regiments and a number of Regulars—about twenty-two hundred men—to meet at his camp on the Grand River near Clinton, Missouri (Ware's Map of the Route from Boonville to Little York). General Lyon needed everything to go smoothly for his plan to work. Procuring horses and mules for a needed supply train was a big challenge. Lyon had difficulty getting enough supplies and reinforcements to enable his cross-country pursuit. Then it rained heavily day and night for several days. The Missouri River climbed up over its banks. Ravines became mudholes. Wilkie reported that the whole country had been "plastered over with mud" anywhere from twelve inches to three feet deep.[359] They had to wait days for the roads to dry up. Lyon was setback by the frustrating rain delay in Boonville and he needed food and transportation. General Lyon was forced to cope with severe inadequacies.

The soldiers were not privy to all the conditions confronting their general and were tired of waiting around. Some of the boys were getting rowdy. When one of the Regular soldiers was paraded "bucked and gagged," Ware's company reacted. The officers' infliction of harsh discipline was a major source of trouble.[360] For punishment, an accused Regular soldier might be gagged and have his arms bound around knees with a stick between. Discipline for the Iowa soldiers was somewhat lax, with extra guard duties or Bible verses to memorize and recite.[361] Soldiers in the First Iowa believed that such punishment for volunteers was just and dignified. But the Regulars resented the volunteers' lack

---

357 Cutrer, 38.
358 Peckham, 293, 294. Sigel arrived in Rolla June 14.
359 Banasik (Wilkie), 96, 101.
360 Piston and Hatcher, 69; Larimer, 49, 50. Jacob thought the Regular Army soldiers were treated worse than mules. They were tied up and whipped for trifling offenses.
361 Lyftogt, 186.

of rigid discipline. The Iowa boys hated the whipping, gagging, bucking, and parading of Regular army soldiers under punishment. Daniel Matson Company E, described disgust at horse whipping or sometimes tying a Regular soldier to the fifth wheel of a caisson to receive one hundred lashes.[362] On this occasion, Eugene's group flocked around the Regular officers and threatened to unloose the humiliated soldier. The U.S. officers responded with fixed bayonets. The boys in Company E left and quickly returned with their own bayonets, eager to show off their skills in fencing with the weapons. The officers of Company E and Captain Matthies, leading the "twin" Burlington German company D, came between the face-off and stopped it.[363]

George Burmeister, First Iowa Infantry (Summer 1861) From copy of a family photograph, with permission of Dolores Rawson, April, 2024.

Eugene Ware, 1866. Kansas State Historical Society (07-02-2024)

---

362 Matson, 60.
363 Ware, 151, 152; See Piston and Hatcher, 70–71, for a description of the harsh discipline imposed by Maj. General Samuel Sturgis on Kansas soldiers.

Lyon had assembled 2400 men in Boonville.[364] It was a bigger camp than soldiers of the First Iowa had previously experienced, though it would not be the biggest. The boys would have taken comfort in the smaller, friendlier contexts of their companies. They built camaraderie playing cards and telling stories, with singing competitions, and mule mischief. They spoke of each other with endearing terms. The soldiers maintained daily duties and morale. Because of their ragged appearance, dignity in the First Iowa was hard earned, but salient. Individual self-respect reflected on the pride and honor of a soldier's unit and the cause for which he fought.[365] It mattered.

Lyon knew his situation was serious. He was desperately hoping to be resupplied. Lyon expected support when they got to Springfield. On July 2 Lyon wrote to Col. Chester Harding, St. Louis Arsenal:

> I hope to move tomorrow and think it more important just now to go to Springfield. My force...will be about twenty-four hundred men. Major Sturgis will have about twenty-two hundred men, and you know what force has gone to Springfield from St. Louis, so that you see what an amount of provisions we shall want supplied at that point. Please attend to us as effectually as possible...I must be governed by circumstances at Springfield...We need here a regular quartermaster and commissary. Cannot something be done for us in Washington?[366]

The next few weeks would test the soldiers' grit even more than before. Their morale and morality would waver. Would they be able to maintain company community under extreme "booming, buzzing, confusion" as a resource for social order amidst ever greater chaos?

---

364 Piston and Hatcher, 58.
365 McPherson, *For Cause and Comrades*, 82.
366 *OR*, Serial 3:388 X; Peckham, 279–280; Harding wrote Col. Thomas, July 5, requesting large amounts of wagon transportation from Rolla, noting the need to take forage for the teams because of the barren, mountainous region. "Please telegraph orders to Quartermaster-General McKinstry." *OR*, Serial 3:390 X.

CHAPTER SIX

FROM BOONVILLE TO SPRINGFIELD

In August and September, 1861 it was still possible to believe in a short war and even envy those who had served.   —Piston and Hatcher

On July 3, 1861, Lyon ordered the cumbersome wagon train and troops out of Boonville. According to one soldier they were headed "to any point where we could lay our hands on the traitor Jackson."[367] An engraved image shows Lyon's forces leaving Boonville, headed for Springfield in southwest Missouri. Scouts looked ahead for the critical sources of drinking water needed to sustain the marching soldiers, the hundreds of mules pulling the wagons, and the horses used by officers, scouts, and for pulling the artillery caissons. Eugene Ware's maps show how their marching routes closely followed rivers and streams.

---

367 O'Connor, 60.

Orlando C. Richardson. "Departure of General Lyon and his Command from Boonville, Missouri for the Arkansas Border." 1861-07-27. Retrieved from The Digital Library of America, https://mohistory.org/collections/item/P0084-1248. (Accessed February 6, 2025.)

Lyon's only chance against the greater forces of Confederates amassing in southern Missouri was to get to Springfield quickly. The First Iowa had been in camp next to the Missouri River for nearly two weeks. Eugene knew they were about to depart because Lyon couldn't wait any longer for supplies or reinforcements. As part of his three-column plan, General Lyon, with his Company B, Second U.S. Infantry, First Missouri Volunteers, Totten's Battery, one hundred unassigned recruits, Captain John D. Voerster's Sappers and Miners, and the First Iowa Infantry, headed for Springfield on July 3.[368] Although the diarists did not mention the company of engineering troops who accompanied them, Wilkie noted the "one hundred Pioneers, on their thighs long, heavy sword bayonets…

---

368 Piston and Hatcher, 13. In January 1861 false reports were sent by telegram claiming the arrival of federal troops which incited secessionists to surround the Little Rock Arsenal. In February Captain James Totten and Company F Second Artillery, were forced to surrender and ordered to Jefferson Barracks in St. Louis. Totten commanded Battery F under Lyon's command. Banasik (Wilkie) 102n161

FROM BOONVILLE TO SPRINGFIELD

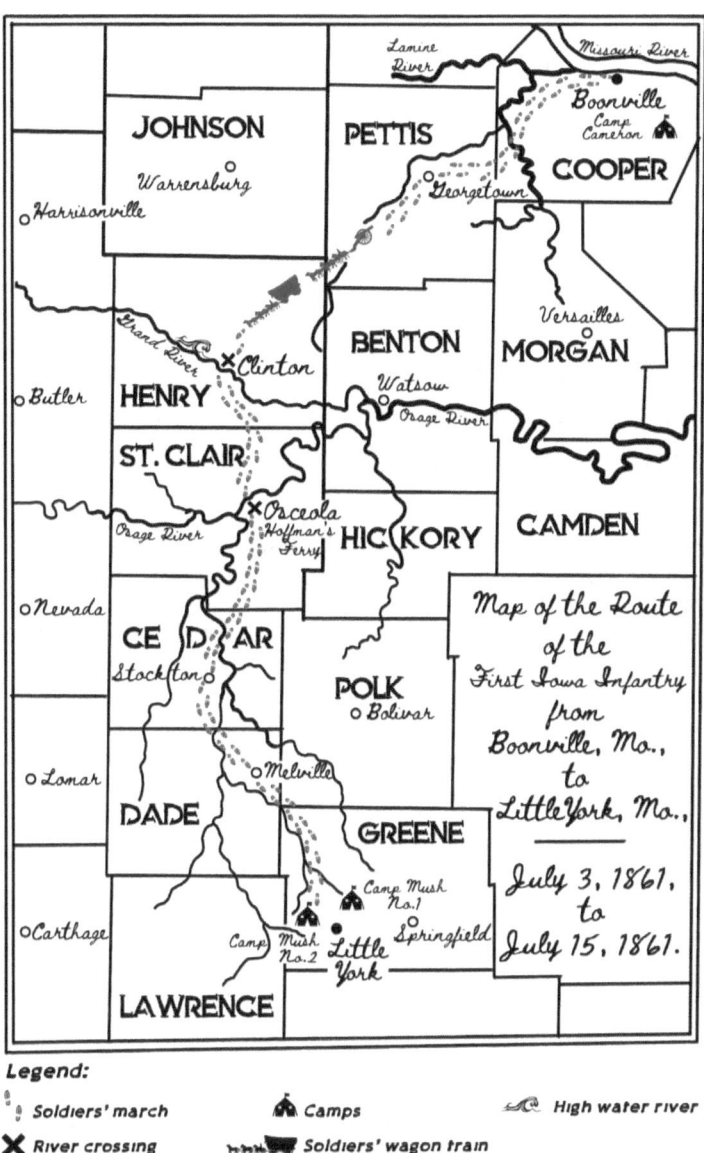

"Map of the Route of the First Iowa Infantry from Boonville, Mo., to Little York, Mo., July 3, 1861 to July 15, 1861." Eugene Ware, The Lyon Campaign in Missouri: Being a History of the First Iowa Infantry, 1861. 1907. (Iowa City: Camp Pope Bookshop, 1991). Icons and Legends added by Shila de Morais, 2021.

across their backs the short but deadly Sharps rifles…and in their hands shovels, axes, and pickaxes."[369] Their purpose was to fell trees, remove obstacles, and assist with crossing rivers and deep ravines.

George Burmeister tells how the troops readied to march: "Sure enough, this morning we were ordered to strike our tents and prepare to start. We left our camp about 7 o'clock A.M. with our regt, the 1st Mo and part of 2nd Mo regts…about 2,500 men."[370] Wilkie describes the scene: "Gen. Lyon, in an old white felt hat, mounted on a superb iron-grey stallion, surrounded by his Body Guard." There were one thousand St. Louis men dressed in blue carrying their "glittering" muskets and a train of wagons two miles long. At the end were a drove of cattle and rear guard.[371] Eugene writes:

> We were filled with rumors…Finally, the number of troops in front of us grew until rumor fixed them at 15,000 drawn up and in camp 100 miles or nearer…Bill Heustis changed it around so that it became 100 troops within 15,000 miles of us, and there it stayed for quite a while. We marched out of Boonville in the mud, with drums beating and flags floating. Old men and good-looking girls in long cavalcades escorted us far out of town on horseback.[372]

George and Eugene both noticed the fine horse-riding abilities of the Missouri women.

Lyon led his troops from Boonville to meet Sturgis.[373] Ware and Burmeister detailed the hot July ordeal. Each man carried a gun, cartridge-box, cap-pouch, belt, bayonet and scabbard, ammunition, blanket, haversack, one day's ration, and full canteen, all weighing about twenty-five pounds. The boys decided to lighten their loads by sharing necessary items.

---

369 Banasik (Wilkie), 102.
370 Burmeister, 07-03-1861.
371 Banasik (Wilkie), 102.
372 Ware, 159. Bill Heustis was Ware's twenty-year-old "veal" jokester friend in Company E.
373 Piston and Hatcher, 41, 68.

Each decided to carry an essential item like a razor, a looking glass, needles, a deck of cards, and so on. The soldiers were united in the courageous goals of wanting to face the enemy and maintain honor—goals which seemed to overcome their unease. Soldiers of the First Iowa Regiment were put right behind the Regulars, who were nicely dressed, finely armed, looked like soldiers and "stepped off with vigor."

> We supposed that it was our duty to keep up with the regulars, and so we trod on their coat tails all day, and so when one of them stopped to tie his shoe he fell back into our ranks at least 200 feet...They did not like our style very well, but we liked theirs...we kept ready to run over them all day long.[374]

When they stopped, the supply wagons were so far behind that there was no wood or water. Eugene wrote that he was too tired to eat, so he joined the men sleeping every-which-way on a hillside. On July 4, there was no celebration. The boys were called up by drums at 3:00 a.m. and on the double-quick, struck down their tents. Instead of a festive parade, they formed a real military procession, "One thousand men from Iowa, commanded by Col. Bates, big powerful men, but ragged and dirty enough to beat Falstaff's recruits all to fits."[375]

Jacob Ritner felt lucky to have been selected to drive the mule team for Colonel Bates's baggage wagon, but he soon found that one of his mules was "the wildest thing in six states. I had rather fight two secceshers every morning before breakfast than bridle that mule."[376] Ware's Company E was detailed to fatigue duty, assisting the drivers of the twelve regimental wagons "when they ran out of profanities." It took enormous strength and effort to pull back on the wagons when going downhill, to keep the wagons from breaking away and crashing, then straining with might to

---
[374] Ware, 160.
[375] Banasik (Wilkie), 102; Larimer, 42. Jacob Ritner wrote that most of the men wore white havelocks from their caps, which, from a distance, made them look like a "drove of sheep."
[376] Larimer, 41, 42.

push uphill and across streams and mudholes. The wheels were often locked to keep the wagons from somersaulting over the teams.[377] The soldiers were thankful for the help of Missouri mules: the mule "has no superior, no equal...He will pull until he drops. He enjoys profanity, likes a joke, and is a good judge of men."[378]

When they arrived at a place called Camp Creek, Burmeister set out with George Aylsworth to buy "eatables." He was fortunate in knowing how to roam over the surroundings to find something to eat, while others were tired and stayed in camp. George told how people in the countryside suffered from the threats of secessionists and hoped for protection. Using his spyglass, he spotted a friendly Union flag and went there to hire as many pies and biscuits as he could. He admired the nearby Germans who stood fast for the Union while surrounded by threatening secessionists.[379] Eugene went with a friend to pick mulberries and buy milk and bread from a distant house. [380]

Lyon, an early riser, had troops up every morning at 3:30 am. On July 5, they started out in rain and mud. They were following the main wagon-road from Boonville which went to Georgetown, to Greenridge and Belmont, and to Clinton. The company wagon sank in the mud to the axles and the mules to their bellies, so the men were forced to lighten the load. Out went most of the tents, and for the rest of the campaign Eugene Ware never slept in a tent. They floundered for twelve miles. "The troops moved off earlier than usual...under excessive heat...we halted near a small creek, we suffered much from want of water and many were sunstruck...Many deep curses were uttered against the general for treating his men like brutes."[381] Lyon had no cavalry at this point, but there were several mounted men in uniform and civilians on horseback. The soldiers

---

377 Matson, 62.
378 Ware, 162–163.
379 Burmeister, 07-04-1861.
380 Ware, 163–164.
381 Burmeister, 07-5 to 07-06-1861.

thought they were scouts. Couriers came in to report that Lyon's troops should meet General Sturgis within twenty-four hours.

Rivalry

The Regular soldiers from St. Louis boasted how they needed to show the shabby volunteer soldiers how to march.[382] However, on July 6, Lyon ordered the First Iowa Infantry to lead the brigade. Colonel Bates, always mounted, led the regiment. The Regulars were marching just behind the First Iowa. This was an opportunity for the First Iowa soldiers: "We passed around the word to give the brigade a run for its money. In an hour there was a gap of half a mile behind us...Every hour we started up 'The Happy Land of Canaan.'"[383] They led the brigade twenty-three miles that day.

Once in a while, Lyon called a halt until the rest of the brigade could close up and said, "There goes that d__d 'Happy Land of Canaan again.'" Eugene wrote "We accomplished one purpose—we wore out the Regulars and gave them to understand that we were the better men." Determination to show off their marching excellence counteracted the embarrassment over their tattered appearance. This was the day Lyon began to call soldiers in the First Iowa Regiment the "Iowa Grey Hounds."[384] Eugene wrote how happy they felt because they could excel in something, but this was also the day the First Iowa formed a great dislike of Lyon. "We never liked him much anyway, and just now he seemed cross and crabbed and to be finding fault with something." When Lyon had to call the First Iowa to a halt allowing other troops to fill the gap, he said that he would not put their regiment in the front anymore.

---

[382] Matson, 61.
[383] Ware, 168.
[384] Lyftogt, 190, quoting Henry O'Connor, who noted that Lyon called them "Grey Hounds" after previously referring to them as "gipsies." There is some discrepancy on the date when Lyon nicknamed them the "Grey Hounds." Ware (157) noted that two companies used "gray" in their titles, the Mount Pleasant Grays and the Governor's Grays of Dubuque.

That was a slap to their pride because the First Iowa had just spent three tough days showing off strength and endurance by outmarching all the other troops: "We were without doubt the champions; nothing and nobody could walk away from us."[385]

The following day Company K acted as guard for the commissary teams, giving soldiers a chance to ride in the wagons. Others in the First Iowa marched behind Lyon's company of Regulars and pushed into their ranks whenever the Regulars stopped to rest. Lyon ordered the Iowa soldiers to keep back. When they failed to follow his order, Lyon called a halt and allowed his Regulars to unload their gear into a wagon so they could march quicker with a lighter load. The Iowa soldiers went right up to the Regulars' wagon as they were unloading their heavy gear, loudly cheered, and sang "The Happy Land of Canaan." They had not liked each other since Boonville. Determined, the men in the First Iowa took turns carrying each other's guns in their effort to keep up with the unburdened Regular soldiers. From his observation point as a driver of Colonel Bates's wagon team, Jacob Ritner described the First Iowa's rivalry with the Regulars as the Iowans ran them down: "Whichever one gets in the lead tries to run off from the other…our regiment has stood it so far much better than the other, which is F. P. Blair's crack regiment."[386] The Iowa soldiers boldly took the chance to demonstrate their excellence. The Regulars felt very offended, but "Nobody disputed our prestige after that."[387]

Major Samuel D. Sturgis and the Kansas soldiers from Fort Leavenworth

Conditions grew worse. There was more marching. The men fast-marched twenty miles and arrived at the surging Grand River, where

---

[385] Ware, 170.
[386] Larimer, 43.
[387] Ware, 174.

they joined Major Sturgis and his troops. Lyon's brigade started cheering as they passed by the Kansas soldiers. They heard how, in April, just a few months earlier, Sturgis and his soldiers had been driven out of Fort Smith, Arkansas, by the rebel government when it seized the U.S. garrison.[388] The Iowa boys were impressed by the Kansas soldiers: "eleven companies of Regulars, all mounted & armed with Sharps or Mainards [Maynard] rifles, & two regiments of three-year men well-armed and equipped for battle."[389] The Kansas troops were about twenty-five hundred strong. Franc Wilkie described the camp scene for the newspaper back home. There were about 6,000 men camping on both sides of the river: "The air full of bugs...everywhere soldiers, wagons, tents, mules, horses, noise, smoke, mosquitoes, wood-ticks, dirty shirts, unclean, unshaven countenances...odor of 100 stables."[390] Jacob Ritner wrote that it was a hot, mean place and "we want to get away."[391]

Eugene Ware recorded details about the difficult Grand River crossing. The entire army, soldiers, wagons, mules, horses, and artillery, had to navigate the river, which was deeper and swifter than the Missouri. The officer in charge of the wagon with the supplies commandeered at Boonville asked whether there were any swimmers among the men. Eugene, who swam the Mississippi River in Burlington for militia training, and one other soldier swam across with lines that they tied to trees. (A third swimmer was carried downstream.) The men could then traverse on the ropes, hand over hand. Ware commented that there were always men who knew how to do everything, felling trees or building a corduroy road across an impassible river bottom.[392] Fires were built to make

---

388 Piston and Hatcher, 13. Captain Sturgis and his troops were ordered to Kansas after Arkansas troops seized Fort Smith in April 1861, just before the state seceded.
389 Branson, 07-07-1861, The Kansas soldiers had been properly outfitted by federal supplies at Ft. Leavenworth, but not all had the fine rifles described by Branson (23). See Piston and Hatcher, 69, for further description of the Kansas troops.
390 Banasik (Wilkie), 101.
391 Larimer, 45.
392 Ware, 175–176.

enough light for the work. All night long the regiment ferried over on flatboats and canoes, hauling artillery, and assisting horses from boats. On July 8, they were not awakened at 3:30 a.m. because they hadn't yet been asleep. The soldiers took pride in the capabilities of other men and in helping each other. The exhausted comrades could think of nothing but coming upon Jackson: "Not fit to lead a blind horse to water. He is a coward as well as a traitor."[393] They remained united in hating the enemy.

U.S. Commander of the West General John C. Frémont

With Sturgis joining him from the west and Sigel cutting secessionists off from the east, Lyon believed he could trap Jackson's troops.[394] But Missouri was not a priority for the War Department, which was more concerned with protecting the Capitol, meeting threats in the East, and safeguarding strategic Mississippi River ports like St. Louis and Cairo. On July 3, 1861, the same day Lyon and his troops left Boonville, the War Department named General John C. Frémont as the ranking officer in the West, but the new commander was in no rush to take charge of Missouri.[395] Lyon and Blair were confident that Frémont would help drive Jackson and Price out of Missouri and guarantee that it remained a Union state.[396] However, Frémont didn't arrive in St. Louis until July 26, 1861, more than three weeks after Lyon left Boonville. He then gave Lyon false hope for support and made himself unavailable to the personal

---

393 O'Connor, 57.
394 Banasik (Wilkie), 106.
395 Piston and Hatcher, 120.
396 Lyftogt, 184; Piston and Hatcher, 121.

messengers sent to him.³⁹⁷ Meanwhile, Lyon's Adjutant General Chester Harding was flooded with troop requests for Cairo and St. Louis, but he sent no troops to reinforce Lyon.³⁹⁸

There were many earthly and human obstacles facing Lyon, and his plan unraveled. On July 9, he received a messenger with news from Colonel Sigel. In Sigel's efforts to halt Jackson's troops, he was defeated at the Battle of Carthage, west of Springfield. Instead of preventing the secessionist Missouri troops from joining the Confederate forces, Sigel had been forced to retreat toward Springfield.³⁹⁹ He needed immediate reinforcement.

Accidents and Casualties

Although Lyon had sent Missouri troops ahead to secure the Osage River crossing, he wanted to quickly reinforce Sigel and needed to put more men on the banks of the river. He selected his "Grey Hounds." He had noticed their speed and endurance during the first high-water crossing and pushed them harder. Lyon ordered the First Iowa to fast-march to the next surging river. The First Iowa struck up another round of "The Happy Land of Canaan" and began another fast march. "This time Lyon sat on his horse and watched them go…Lyon did not smile when he was pleased—he just pulled his chin whiskers with his mouth half open."⁴⁰⁰

---

397 Cutrer, 44–45. When Fremont arrived in Missouri July 26, he reported being shocked by the Missouri secessionists who were in active rebellion against the Federal Government. "Frémont later stated that, because Lyon 'had saved Missouri from secession,' he had left Lyon's movements to his own discretion. 'To any other officer in his actual situation, I should have issued peremptory orders to fall back upon the railroad at Rolla." Frémont added that he had made "every possible effort to reinforce Lyon."; For divergent opinions of Gen. John C. Frémont, compare letters and commentary from John P.C. Shanks, *Vindication of Major General John C. Frémont Against the Attacks of the Slave Power and Its Allies*, (Washington, D.C.: Scammell & Co.,1862), with Peckham, Full text available https://archive.org/details/vindicationofmaj00shanrich/page/n3/mode/2up.

398 Peckham, 253; Snead 166.

399 Cutrer, 39. On July 5 Sigel's forces engaged Jackson as he was moving south, intending to rendezvous with Confederate General Ben McCulloch who had entered Missouri from Arkansas.

400 Ware, 184.

The crossing was about ten miles southwest of Osceola.[401] The men marched twenty-five miles and suffered from heat and thirst. But the news that Jackson threatened the federal garrison at Springfield, as Burmeister wrote, "inspired us with courage, and we marched over tough country with little rest during the day."[402] Several had dropped back and formed a group at the rear. Most of the regiment got in at 6:00 p.m. indescribably tired. The First Iowa soldiers had started twenty-three hours behind the Missouri regiment and arrived only four hours behind them. Support for each other was a key to performing this extreme feat. They were so tired that they needed a few hours each on his own to recover. Challenges like these exhausted the soldiers but also gave them mutual empathy. They shared the knowledge of how their courage and ability to endure had been pushed to the limit.[403]

The Osage River was bank-full, and Eugene was determined to go in and cool off:

> Every muscle was aching and every nerve was on a quiver...I felt lonesome, and did not want to talk... I stuck my bayonet, fixed to the musket, down into the ground, and took off what few clothes I had and hung them on the gun. I passed a six-foot snake in a bush that had been driven out of his hole by the water and I shook him out, but could not kill him. I then got into the water and sat in it up to my chin until I got cooled off...went back to the company line. The boys were lying around on the ground; some were sleeping, some were smoking and some were eating, but none were talking. We had no roll-call, no guard-mount, no bugling; it was everybody for himself.[404]

---

401 O'Connor, 56.
402 Burmeister, 07-11-1861.
403 McPherson, *For Cause and Comrades*, 163.
404 Ware, 185–186.

The men were too depleted to maintain unity and order, but at 3:30 a.m. the next morning (July 10), the regiments set to work to cross the Osage. Troops had to fell trees to cover washouts and dig new roads for the coming teams. Teams were coming up to cross all day. It took two days for the teams, cattle, and rear guard to make the second high water crossing. Men dropped. There were accidents and casualties, and there were men who couldn't take life any longer.

> There were several men lost at this point. Four men overcome with heat died. Another man was killed in the felling of trees. One was accidentally shot. One man was on the ground asleep, when an army wagon…ran over him and broke his neck. Two men were missing…A soldier intending suicide jumped overboard (from a ferryboat) and did not come up again; another jumped after him.[405]

Burmeister's Company K was sent on scouting expeditions along the river where he found hostile rebel supporters. He described rough, unhealthy country. George entered the house of a secessionist who tried his best to frighten him with lies of enemy plans. He told how long it took to cross the rivers with such large forces. Company K was taken over the Osage River during the night before they were finally permitted to rest.[406]

It had been a grueling week since Lyon's troops left Boonville. The Iowans' families had come through hard times, and as heirs of the pioneer spirit they could overcome difficulties.[407] But they had never faced anything like those yet to come. Eugene described his wardrobe. He had no socks for his hard, stiff shoes, and Mace suggested filling them with soap, which he did to his great relief. He had a black, well-worn hat, a slate-colored woolen shirt, and trousers. He had shoestrings made of buckskin, a large, red-bordered pocket-handkerchief that featured a

---
405 Ware, 187.
406 Burmeister, 07-10-1861.
407 Baker, 4.

blue steamboat plying up a yellow river. When marching, he put the ends around his hat and let it hang down to keep the sun off his neck. He carried his diary in his pocket, with a piece of lead pencil, a rusty knife and a plug of tobacco, plus a small wad of Missouri money.[408]

Extreme Marching

Thus, Eugene was outfitted as Lyon's entire combined army, having crossed the Osage, started out on July 11, expecting a rebel army everywhere. They marched through the night, for almost twenty hours, hoping to help Sigel fight the enemy. They marched across rocks, steep Missouri hills and gullies deep enough to snap wagon axles. George writes sparse details about the agonizing conditions:

> At dawn our forces rested near a creek where nearly every one soon disappeared in the brush and...fell asleep...It is said we marched 46 miles in a day and night.[409]

They stopped in a town where storekeepers had killed two of their men. They heard that Jackson had left for Arkansas to keep out of their reach and they started out again, among friendly people. It was hot and dusty. They passed through prickly pears and thick timbers, without water or rest until midday. They marched another 20 miles. Wilkie described the timber as the "deepest" kind:

> forcing us to grope our way through a darkness deeper than that which fell upon Egypt...We went climbing up hills almost perpendicular...now plunging down others to be met at the bottom by swift streams that came up to the men's waists...Rough strata of rocks cropped out at every step. Huge stumps stood in the way, breaking the skins of the men and catching the axles of wagons. For the first

---
408 Ware, 191–192.
409 Burmeister, 07-12-1861.

few hours a number of cheery choruses rang out through the woods...but these grew fainter and less frequent, till midnight, when we plodded on in silence.[410]

Jacob Ritner described how he drove the mule team all night on a road that was a mass of rock: "the poorest, rockiest, meanest, most God-forsaken country I ever saw."[411] William Branson Company C admitted, "I am nearer worn out this Friday than I ever was in my whole life."[412] When they camped near Melville, George went with William Eckles to hire more baking. Sharing the bread with others made a "fine night" for Burmeister. He was then ordered to go back into town and bring back any straggler soldiers from the regiment. Even after learning that soldiers had been killed by nearby rebels, the First Iowa men continued to sing as they set out. They sang every day, every hour "The Happy Land of Canaan." Their trademark song could be heard for miles. Captain Matthies of the Burlington German company came up and said, "You should that singing stop. You will your strength lost."

They kept marching. "If a man stumbled and fell, he did not get up again...When one of our men broke down...we had to pull him to the side of the road so that the artillery would not run over him." Marching next to Ware was Samuel Chapman. He had one black eye and one blue eye and was a "tall, slim, whalebone of a lad."[413] In order that neither would fall down they held hands, and, when one stumbled, the other yanked him up. They changed sides and hands, shifting muskets side to side. They led the company. Bill Heustis said, "I wish I had stayed at

---

410 Banasik (Wilkie), 111. Wilkie at times exaggerated his reports for the readers back home.
411 Larimer, 46.
412 Branson, 07-11-1861. (p. 30)
413 Matson, 52, 55. Daniel Matson and Samuel Chapman were friends in Yellow Springs Township, Des Moines County, and walked together to Burlington (the county seat) to enlist in Company E. Daniel Matson worked for and lived with the Rankin family in Yellow Springs Township. Matson described Samuel as a "big raw-boned scrapper" and good at books; Banasik (Wilkie), 289. Samuel Chapman later became a judge in Nebraska.

home and sent my big brother." Eugene described Heustis as tall, lean, and tireless as the wind. He was the wit of the company. Because Eugene Ware was also tall and thin, Bill would say, "See old Link a-standing up there, six feet high and six inches square."[414]

"Running a race with hunger as well as with Price and Claib Jackson"[415]

When they got into camp about noon, only thirty-two company men made it in together. The men, barely able to stand, were happy to see each straggling soldier as he arrived into camp. They hugged each other before dropping. There was no more coffee, only mush and warm water from the creek to drink, and more men sick with diarrhea. When Lyon ordered a halt near a small stream, men dropped and slept anywhere and everywhere on brush heaps or on wagon tracks. The men, barely able to stand, were happy to see each straggling soldier as he arrived into camp. That night, Eugene was detailed on guard duty. He was hungry and ate a raw bacon sandwich. Eugene bemoaned how the rebels had emptied the smokehouses and had taken all the beef in the area. Missouri farmers' home-smoked pork was an important source of supply. When he went to headquarters, Eugene heard that all the regular rations that had been brought along were finished. The wagons were empty. He realized that they were worse off than ever.[416]

All for Naught

Soldiers believed they were getting close to Jackson. They stumbled on, sometimes in darkness, until they fell asleep before hitting the ground. Soon after daylight on July 12, a messenger arrived with information that

---

414 Ware, 194–195, 197.
415 Ware, 198.
416 Ware, 198.

Colonel Sigel was no longer in immediate need of help.[417] Part of Sigel's infantry forces were surrounded at Neosho by hundreds of mounted Arkansas Rangers and surrendered on July 5.[418] Sigel had safely retreated to Springfield. The Iowa soldiers thought that Lyon's troops would pursue and capture General Price before he could be reinforced from the south, but the rumored reports about McCulloch had proven true. The Confederate general was convinced by Jackson and Price that it would be catastrophic if he didn't enter Missouri quickly.[419] McCulloch's troops had entered the state in early July after his meeting with Price at Cowskin Prairie.

The nearly fifty miles and forty-eight hours of miserable forced fast-marching through rugged deep gorges, woods, fallen timber, and swampy sloughs to help Sigel was in vain. The Union troops had marched in extreme summer heat, humidity, rain, and mud while lacking adequate food, arms, and clothing—as well as accurate information about enemy strength and their terms of duty. They faced the back-breaking work of two high-water river crossings. The Iowa soldiers were angry: they blamed their officers for brutal treatment and mismanagement, and their commanding officer, Brigadier General Lyon, for giving preferential treatment to other regiments. They were often ordered to march "for we know not where."[420] Wilkie estimated the distance made from July 3 to 13 to be two hundred miles.[421] For the remainder of the summer of 1861, soldiers of the First would follow the orders of General Nathaniel Lyon. As their commanding officer, Lyon was crucial to the history, morale, and cohesion of the First Iowa men. Would his leadership weaken or strengthen company community?

---

417 Banasick (Wilkie), 112.
418 *OR*, Serial 3:38, Captain Joseph Conrad, Third Missouri Infantry, to Col. Sigel.
419 *OR*, Serial 3:39, Ben McCulloch to Hon. L. P. Walker, July 5, 1861; Brooksher, 116.
420 William Branson Diary, 06-18-1861 (p. 11). Branson, from Ohio, enlisted in First Iowa Infantry Company C while visiting Cedar and Muscatine counties. He wrote brief notes in his diary mostly about weather or notable events, and often expressed confusion: "we know not."
421 Banasik (Wilkie), 112.

Nathaniel Lyon, General, 1862
Steel Engraving from a photograph. Missouri Historical Society Photographs and Prints Collection (P0084-0865)

The exhausted Iowa First soldiers gave up hopes of a fight, but instead of complaining about the unnecessary hardships, Eugene and George noted their disappointment about not getting into a battle. The marching slowed until they reached Springfield where some of the soldiers took their frustration out on each other.[422]

---

422 Banasik (Wilkie), 112.

CHAPTER SEVEN

JULY 13 TO 28, 1861

The boys wanted to fight and they wanted
something to eat.   —Eugene Ware

Lyon rode into Springfield July 13 and found that his requests sent from Boonville asking for supplies and reinforcements had not been fulfilled. Eugene Ware thought there was no one in Rolla with enough sense to send them. It isn't exactly clear what happened to the ordered supplies, but there is speculation that Quartermaster Justus McKinstry confiscated them in retaliation for Lyon's tendency go around him and ignore official military regulations. McKinstry received direct orders from Washington on July 6 to send the supplies, but instead he discharged the ordered transportation. Without wagons, supplies could not be forwarded from Rolla to Springfield. McKinstry told Dr. Frank Porter, who made a personal appeal on Lyon's behalf, that it was impossible to supply transportation.[423] In his letter to Lyon July 21, 1861, Adjutant General Chester Harding

---
423 Phillips, *Damned Yankee*, 225; Peckham, 317, 318. Dr. Frank Gibson Porter was a well-respected man who served as surgeon for Missouri Union volunteers. Porter made an appeal to McKinstry, who showed little concern, so he took his request directly to Frémont, who responded that if Lyon intended to fight the enemy at Springfield, he must do so on his own.

explained that it was embarrassing mismanagement of transportation.[424]

The First Iowa soldiers felt thwarted as they faced an additional twenty-mile march to their camp at Pond Springs west of Springfield, near a little stream on the edge of a prairie. When one of the disappointed boys grumbled, Corporal Bill (Fuller) threatened to lick him. James Drealard objected, and they went at it. Others formed a circle, waiting for their turn, until there were half a dozen free fights.[425] In the melee, Eugene's trousers were wrecked so badly that as he marched, he was "stepping outdoors."

The next day while foraging for food, Eugene and Corporal Bill came across a deserted log cabin with a clothesline bearing a pair of heavy, butternut-colored winter trousers. The reddish-brown color came from local dye made from the bark of butternut trees. A darker dye came from walnut hulls. After a brief argument with himself, Eugene decided that he should take the pants from the absent rebel owner.[426] Eugene took needle and thread to his newly acquired trousers, "reefed them in" at the waist, shortened them and cut an Indian-type fringe up and down along the seams.[427]

After arriving at his Headquarters of the Southwest Expedition in Springfield July 13 1861, Lyon described the situation in his letter to Col. Chester Harding:

> Sir: I have about five thousand men to be provided for and have expected to find stores here as I have ordered…I shall endeavor to take every due precaution to meet existing emergencies, and hope to be able to sustain the cause of

---

[424] Ware, 205; Lyftogt, 190; Peckham, 306–311, n.314. Although Harding had ordered Lyon's requested arms, but unbeknownst to him, ammunition, and provisions were lying for weeks at Rolla. Peckham tells of Lyon instructing a messenger "by no means to expose his plans to Quartermaster McKinstry" who would do everything to obstruct. Peckham had no facts to prove McKinstry's ill feelings toward Lyon, but states that he had been assured by others of his attitude.

[425] Ware, 201. Third Corporal William J. Fuller, 21, Burlington Company E.

[426] Ware, 204. The women in southwest Missouri died their yarn with walnut or butternut bark and using handmade looms, wove it into cloth which they dyed again. It was durable and called butternut.

[427] Ware, 207. "Reef" was a term used by sailors to take or roll in a portion of sail.

the Government in this part of the State...Please telegraph to McClellan and to Washington anything in this letter you deem of importance...Shoes, shirts...etc., are much wanted...in considerable quantities.[428]

Since Boonville, Lyon had asked his assistant Major John M. Schofield to write some of his letters. Schofield wrote to Col. Harding, July 15, 1861, "General Lyon is now here with about seven thousand men. Of these fully one-half are three-months' volunteers, whose term of service has nearly expired, the latest expiring on the 14 of August." Schofield, speaking for Lyon, suggested alternative scenarios for protecting Cairo and St. Louis by shifting troops. "Unless the Government gives us relief speedily, our thus far successful campaign will prove a failure."[429] The letters reveal Lyon's bold thinking and assertiveness, not always appreciated by superior officers. No reinforcements came.

Lyon's army occupied a series of camps outside Springfield. The First Iowa Regiment had mush three times a day, sometimes with boiled beef, and called the place "Camp Mush." They constantly heard rumors about the vast numbers of nearby enemy. There were men, women and children continually coming through camp, some of whom were spies. Nothing could prevent them from riding through camp to learn details of Lyon's numbers and arms.

The water in the springs was running low and warm, and wells were nearly drawn dry. The camps were filthy, and men began to contract typhoid. The Springfield hospital was packed. Colonel Bates became ill, and Lieutenant Colonel William Merritt took command of the First Iowa

---

[428] OR, Serial 3:394, X, letter from Lyon to Col. Harding; Peckham, 299.
[429] *OR,* Serial 3:396, X, letter from Schofield to Col. Harding; See also Peckham, 265–312 for letters written by Lyon and Schofield requesting reinforcements and supplies, June 27, July 1, 2, 13, 15, 17, 26, 27; According to McElroy, *The Struggle for Missouri* (108), Schofield was a loyal Douglas Democrat who didn't express opinions on slavery or secession. According to Banasik (360), Schofield took leave of absence as a physics professor, became Lyon's Chief of Staff, and later became a "cautious" Union brigadier general and commander.

regiment. Many in the regiment had no shoes, or just leather soles tied on with strings, but officers expected them to march on rough roads, across rocks and stumps. Soldiers knew if they went home whipped, they would never be able to explain it.

Lyon received an order from General Scott, Commanding General of the U.S. Army, asking for five companies from his Second Infantry to be sent East. Lyon responded in a July 17 letter to Col. Townsend that if he complied, Ft. Leavenworth would be unprotected and that he would be unable to proceed. Townsend served in Washington in the Adjutant General's Corps. Lyon wrote that there should be troops from North, Middle, or Eastern states more readily available. "It seems strange so many troops must go on from the West, and strip us of our means of defense…it can only be victim of imbecility or malice…Cannot you stir up this matter and secure us relief?"[430] We don't know if Lyon's insults rumored their way back to General Scott.

The soldiers had enlisted for the chance to show courage and patriotism. Fighting could bring honor to their companies and to their home communities. But now the soldiers feared that they would be sent home before fighting the rebels. Terms for many of the Missouri three-month volunteers expired between July 22 and July 28, and it was a subject of camp talk. The First Iowa soldiers had been mustered into federal duty May 14, 1861, for ninety days, thus due to be mustered out the week of August 14. But it seems the Iowa soldiers didn't understand their terms of duty. They thought enlistment was the same as muster. Without clarification, it could well have been confusing as the boys enlisted on different dates in different places.

---

430 *OR* 3:397 X. July 17, Lyon to Harding; Peckham, 303, Letter to Colonel Edwin Townsend, July 17; "The Generals and Admirals: Winfield Scott (1786–1866)" *Mr. Lincoln's Whitehouse*. https://www.mrlincolnswhitehouse.org/residents-visitors/the-generals-and-admirals/generals-admirals-winfield-scott-1786-1866/. Winfield Scott retired November 1861, just a few months after Lyon received this order. At the time Scott was infirm, vacillated in giving advice and complained that officers were not sending him reports. After a long, distinguished career, he was no longer capable of providing the organizational skills needed for the Army in 1861. Historian Russell McClintock characterized him as an "insufferable political busybody." "Mr. Lincoln's White House." https://mrlincolnswhitehouse.org.

It seems astonishing that the officers were also confused about their men's term of duty, or they simply failed to clarify this very important point for soldiers of the First Iowa. Eugene thought the muster date of enlistment for three months began on the day the company was accepted by the state, April 20, 1861.[431] It's clear from Schofield's July 15 letter that General Lyon knew the Iowa regiment's muster out date of August 14.

This was yet another source of buzzing confusion and frustration for the soldiers. When they were corrected, they thought Lyon was trying to bully them into staying and fighting. Lieutenant Colonel Merritt asked the men to vote on staying even if their terms of duty were over. The soldiers knew Lyon wanted to fight and they knew the odds were against them, but honor mattered more. Ware admitted that there were some dissenters as the boys believed their time was up on the coming Saturday, but "Bill Fuller said he could lick any two men who wanted to go home." After the men talked it out Eugene said it boiled down to one proposition, "We want to go home mighty bad, but not without a fight." When Colonel Merritt put the question to a vote, they chose to stay and fight. Franc Wilkie wrote his news report from camp: "If their times were out today, and tomorrow and there were a certainty of meeting Jackson, or even next week, every man would willingly stay, but they will extend the time of service under no other circumstances."[432]

"Hard Times"

George complained about the rain, the half cracker per meal, and the person who stole his chicken from over the fire. Frustrations were made worse by mosquitoes, ticks, lice, and "jiggers" (chiggers, or cheagers). The soldiers boiled their clothes, cut each other's hair down to the cuticle, and were kept busy trying to scrape off bugs and treat the bites. Eugene admitted, "The man gets homesick and dispirited, then everything seems

---
431 Ware, 78, 211, 226.
432 Lyfgogt, 192; Ware, 211; Banasik (Wilkie), 114.

to take hold of him...then his courage breaks its halterstrap...I had myself been figuring up if glory was not too expensive, and if it were not worth much less than it cost."[433] George wrote, "I am well contented to 'stand still and see the salvation of the Lord.'"[434] This was a rare statement in the diaries, as neither George nor Eugene made other references to God. On July 17 the soldiers had crackers for supper.[435]

After the nation's financial panic of 1857, a song originated called "Hard Times" with the verse "O Crackers come again No More." Leonidus Fowler, a musician in Company C, wrote a new verse which became a favorite song about crackers (later known as hard tack). The First Iowa Regiment came up with the revised song about crackers which was taken up by other soldiers and sung in regiments across the country. By mid-July the Iowa soldiers ended the song with "You were old and very wormy, but you're pie beside that mush. O crackers, come again once more."[436]

The troops were now mostly inactive, lying around grumbling. It seemed as if there would be no fight. They heard that the enemy was camped forty miles away in rebel country, being well fed. Soldiers found fault with Frémont for not hurrying things up and supplying their needs. Eugene writes how they disliked General Lyon:

> He never seemed to sleep any, he never smiled, he always appeared nervous and irritated, and he never had a pleasant word for anybody. We made up our minds that he did not care much for us and we did not care much for him.[437]

Burmeister notes minimal details from camp near Springfield:

---

[433] Ware, 181.
[434] Burmeister, 07-16-1861.
[435] Banasik (Wilkie) 128. Soldiers were given two or three crackers, two cups of coffee, some beef or pork, and sometimes rice or bread for a day's food, unless they were on half- or quarter-rations.
[436] Ware, 218–219; John D. Billings, *Hardtack and Coffee or the Unwritten Story of Army Life* (Boston: Smith and Co.,1888), 58–59.
[437] Ware, 216.

An execution of a soldier took place in the 1st Regiment [Kansas Volunteers] who was found guilty of murdering a comrade...This was a miserable day for standing guard since it's almost constantly raining...We are receiving about one half cracker per meal. Soldiers steal...I was pretty successful in buying pies and milk and had a glorious time. But as I returned to camp I was informed that I was on guard duty for the next twenty four hours for being absent from battalion drill. So what I gain on one side I lose on the other.[438]

Lyon in a Peck of Trouble

This was a time of uncertainty, with little hope, and the soldiers were critical of their superiors. Order within the ranks was breaking down. Eugene says they were "inactively going to pieces" and felt that they would soon "all be either starved to death or captured."[439] He writes, "That's the way it is in war—the artillery horse eats the wheat and the women and children go hungry."[440] Early on the morning of July 19, a terrific storm began with "cyclonic" winds and heavy rain falling like ropes. Horses ran away and wagons were blown over. Soldiers stuck bayonets into the soil to keep gun barrels dry and to avoid attracting lighting. Eugene writes about his depressed state after the storm:

> It [the lightning] cut through the air with a siz-z-z. We smelled it...I saved my diary by turning a mess pan upside down and putting my diary with its oilcloth case on the mess-pan, and then turning another mess pan down over it and sitting on the mess-pans...Everything was so wet we could not make a fire...Our mess ate raw dough...The want of food, clothing and tents made itself felt in a longing to

---
438 Burmeister, 07-14 to 07-16-1861.
439 Ware, 219.
440 Ware, 236.

get out of the service.[441]

George said they were lying in a bed of water. Wilkie described the situation for people back home: "General Lyon is in a 'peck'—better perhaps a bushel—of troubles."[442] Wilkie reported how many of the Missouri soldiers' terms were expiring, and that without provisions nothing could be done. Everything was favoring Jackson.

Despite the gruesome situation, the Iowa soldiers entered an abandoned mill where Eugene found a copy of Elijah Burritt's *Geography of the Heavens and Class Book of Astronomy*. They used it as a guide for picking a favorite star or constellation to watch for hours as they tried to sleep outdoors on the cherty ground while looking up at the night sky. They all knew the names of the larger summer stars. Eugene's favorite constellation was Corona Borealis: "We talked over how little man was and wondered if we would ever know any more about it."[443]

Expedition to Forsyth

As Lyon's forces were thinning, nearby secessionist forces were uniting and growing stronger. Lyon's prospects looked dismal. But when he heard about a Confederate recruiting camp near Forsyth (Ware's map, p 162 July 20, 2861 to August 10, 1861), Lyon ordered Ware's Company E, Burmeister's Company K, and four others from the First Iowa toward a potential battle under command of General Sweeny and Lieutenant Colonel Merritt. Before knowing the reason for their orders, six companies of the First Iowa had to march several miles from their camp over hot, open prairie back into the main camp in Springfield where they hoped to be "shod up and marched home."[444] "It was a noisy camp of six thousand men, and over two thousand horses and mules, drums beating, fifes squealing, horses neighing,

---
441 Ware, 224–225.
442 Banasik (Wilkie), 114.
443 Ware, 226–227, 262.
444 Ware, 226

mules braying, men singing, swearing, everything but praying."[445] There was mail from home, some a month old. Eugene's father had sent two five-dollar bills which he shared with two of the boys "who were busted and had not heard from home."[446] Eugene took them along for a restaurant meal. In town, the men had access to newspapers and read how politicians were making Lincoln's job hard. The North remained divided in support of Lincoln. Eugene explained how many citizens wanted Lincoln to act faster and blasted him for being too slow. Others wanted him to move slower and blasted his quickness. The president was caricatured and abused:

> He was smooth-shaven before election and during his contest with Douglas. There was a virility about his unshaven face which attracted attention. It set a man to guessing...It was unusual; it was coarse; it had no lines of weakness...Whiskers changed this: He was as much concealed by them as if he wore a mask...Looked weak.[447]

Abraham Lincoln, Presidential Candidate
Platinum print likely made by George B. Ayres from a negative taken in Springfield, Illinois, By Alexander Hessler on June 3, 1860. Cleveland Public Library Digital Gallery (Accessed 02-24-2025)

---

445 O'Connor, 54.
446 Ware, 229; Banasik (Wilkie), 126. Quartermaster Guelich of the First Iowa arrived from Hannibal with mail and newspapers.
447 Ware, 118, 249.

President Lincoln ca. 1861
by Austin Augustus Turner for D. Appleton and Company
Lincoln Financial Foundation Collection, Allen County Public Library,
Fort Wayne, Indiana (Accessed 02-24-2025)

On July 20, the Iowa troops were called out to march. Eugene ate well, cleaned up, and expected to be headed home, but instead started marching south: "We were all the time wondering what was up…It was evident we were not going home."[448] The company wagon carried wheat loaves of bread as "big as buckets and with shells as hard as a turtle." If a fight was coming, men in the First wanted to celebrate with their regimental anthem and started up "The Happy Land."

George said their destination was unknown, "Such is the ignorance of the common soldier." He describes the expedition with the six Iowa companies, the Second Regiment Kansas Volunteers, and two cannon:

---

448 Ware 229–230.

The weather was exceedingly hot and the men complained very much on account of being marched too fast without having sufficient rest and water...We encamped near a beautiful stream called the James River, having marched 18 miles. The country is very mountainous...We passed through a small town called Ozark...A number of the needy were supplied with boots and shoes from several stores...I acted as clerk but I think many things were taken out without being reported to me...The boys were treated to a good drink of whiskey, some got a little too much.[449]

They had to ford the steep-banked Swan Creek which was running with chest-high water.[450] Both soldiers noted General Sweeny's order to march the next four miles to Forsyth on the double-quick, which was as they were drilled, 165 steps a minute and 28 inches to the step.[451] The unwelcome order came after they had marched twenty-some miles in rain and mud, without sleep. The Missouri rebels avoided the Union soldiers. As some of the State Guard troops escaped, they warned others in Forsyth, where there was just a brief fight.[452] Later, when the Union troops camped, they understood the dangerous situation because officers ordered extra guard protection. Each regiment was guarded, and another line of defense was added around the whole camp, with pickets beyond.[453]

Despite the danger, fear, and exertion, as if astonished, the Iowa soldiers noted the rivers and streams in Missouri. George tells how "In crossing these (streams) our shoes filled with sand and water...We crossed one little creek twenty-two times." He describes the clear streams

---

449 Burmeister, 07-20-1861 to 07-22-1861.
450 Banasik (Wilkie), 122; Ware, 237.
451 Ware, 237.
452 See Brooksher, "Sortie to Forsyth," 127–139, and Piston and Hatcher, 125–130, for details on Forsyth.
453 Ware, 238.

like crystal, the most beautiful he ever saw. Eugene writes: "They had a crystalline flash and beauty that enchanted us…They were running with water as pellucid as air and sunlight."[454]

"We swallowed our scruples"[455]

The soldiers didn't feel that they had accomplished a mission. The time and energy spent looking for a real fight at Forsyth and not getting one was frustrating and depleting. Social order was dissolving. The soldiers felt they had earned spoils from the rebels, so they took out some of their frustration by pillaging boots and other goods from secessionist stores. They acquired some beef and had a good square supper. Sweeny reported their capture of valuable horses, mule and horse shoes, arms, camp furniture, sugar, salt, and hats.[456] Wilkie wrote that the skirmish was important because it broke up a force of four hundred men who had been drilling in the strongly secessionist region.[457] George commented on how easy it would have been for secessionists to rout them if they'd had better leadership. Forsyth was between two perpendicular cliffs. If the rebels had defended the pass which entered the town "we would have suffered severely."[458]

On the march back to Springfield, the boys were not sure why they were not surrounded: "The rebels rode all around us all day."[459] The return was only fifteen miles which for them "was not a full day's work," but it was over rocky, abrasive land, which cut through many boys' shoe soles. Resourceful soldiers made moccasins out of deerskins. Others tied gunny-sacking over their soleless shoes. George describes the fatiguing march and the miserable fare, some boys without shoes and clothing.

---

[454] Ware, 245; Henry O'Connor Company A also mentions the beauty of the Ozarks and tells how the soil they slept on was full of limestones, 54.
[455] Ware, 253.
[456] *OR*, Series 1, Vol. 3:44–45, Report of Brig. Gen. Thomas W. Sweeny.
[457] Banasik (Wilkie), 125.
[458] Burmeister, 07-22-1861.
[459] Ware, 245; Burmeister, 07-24-1861.

"All this we bear knowing that we are serving our country."[460] The troops arrived at a temporary camp on Unionist John S. Phelps's farm, where his wife, Mary Whitney Phelps, provided food and water to the soldiers. Congressman John Phelps was the elected colonel of the Greene and Christian County Home Guards and he provided scouting intelligence to Lyon.[461] The Iowa soldiers marched another 12 miles from Springfield before they rejoined the others in their regiment on July 26. They were cheered as they arrived.

Officers continued to drill the soldiers twice a day over prairie grass, weeds, rocks and bushes.[462] A commissary arrived from Rolla, but they still had coffee for dinner. Posters were up for re-enlistment, but George knew of few who were interested. He felt tired.[463] They were exhausted and hungry, yet George describes uncomplaining men. He spent fifty cents for pies and buttermilk to share with friends Adolph and Hugo Schuster.[464] Eugene, however, wrote that after his boys were given some fly-blown putrid beef, they raised hell until the lieutenant intervened and told them, "We must not lose our grip" nor dishonor the regiment. Eugene agreed, "The country needed saving and needed it bad."[465]

Food has a central role in the diaries, it was worth describing. Lyon's officers ordered soldiers not to forage, and threatened them with being shot or getting extra guard duty. But hunger trumped the threats. George

---

460 Burmeister, 07-24-1861.

461 "John S. Phelps Papers," Community and Conflict The Impact of the Civil War in the Ozarks. John Phelps was a long-term con-gressman and was later appointed by President Lincoln as the military governor of Arkansas. He became the governor of Missouri in 1876. Mary W. Phelps often fed soldiers and cared for Lyon's body after his death. https://Ozarkcivilwar.org/archives/3549.

462 Branson, 07-26-1861 (page 46).

463 Burmeister, 07-25-1861. There is discrepancy in estimates of the distance between the First Iowa's camp and Springfield, from 12 to 15 miles. This might have been because they changed campsites, camping once at Phelps's farm. John S. Phelps was from Springfield, a Democrat, slave owner, and a loyal Unionist.

464 Burmeister, 07-27-1861; Hugo and Adolph F. Schuster are listed as members of Company A, in Blair's First Missouri Infantry. The Schusters were family friends from St. Louis, where the Burmeister family lived before moving to Iowa. George stayed with them after the retreat to St. Louis, before he returned to Iowa.

465 Ware, 254.

made an effort to describe his foraging successes, where he often found mulberries. Eugene writes about a melancholy day when all that kept them from going to pieces was drinking blackberry root "decoctions."[466] George could sometimes purchase milk, buttermilk, biscuits, pies, cornbread, or with special luck, a chicken. Matson described how local citizens heard that soldiers had money and came into camp with overpriced wheat bread, pies, melons, and peaches. Eugene wrote of the special times when Mace boiled whole grains of wheat, roasted green ears of corn, made corn pone in hot embers, or lob-scouse in their small iron bake-oven.[467] He noted when a comrade in the woods shot a razorback to roast over the fire. Both boys were fortunate to receive a few dollars in their sparse mail from home which allowed them to buy food items which they shared with friends.

General Lyon learned about the July 21 Union defeat in the Battle of Bull Run at Manassas, Virginia. The news about Bull Run was disheartening. Eugene thought it was not all surprising because the South had prepared early for war and had the best arms and choice of the old Regular Army officers.[468] Lyon heard from Colonel Harding of southern troops crossing over from Tennessee and coming north from Arkansas to Pocahontas, in southeast Missouri. Harding wrote that Frémont would arrive soon, and that U.S. forces had been sent to protect northeast Missouri, St. Louis, and Cairo.[469] Harding assured Lyon that Frémont would take vigorous measures to support his efforts, but Lyon understood the news to mean there would be no reinforcements for him. He finally had to face the truth. Lyon had for too long believed Frémont's few assurances.

The Blairs, Lyon, President Lincoln, and the head of the U.S. Army had made a terrible mistake. Because they knew Frémont could be trusted

---

466 Matson, 61; Ware, 267.
467 Ware, 284. Lob-scouse was made from mixing crackers (hard-tack), bacon, pork or beef fried in fat and added to the pot.
468 Ware, 248.
469 Peckham, 306–311. Letter from Harding to Lyon, July 21, 1861.

as a loyal Unionist, they had appealed for his assignment as head of the U. S. Army's Department of the West. They did not anticipate how his ego, ineptitude, and personal political agenda would put Missouri at such great risk. Eugene Ware hated him for being vain and incompetent and called him "an empty, spread-eagle, show-off, horn-tooting general."[470]

Wilkie described the Iowa troops as physically demoralized, squalid, ragged, filthy, and the laughing stock of the whole army.[471] Eugene described men so morose they stopped playing cards. He said twenty percent of the men were sick, blaming it on the constant diet of cornmeal. July 27 was another day of uncertainty, the men were told to be "ready to march at a moment's notice, our destination not known."[472] Lyon's troops slept on arms, on high alert. On July 28 they had nothing but coffee and mush. The boys called the site "Camp Mush number 2." They were fighting each other. Company E was withered down to about seventy-five men. One night as they dropped onto the ground to sleep, they looked up between the stars and "tried to look beyond them and see what kind of a roof there was over it all." They knew Lyon was hoping to find General McCulloch and his Southern soldiers from Texas and Arkansas before they could unite with Price and Jackson, but Lyon didn't know where the enemy was. "Lyon always looked worried and mad. He was sleepless and constantly on the go…Heustis said: 'Old Lyon is busier than a snake doctor.'"[473]

Eugene noted how each region in Missouri seemed to differ in their loyalties. Forsyth was fiercely secessionist, but west along the James River and the west part of Taney, east part of Barry, and all of Stone

---

[470] Ware, 248.
[471] Banasik (Wilkie), 128. Wilkie claims new uniforms were lying in Quincy, because the Second and Third regiments "hypothecated" them for the freight on their own uniforms.
[472] Branson, 07-27-1861 (page 47).
[473] Ware, 267, 259–261. A snake doctor was a term used for dragonfly.

Counties seemed to be loyal to the Union.[474] He noticed how loyal Union volunteers in the Springfield Home Guard wore homespun butternut-colored clothing that looked much the same as that worn by Price's nearby secessionists.

---

474 Ware, 239. Eugene came to realize that the strongest secessionist feeling was in mid and northern Missouri where most of the slaves were owned.

CHAPTER EIGHT

"TOO LATE"

rain
running gushing water

Missouri River
Grand River   Osage River
Muddy Creek   Moody Creek   Tebo Creek
Pond Creek   Pomme de Terre   Pond Springs   Pickerel Creek
Little Sac   Sac   Swan Creek   Camp Creek   Clear Creek
Niangua   Dry Branch   Basin Fork
Finley River   James River   White River
Gasconade

crystalline   springs   pellucid
Dug Springs
Dry Creek
Wilson's Creek

By the end of July, General Lyon knew that General Ben McCulloch agreed to join Price's campaign. Jackson's messengers had convinced McCulloch that Lyon would soon have 9,000 troops, in addition to Sigel's forces of 3,000, "with intention to enter this state (Arkansas) and the Indian Territory."[475] Without full orders to do so, McCulloch made an invasion of the U.S. with rebel forces. It was an aggressive plan to force Missouri into the Confederacy with troops from Texas, Arkansas, southern Kansas, and Louisiana. The movements of Confederate soldiers were reported in the Springfield newspapers. In his July 29 letter to the Dubuque *Herald*, Franc Wilkie reported that intelligence from Camp Walker (Arkansas) confirmed a secessionist plan to attack Springfield, with detached parties slowly advancing.[476]

General James Rains of the Missouri State Guard was near Dug Springs, General McCulloch a few miles behind, and Brig. General Nicholas Bartlett Pearce, commander of Arkansas State troops, was on the Springfield Road north of Cassville.[477] Rebel pickets were engaging with Lyon's pickets. McCulloch hoped to catch Lyon in a trap of his own by luring him between two steep ridges where his troops might pin down Lyon's troops from above. To that end, he would "dangle" General Rains's Missouri cavalry in front of Lyon.[478]

On July 30, the boys lay around all day in the hot sun with nothing to eat but mush. Eugene said there must have been twenty fights that day: "Some of the boys got off their balance" and wanted to march to Rolla.[479] Jacob Ritner wrote to his wife that they were the "most ragged set of men I ever saw. Some are nearly naked."[480] George remained steadfast:

---

475 *OR*, Series 1, Vol. 3:600, Ben McCulloch to Hon. L. P. Walker, June 29, 1861; Cutrer, 42; Brooksher, 112; Snead 230. McCulloch was ordered to conciliate and protect the Indian Nation. He could control Ft. Scott, but was reminded by his superiors, more than once, that Missouri was still in the Union, and he could cross the border only if it aligned with his primary responsibilities. Jefferson Davis was scrupulous about states' rights and rules of the Confederacy. He would not give authority to enter the state until a Missouri Confederate legislature requested it. General McCulloch decided to move against the federals; Piston and Hatcher, 106, 134, 157, 158; Brooksher, 149. McCulloch moved troops to Wilson's Creek August 6 and 7.
476 Banasik (Wilkie), 127.
477 Banasik (Wilkie), 138n255, 139n256.
478 Cutrer, 46.
479 Ware, 264.
480 Larimer, 50.

> I had a grand washing day. Everything went smoothly till midnight when the alarm of an attack was given. Co. K was first under arms and a great battle was expected, but soon this expectation vanished like a bubble, the alarm was false…I sleep in the open air and enjoy the pleasant breeze and the silver rays of the moon unmolested.[481]

When it seemed that the situation could not get worse, scouts told Lyon that the enemy was advancing on Springfield in three columns. General Lyon called out nearly his entire army to march straight at what he believed was the strongest, largest, advancing column of the enemy.[482] Neither the captains nor officers knew their destination. None of the officers seemed to know where they were going. Eugene said they were ordered to start at 2 o'clock. The soldiers hoped they were heading for Rolla to be mustered out: "We all thought we were headed home until the turn was made."[483] Finally, at 6 o'clock the troops headed south.

Dug Springs and the Rebel Camp near McCulla's Store

On August 1, the men marched into the night until they fell asleep in the middle of the road. They again moved out early on August 2, in extreme heat with no water, many men dropping before they reached Dug Springs, a source of water in Christian County south of Springfield. Eugene's company and one other from the First Iowa acted as skirmishers until they heard a bugle to "rally by company." The bugle rally was an order to prepare fixed bayonets to resist a cavalry charge.[484] The troops skirmished at

---

481 Burmeister, 07-30 to 07-31-1861.
482 Rombauer, 308–309; Banasik (Wilkie), 130; See Brooksher, "Rain's Scare," 152–164, and Piston and Hatcher, 140–144, for details of the Dug Springs skirmish.
483 Ware, 270–271; William Branson Company C, wrote that many rumors were circulating around camp and they would soon be heading home; there was intense excitement because Jackson was advancing on Springfield; there were false alarms, and they never knew where or when they were marching (8-6-61) (pages 58– 60).
484 Ware, 274.

Dug Springs and pushed General James S. Rains into panicked retreat. They engaged again briefly on August 3 before the Missouri secessionist troops retreated further to join McCulloch's troops.[485]

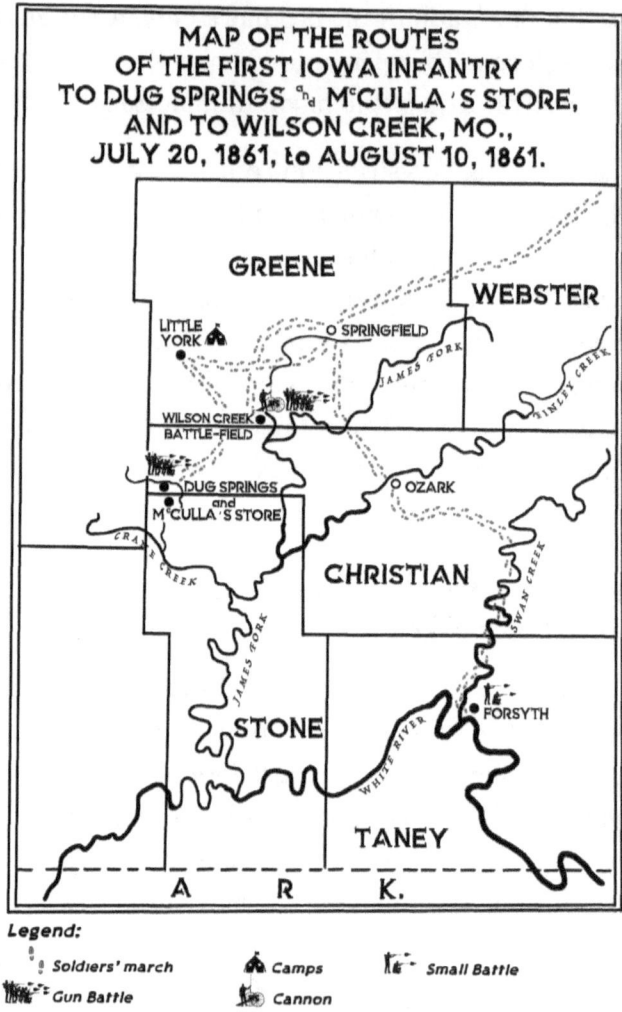

"Map of the Route of the First Iowa Infantry to Dug's Springs and McCulla's Store, July 20, 1861 to August 10, 1861." Eugene Ware, The Lyon Campaign in Missouri: Being a History of the First Iowa Infantry, 1861. 1907. (Iowa City: Camp Pope Bookshop, 1991). Icons and Legends added by Shila de Morais, 2021.

485 Cutrer, 46.

Butternut Confusion

Lyon had little information about enemy location and had ordered his troops to probe and set up defensive positions. As it happened, General Rains and his Missouri State Guard troops unknowingly rode into those positions, then fled in panic.[486] In blistering heat, Lyon continued pursuit towards a secessionist camp with horses in the valley near McCulla's store. In these two skirmishes the Iowa soldiers were to the right of Lyon's command, but the enemy retreated before the Iowa unit was sent into action. Small groups of unaware secessionists came riding very near the Union troops who didn't recognize them as the enemy. The rebels wore butternut-dyed clothing which looked much the same as the local Union Home Guard volunteers. One squad of about sixty rode directly in front of Lyon and his staff. The secessionists themselves were confused, supposed the Union troops were theirs, and rode openly into Union forces. Some were taken as prisoners, but most rode away as soon as they realized the mistake.[487]

Companies in the First Iowa were the leading unit for three miles, until they came to the rebel's abandoned camp. There were piles of forage, oats and corn, smoked hog heads (jowls), cured beef and pork, and a few hats, shoes, and socks. Eugene carried away a jowl on the tip of his bayonet. The soldiers took what they could, filled their canteens and started the return march through woods and brush. A few secesh were hidden and would jump up and run. "Little Baldy got two at once, both bigger than he was."[488] George described the extreme heat, thirst, getting a piece of bread, and said they came close to the enemy and almost got a fight. McCulloch and Lyon both pulled back. To the Iowa men, the action seemed incomprehensible, because Lyon was chasing an unknown. George writes: "We were constantly on alert…Our company and Co. G acted as rear guard for the entire train of 200 wagons." On the march

---

486 Piston and Hatcher, 147–150.
487 Banasik (Wilkie), 137, 138.
488 Ware, 281.

back "some poor fellows came near dying."[489] The pork jowl was stolen from Eugene's bayonet, but he couldn't shake off the lasting image of a cavalryman and his saber, dripping with blood. The strong impression was a reality check: "This is the real thing, the real, sure enough war."[490]

Dug Springs was another unsatisfying skirmish for troops who so desperately wanted to fight. Bill Heustis said, "they're afraid and we wasn't." A frustrated Eugene writes: "The enemy evidently intended that we should not sleep and they did not intend either that we should have a fight...We were in a semi-fortified position and also in a state of siege."[491] The experience gave the soldiers great confidence in the Regular Army officers. From then on, their admiration for the Regulars grew, including Lyon. They did not like him but had great confidence in him.[492]

The troops started back feeling that the expedition had been a failure, but not fully understanding why.[493] General Lyon lacked adequate intelligence, but learned from the skirmishes at Dug Springs and McCulla's store that there were close concentrations of enemy troops. He was frustrated. The enemy kept just out of Lyon's reach until he retreated and then they came in close. In perhaps a final effort to grab the attention of his superiors, Lyon wrote a report on August 4 from McCulla's store, confiding his worry:

> I fear much my inability to retain position in Springfield, for the enemy, mostly mounted and very numerous, will cut off means of obtaining flour. I should still hope to retain Springfield...but for the expiration of the term of the three-months' volunteers...by which my force will be reduced to about 3,500 men, badly clothed and without a prospect of supplies. Prudence seems now to indicate the necessity of withdrawing...I have given timely notice of my danger, and

---

489 Burmeister, 08-02 to 08-03-1861.
490 Ware, 275–276.
491 Ware, 276, 284.
492 Ware, 284, 293.
493 Ware, 287.

can only in the worst of emergencies submit to them."[494]

Rather than be drawn farther away from Springfield and concerned that the town might be attacked while most of his troops were gone, Lyon returned. The retreat was hot and miserable, with thick, yellow-brown dust kicked up by marching troops and wagons, filling eyes, ears, and mouths. The horses and drivers suffered the most.[495] The sense of danger and fear only worsened over the next few days.

"We know not at what moment."[496]

George's entries describe the return to camp, fear and anxiety from false alarms, lack of sleep, and not feeling well:

> We camped where the pure crystal water gushed from the mountain… It seemed impossible sometimes to endure heat, dust, thirst and fatigue, yet we firmly persevered, and finally conquered all these…Our company was ordered out at 9 o'clock pm…trying to find our position as picket guard…The order to strike tents was given…The enemy is advancing.[497]

Lyon's soldiers regrouped in camps on August 5, and William Branson moaned: "It is impossible for me to describe the hardships and sufferings we have passed through since we left Iowa."[498]

On August 5, General Price told General McCulloch that Lyon was preparing to leave Springfield and that they needed to attack. Price was going to fight Lyon with or without McCulloch. There was animosity between the two leaders over rank and leadership roles. Price believed he should be in command because of his earlier experience and ranking as a

---

[494] *OR*, Series 1, Vol. 3:47–48, Report of Brig. Gen. Lyon to Capt. John C. Kelton, August 4, 1861.
[495] Banasik (Wilkie), 138; Rombauer, 310; Piston and Hatcher, 144, 145; Ware, 291.
[496] William Branson repeatedly writes "We know not."
[497] Burmeister, 08-05 to 08-06-1861; William Branson wrote how Moody Springs was the "strongest, nicest water I ever saw." 08-04-1861 (p.55).
[498] Branson, 08-05-1861 (p. 56).

U.S. brigadier general in the Mexican War. He spoke condescendingly to McCulloch. However, Sterling Price was no longer a U.S. officer nor was he yet a Confederate major general. He was Missouri's former governor, the state's Commissioner of Banking, and Jackson's appointed general for the Missouri State Guard. General McCulloch (C.S.A.) demanded that he should be in command of the troops, and Price reluctantly agreed. Although McCulloch was uncertain as to how much he could trust Price, he agreed to camp at Wilson's Creek on August 7.[499]

The citizens of Springfield, fearing rebel victory, began to leave while they could. On August 8 aids were galloping in and out of Lyon's camp with messages. Lyon ordered an attack but soon countermanded it, much to the disgust of the soldiers. George wrote that the alarm was a shameful ruse, circulated by some of the home guards with fearful imaginations. But one of Lyon's own captains had also raised an alarm which caused the general to send out troops.[500] George was excused from duty because of a painful abscess on his left knee and was put in charge of the hospital that night.[501]

Truth or Rumor?

Eugene sent his diary home by an express company that was doing business in Rolla.[502] A supply train arrived from Rolla, escorted by two soldiers from each company of the Thirteenth Illinois Infantry and Home Guards.[503] Rumors magnified the numbers of enemy which surrounded them; these ranged from 15,000 to 30,000: "Private soldiers with no

---

[499] Shalhope, 174; Cutrer, 46.
[500] Piston and Hatcher, 169, 174.
[501] Burmeister, 08-08-1861.
[502] Ware, 304. Eugene noted that it was his great fortune to learn the diary arrived safely to his Burlington home.
[503] Ware, 303, writing on August 8; Branson, 08-06-1861. Branson states the supply trains arrived August 6; *History of the Thirteenth Regiment,* 58. Lyon ordered Colonel Wyman and the Thirteenth Illinois Infantry to guard supplies and railroad terminus at Rolla. Two men from each company under Captain James Beardsley, Company D, started out on August 3 from Rolla with supply wagons, coming the 120-some miles to Lyon's camp in Springfield. "Our men participated as volunteers in the great Battle of Wilson' Creek."

means for verifying reports did not know what to believe."[504] Wilkie learned that large secessionist forces had gathered in southwest Missouri for an attack on Springfield.[505] They had roll call every hour to keep men close together and after sundown bivouacked in line of battle, then soldiers laid down in rows with their guns. It is hard to imagine the toll taken by anxiety, fear, and false alarms. Eugene wrote that the two most nervous men were General Lyon and "Corpular" Mace. Mace told them that they were in trouble. Eugene thought that he was somehow connected to a negro grapevine of surveillance information.[506] Mace seemed to know where all the rebel regiments were camped and said whoever got him would be two thousand dollars ahead. He disappeared.

Camp talk carried more hearsay. The Iowa soldiers heard that if they would stay Lyon could go to battle, if not, there would be a retreat to Rolla: "We would not spoil a fight if there was a show for one; we did not want to take the responsibility of a retreat and did not want to march off to the sound of booming cannon in our rear…If we were to have a fight, we wanted it quick."[507] They did not expect to get through the night without a fight. The lieutenant asked Ware if he could take the place of Corporal "Churubusco" who had taken ill, and Eugene was immediately detailed with twelve men for picket duty. Occasionally a secesh (who were very good sharpshooters) came near enough and picked off a picket man.

Despite weeks of incertitude, General Lyon now fully understood that enemy troops had united and intended to take Springfield. He knew with certainty that nearly half of his volunteer soldiers had mustered out and returned to St. Louis and that no reinforcements were coming. Most of his remaining soldiers were poorly fed or ill-equipped. Soldiers in the

---

504 Ware, 302; Branson, 08-07 to 08-08-1861 (p. 60). "Messenger arrived saying enemy of 20,000 advancing."
505 Banasik (Wilkie), 140.
506 Ware, 260–261, 290. Mace was terrified of being caught by Confederates and sold back into slavery. He left the camp and reappeared after the soldiers arrived in St. Louis, where Eugene and friends paid him and said their good byes. Ware, 304, 347.
507 Ware, 295, 296.

First Iowa Infantry remained in the expectancy of a fight. They would not leave without Lyon, and Lyon would not leave until it was absolutely demonstrated that he could not stay. But "It was too late to retreat—it was too late to stay." [508] Lyon was in a lose-lose situation.

---

[508] Peckham, 104, 324, 331,

CHAPTER NINE

A STORM WAS BREWING

You may nurse a viper and get stung by it…but you shall not obtrude your viper on us.
—Nathaniel Lyon, October 27, 1860, letter written to the *Manhattan Express*

On the night of August 8, the distant night sky was lighted up with campfires of the enemy. Two additional Missouri companies from Lyon's army, the Third Missouri Volunteers and the Fourth Reserves, mustered out and left for St. Louis August 9.[509] Refugees were pouring into Springfield describing great numbers of enemy in the countryside, and many citizens deserted the town.

Lyon sent sick soldiers with them. George was asked by Captain Cook to remain in town but to not attempt the battle because of his painful abscess which would prevent him from marching: "I feel bad because I could not take part."[510] Burmeister, like Colonel Bates, who had fallen ill, did not join the march to Wilson's Creek, where the battle took place August 10.

---

509 Rombauer, 313.
510 Burmeister, 08-08 to 08-10-1861.

Frémont sent a letter to Lyon August 6 by special messenger, but it didn't arrive in Lyon's camp until August 9. He advised a retreat, but it was too late. Lyon responded in what would be his last letter, that he would try to hold his ground. A retreat could mean huge losses of men, artillery, and transportation:

> I find my position extremely embarrassing and am at present unable to determine whether I shall be able to maintain my ground or be forced to retire…If the enemy move to surround me I must retire…I may… endanger safety of my entire force with its valuable material."[511]

Lyon knew he was greatly outnumbered, and there would be great losses in a fight. He was down to three thousand seven hundred men who were mostly marching infantry soldiers. Franz Sigel had one thousand four-hundred troops. The combined Confederate and State Guard forces were strong and advancing nearby. Lyon feared the enemy, with many more soldiers and at least four thousand cavalry and mounted riflemen, could surround them, their weapons, many valuable wagons, and supplies in a slow, 120-mile trek to Rolla.[512] Lyon would have despised the idea of surrendering to Price and the Confederates, especially if he was still fuming over how some of the enemy troops were using federal weapons taken from U.S. arsenals. He surely felt a vise tightening around his small army. Lyon readied for a retreat because it seemed unavoidable, but he soon decided that a fast and vigorous shock to the rebels was an option. Lyon hoped the surprise might prevent or delay the enemy from attacking the retreating Union troops. He made a final choice and ordered the shocker.

Lyon's decision to attack remains a matter of interpretation. Some suggest this was a pathological judgment, others that it was the best

---

511 *OR*, Series 1, Vol. 3:57, Report of Brig. Gen. Lyon to Maj. Gen. John C. Frémont, August 9, 1861; Peckham, 324; Ware, 309; McElroy, *Struggle for Missouri*, 157; Banasik (Wilkie), 139n256. Wilkie reported that Lyon decided to fight at Wilson's Creek to halt the rebel advance and to save Springfield.

512 Peckham, 524.

possible option given the situation. Captain Joseph B. Plummer, who led a battalion of Regulars in Lyon's advance on the enemy, reported that citizens urged Lyon to stay and not retreat from Springfield.[513] Lyon did not want to wait for the enemy to attack. The officers advised retreating, but Lyon worried about the dangers of his marching troops becoming surrounded by mounted troops. Wilkie thought the officers were ready to retreat and did not show the same loyalty as Lyon because of the government's disregard for their needs.[514] Lyon argued that putting up a stubborn fight could better guarantee security for a retreat. It's likely that Lyon made the plan after receiving information that the enemy was expecting reinforcements within a few days from Hardee's Confederate column approaching from the southeast.[515] The officers did not object to his final decision, but they did object to Sigel's plan to use his German troops to independently flank the enemy from a different direction.[516] Lyon's agreement with Sigel's plan remains poorly understood.

Historian Phillips speculates, and Piston and Hatcher concur, that because of Lyon's shifting plans and temperament, he was unstable and made his final decisions because he needed to fulfill his goal of punishing the enemy.[517] However, considering the circumstances, some degree of indecision and anxiety seems reasonable. General McCulloch was also wavering under lack of clear authority from the Confederate command and the heavy responsibility of sending men into battle with imperfect information. He had earlier ordered an advance on Lyon, then pulled back when intelligence reported that Lyon wasn't there. One of his greatest

---

513 Peckham, 383, 384, 386. When asked by the Committee on the Conduct of the War if the battle was better than waiting for reinforcements Captain Plummer (later Colonel then Brigadier General Plummer) of the Regulars answered, 'Yes, Sir, a thousand times." When questioned about the rationale of fighting against the odds, Plummer answered, "an attacking force has an advantage, in moral effect also giving them courage, while falling back is intimidating."
514 Banasik (Wilkie), 142.
515 *The Clinton Herald*, Saturday, August 17, 1861. "Report from Rolla, August 13."
516 Piston and Hatcher, 177.
517 Phillips, *Damned Yankee*, 248; Piston and Hatcher, *Wilson's Creek*, 174, 178.

challenges was getting reliable information about Lyon. After the battle, McCulloch reported that he relied on the Missourians for accurate scouting reports, "owing to their knowledge of the country...This they repeatedly promised, but totally failed to furnish."[518] Incomplete reports were confusing, even to experienced army officers.

Lyon's idea was giving it all they had before the enemy could coordinate their advantage.[519] Sweeny agreed, as did Surgeon Florence M. Cornyn of the First Missouri Volunteers (U.S.), saying a retreat would be impossible against the Confederates' much greater cavalry and speed. Lyon would not surrender without a struggle and did not expect a victory, but wanted to retreat to Rolla through a "crippled foe." [520] Did Lyon believe that a surprise attack was possible? How much did he know about McCulloch's planned attack on Springfield? Lyon's scout came in to report that indeed McCulloch's forces were united with those of Rains and Price.

John M. Schofield reported just after the battle, that the enemy was continually receiving small arms and artillery from the South while Lyon's own numbers were diminished from discharges and "wasting from privations." He noted how people coming in from the countryside and Home Guards reported numbers of advancing enemy, and there were false alarms. Because they had received no reinforcements, Schofield wrote that Lyon had forebodings about needing to either abandon portions of southwestern Missouri and southern Kansas to the enemy or face the total destruction of his army. He stated that Lyon planned the attack on Wilson's Creek during the day on August 9.[521] In his autobiography published thirty-two years after the Civil War, Schofield criticized Lyon's decision to fight at Wilson's Creek and found fault with many of his fellow officers.[522]

---

518 Shalhope, 173; Piston and Hatcher, 157.
519 Lyftogt, 196; Ware, 339.
520 Peckham, 324, 327.
521 *OR*, Series 1, Vol. 3:57–59, Report of Maj. John M. Schofield, August 20, 1861.
522 John M. Schofield, *Forty-Six Years in the Army* (New York: The Century Company, 1897), 40, 42–47.

"The Campaign in Missouri – the Dark Side of War – Refugees from Southern Missouri, Driven from their Homesteads by the Rebels, Camped near Gen. Sigel's Division at Rolla." 1862. (Unknown). Retrieved from the Digital Public Library of America, https://mohistory.org/collections/item/P0084-1270. (Accessed April 20, 2025.)

Lyon's Bit of Luck

Unbeknownst to Lyon, his officers and men, was a remarkable synchronicity of events. Not far away, at nearly the same time as Lyon made his decision to attack rather than retreat, Confederate General Benjamin McCulloch agreed to Jackson's and Price's demands and ordered an August 9 attack on Lyon at Springfield. Sterling Price was leading forces of the Missouri State Guard.[523] Although McCulloch neither liked nor trusted Price, he was encouraged after receiving information that Confederate General Gideon Pillow was advancing into Missouri from

---

523 Piston and Hatcher, 134, 161.

the east.[524] But a storm was brewing that day, and it began to rain on McCulloch's troops. Heavy rain would damage ammunition. Instead of advancing on Springfield, McCulloch's forces remained in camp near Wilson's Creek.[525] Price ordered the pickets to be brought in.[526] The rebel troops were sleeping in the drizzle, confident of attacking Lyon's troops in Springfield the next morning.

That same night, August 9, Lyon ordered his soldiers to fall in. He ordered Lieutenant Colonel William Merritt to have the First Iowa Regiment in line by 6:00 p.m.[527] Would the exhausted First Iowa soldiers who had marched so many miles and claimed, at times, to hate Lyon, fall in line to fight for him? On his dapple-gray horse, Lyon rode by each company giving them practical, but not inspirational, advice. He told Company E to fire low, not higher than the enemies' knees, and to wait until they were close.[528] Eugene said how the boys in his company "had that strange confidence in an officer who they believe understands his business."[529] Making little noise in the dark, Lyon's troops marched towards the enemy forces. Horses' hooves and artillery wheels were padded, under orders for silence. Seventy men from Ware's company marched at night and quietly discussed how they wanted their coffins decorated. Officers later reported that Lyon said he had great confidence in his little army, who, "one on one, could not be whipped."[530]

The Battle of Wilson's Creek

Lyon's surprise attack on the combined enemy forces at Wilson's Creek began at dawn on August 10, 1861. Franc Wilkie wrote that a few min-

---

524 Brooksher, 160; Piston and Hatcher, 148. The authors state that although Snead witnessed dramatic conflict between Price and McCulloch, this written account by Snead cannot be trusted.
525 Piston and Hatcher, 161, 162; Shalhope, 176.
526 Piston and Hatcher, 312.
527 Lyftogt, 198.
528 Ware, 310.
529 Ware, 312, 315.
530 Peckham, 332.

utes after 5:00 am, the boom of artillery was heard in Springfield. He arrived on the scene of battle after much of it had been fought. Wilkie reported that as he approached, "The whole earth was shaken with one tremendous continuous peal that seemed the prolonged howl of a hundred thunder-storms mingled in one."[531]

According to Eugene Ware, the cavalry, artillery, and infantry marched in companies to their battle lines. Two pieces of Totten's artillery were run up between Company E and the one to their right. A body of perhaps one thousand enemy advanced in a meadow, until the batteries turned on them. For a while the enemy were stunned and confused, then rallied and advanced. The firing began. "How long it lasted I do not know. It might have been an hour; it seemed like a week; it was probably twenty minutes."[532] Eugene said that he was not able to give an accurate account of the charges and counter-charges on the slope of that hill, except to say that they kept coming.

Piston and Hatcher note that Burlington (twin) Companies D and E were used as skirmishers to the left of DuBois' Battery. The First Missouri Infantry and the First Kansas moved toward the south bank of a ravine which held the enemy. The First Iowa anchored the left of the Union line. To the rear, the Second Kansas regiment was held in reserve. When Rain's division of one thousand Missouri State Guard moved towards them, Lyon ordered the Second Kansas forward. Captain Totten moved farther to the front and right with two guns for support and fired into the enemy's artillery. The Union line fired into the enemy until rebels charged against the artillery. Soldiers on both sides shot furiously until they could no longer see through the dense smoke. Eugene described a continual movement of troops, the difficulty of hearing orders in the din of fierce fighting, and confusion. He thought the most stubborn

---

531 Banasik (Wilkie), 143; Burmeister 08-10-1861. George could hear the rapid cannonading. He tells how news was regularly coming into Springfield reporting on the progress of the battle.
532 Ware, 319, 320.

fight came from a detachment of Louisiana troops who were using nice, rifled muskets which had been taken from the U.S. armory in Baton Rouge. After repulsing them, the Iowa soldiers found many dead soldiers wearing heavy brass belt plates with pelican emblems worn by the Baton Rouge Pelican Rifles.[533]

In the constant noise, smoke, dust, and chaos of fierce volleys, there were failed assaults and pullbacks. Some soldiers heard orders while others could not, sometimes resulting in misaligned companies. At some point, the Rolla detachment from the 13th Illinois Infantry, led by Lt. James Beardsley, Company D, fought in the battle with the First Iowa.[534] There is agreement that, for a long while, the Union center was the target of the Rebel offensive, and it was held by Totten's battery, Steele's command, and the First Iowa.[535]

Both sides were engaged about four hours when Lyon ordered the First Iowa to move right to defend a vulnerable gap in the Union line. At the same time that the Second Kansas was moving up, soldiers in the First Iowa asked if Lyon would lead them. Eugene wrote that Lyon was killed leading their regiment's charge when the general was not in front, but on the right end of their line. Lyon was shot after shouting, "Come on my brave boys, I will lead you forward!" It remains unclear which soldiers, exactly, heard his last words. Eugene believed that Lyon's last words were meant for the First Iowa and that it was undisputed until quickly changing narratives claimed the same position for the First Missouri and Second Kansas. He writes, "History has tried but cannot rob us of this."[536]

---

[533] Ware, 321, 322; Piston and Hatcher, 283. See p. 4–5 for brief discussion of the Pelican Rifles.

[534] Piston and Hatcher, 80, 242, 262.

[535] Piston and Hatcher, 275, 280; Bearss, 129; Brooksher, 190; Ware, 330, discusses Schofield's and Sturgis' reports which note the centrality of the First Iowa Infantry in the battle.

[536] Ware, 332–333. Ware gives various reasons for the false reports, noting that the official report of the Second Kansas says nothing about it. Another account was given by a wounded soldier who was taken off the field before the event happened. See Piston and Hatcher, 264–268. In Merritt's report, he confused the left and right flanks. The error was repeated in reports by Sturgis and Schofield and caused newspaper controversy, 378n8;

Confederate cavalry was sighted in the rear to their right and charged the Union artillery from the back. "We were ordered to face about and step forward to meet them" in round squads of 15–20 men, as they had been drilled. The First Iowa kept firing and awaited the cavalry approach with fixed bayonets, then the Union artillery turned them away.

General Sigel, who had convinced Lyon to divide his force, successfully divided the rebel forces for a short time before he was routed. Eugene thought that Sigel wasn't whipped until after he had whipped the enemy's lower camp. Unfortunately, Sigel's failure was unknown by the rest of the Union forces. Sigel's troops were of no use to Lyon after their mid-morning defeat, leaving Lyon's army to hold the Union line with fewer than 4,000 soldiers. They held off two assaults and maintained the high ground. They had left Springfield about fifteen hours earlier and believed the enemy might number as many as twenty thousand.

At about 10:30, the Missouri State Guard and Arkansas soldiers made a third assault. DuBois' battery and the nearby infantry line stopped it.[537] Word passed along the lines that Lyon had been killed. Finally, the enemy artillery ceased firing and there was a lull. During the pause, Major Samuel D. Sturgis ordered the Union retreat. Eugene thought they were the last off the field, and no shots were fired after them: "In front of us and down in the meadow and around the burned supply trains were a large number of killed Confederates, and none anywhere to be seen with weapons in their hands."[538]

The Iowa boys had no idea the day had gone against them, because as Eugene noted, they were "hard to dislodge." Ware described how each company was a little army and how "each company inspired itself."[539] The Iowans left the field with the certain belief that they had indeed struck a blow because the rebels were crippled enough to pull back when they

---

537 Piston and Hatcher, 268, 274, 280.
538 Ware 322–328.
539 Ware, 332.

could have demolished the smaller retreating force.

Captain Gordon Granger, who believed they were on the verge of victory, pleaded with Sturgis not to order the retreat, saying "But they have burned their trains."[540] Captain John B. Plummer later reported that after seeing the enemy wagons burning, he assumed that, from his perspective, the Confederates set the fires to keep them from falling into enemy hands.[541] A Confederate soldier wrote that from their position on high ground, they could see Churchill's (the First Arkansas) camps, tents and wagons on fire.[542] Bearss writes that stragglers from Sigel's troops set fire to abandoned wagons.[543] Eugene writes that five acres of wagons were set on fire by Totten's shells: "How could they pursue us? It was a great sight to see their wagon train burn...I saw it all; I watched every shell, and the smoke rose in a heavy black pall over the landscape."[544] Henri Lovie's onsite drawing of Lyon's death for *Leslie's Illustrated Newspaper* documented the burning Confederate

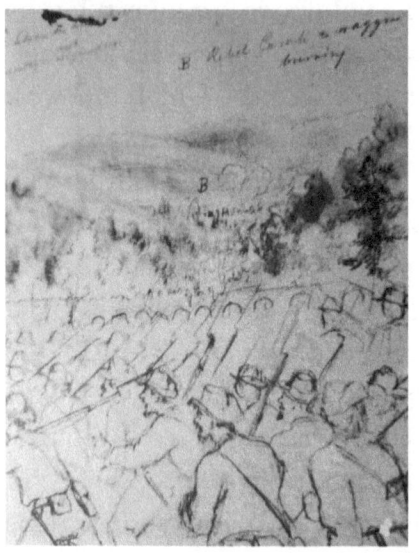

Detail from Lovie Sketch with notes about rebel train burning and showing the First Iowa Infantry fighting for General Lyon at Wilson's Creek

---

540 Brooksher, 223.
541 Peckham, "Committee on Conduct of War, January 9, 1862." Would the southern forces burn their own wagons if they believed they were winning the battle?
542 Piston and Hatcher, 93, 275. Thomas J. Churchill organized and was elected colonel of the First Arkansas regiment. He was later elected governor of Arkansas.
543 Bearss, 72.
544 Ware, 335.

wagon trains.[545] His sketched notes read: "B. Rebel Camp and wagons burning" and "Iowa Reg. marched up and formed for bayonet charge." Lovie's drawing shows the First Iowa Infantry next to the dying general.

There is speculation about the lack of Confederate response to the Federal retreat. Arkansas Brigadier General Nicholas Pearce reportedly said that his officers "were glad to see him (the Union enemy) go."[546] According to historian Thomas W. Cutrer, the risk of pursuit was too great for the Confederate general: "McCulloch was commanding an army as disorganized by victory as his enemy was by defeat."[547] Piston and Hatcher conclude that after the battle, McCulloch and Price agreed not to pursue the Union Army because of their own troops' exhausted condition and shortage of ammunition.[548] Fresh antagonism soon broke out between the two men after Price made his report the first to be printed in the Springfield papers. His account ignored McCulloch's leadership and implied that the Missouri State Guard were solely responsible for defeating Sigel.[549] McCulloch reported to the Adjutant General of Confederate States a great victory against forces about the same in numbers as theirs, about nine or ten thousand strong, and possession of Springfield, with enemy in full retreat toward Rolla. To L. P. Walker, C.S.A. Secretary of war, he wrote "Nothing could withstand the impetuosity of our final charge."[550] McCulloch did not mention that after Sigel's mid-morning rout and retreat, about 4000 Union soldiers held off repeated assaults by the combined Confederate and State Guard troops, nor that he did not take possession of Springfield until after the Union troops and the very long wagon train were safely gone.[551]

---

545 Joshua Brown, *Beyond the Lines: Pictorial Reporting, Everyday Life, and the Crisis of Gilded Age America* (Berkeley: University of California Press, 2006), 32, 55, 56; Henri Lovie's sketch was made with visual notes and comments, "Death of General Lyon, August 10, 1861" The New York Public Library Digital Collections..

546 Bearss, 135; Brooksher, 224; Piston and Hatcher, 286.

547 Cutrer, 50; Ware, 334, quotes the official report by the Colonel of the Louisiana Pelican Regiment: "My men were too exhausted to make a successful pursuit."

548 Piston and Hatcher, 308.

549 Piston and Hatcher, 312.

550 *OR*, Series 1, Vol. 3:107, Ben McCulloch to Hon. L. P. Walker.

551 Banasik (Wilkie), 156n301, n302. Wounded soldiers were left in Springfield under the care of four soldiers.

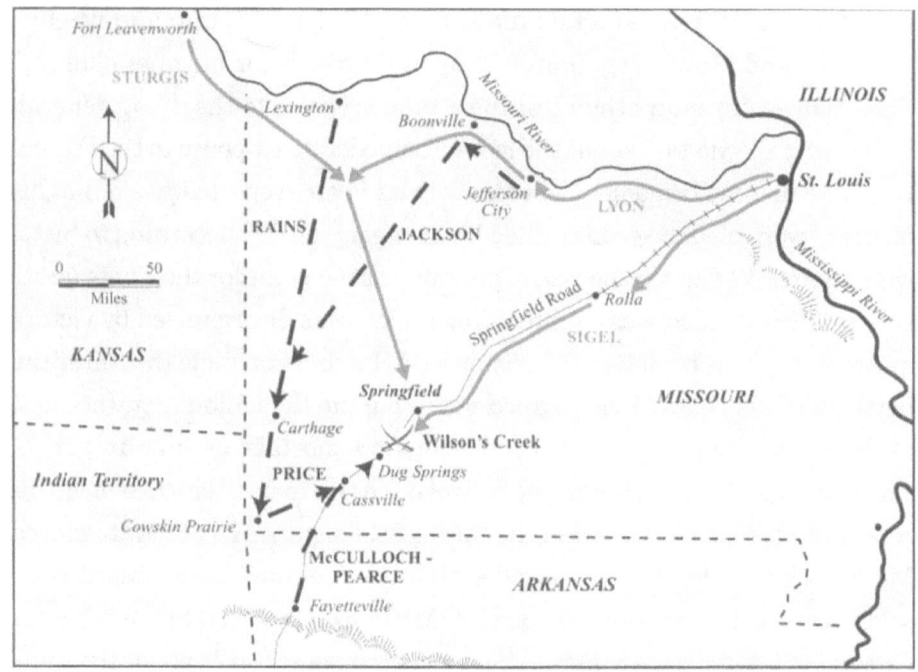

Routes to the Battle of Wilson's Creek
Map from the National Park Service 2/9/2021

The greatest cost of Lyon's campaign was that, like the Union general himself, many of his fighting soldiers and officers and those of his enemy fell at Wilson's Creek, "face to the front."[552] Eugene Ware survived the battle, and George Burmeister survived the knee infection. Lyon's remaining army was not pursued, not that day or during the next week as they slowly marched yet another one hundred rugged miles before arriving in Rolla.

---

552 McElroy, *The Struggle for Missouri*, 51. McElroy used the phrase "face to the front," to describe Lyon's death at age 42; The First Iowa Infantry lost 154 soldiers, total casualties (killed, wounded or missing); 80 total casualties from Plummer's Regulars First U.S. Infantry; 55 from Second Missouri Infantry; 7 from Kansas Rangers and Co. D. U. S. Cavalry; 11 from Totten's Artillery; 293 from Third and Fifth Missouri; 61 from Companies B and E, Second U.S. infantry Regulars and Recruits; 284 from First Kansas Infantry; 70 from Second Kansas Infantry; 295 First Missouri Infantry. Piston and Hatcher, 337–338.

The Union Retreat

George did not want to be left behind with the injured soldiers, so he tried walking with the retreating troops, but had to use a wagon for some distance. They continued to march after dark, expecting the enemy to pursue: "We did not suppose that anyone would be so fortunate as to reach Rolla alive." There were rumors that Confederate General Hardee was ahead with 10,000 troops to cut them off. They passed through Lebanon where George was able to purchase something to eat. On August 14 the official U.S. terms of duty expired for soldiers in the First Iowa Infantry. There were boys who refused to march in ranks or perform any duties: "Some blame General Lyon for engaging the enemy with such awful odds against us, yet I admire his policy." George thought they gained more than they could have with any other plan and writes how a timid retreat could have been annihilation and probably have opened the way to St. Louis. After marching through deep ravines and dark hollows, on August 16 they crossed the rapidly flowing Gasconade River where the water was up to George's breast. He held clothes, his gun, and accoutrements over his head. Some soldiers were carried downstream and had to be rescued by horsemen. When the troops got to within seven miles of Rolla they stopped for dinner, then kept going knowing they were headed home. They arrived about 11:00 p.m.[553]

On August 17 soldiers in the First Iowa gave up the old muskets and received new uniforms with a coat, pants, and shoes. George took a wash, threw away his rags, and put on his new clothes. They got onboard the railroad cars about 10:00. In St. Louis George was welcomed by family friends, the family of H. E. Schuster. On the 19th he went to the North Market and found his brother Charles, who was working in the city. The next day George took a ride in the new railroad cars which were being

---

[553] Burmeister, 08-11-1861; Eugene Ware, 344, describes crossing the Gasconade, Roubidoux, Big and Little Piney Rivers.

used in St. Louis. Recruiting offices were open all over town. George visited the Arsenal where most of the regiment was camped. He thought it was a filthy, contaminated atmosphere. Soldiers in the First Iowa Infantry were mustered out of service on the 21st and received pay on August 23, after which most companies departed for home.[554] George remained in St. Louis and on the 28th attended the funeral procession of General Lyon, which was conducted by Franz Sigel and attended by General Frémont and his staff.[555]

George was determined to find gainful employment in St. Louis. He enrolled in Jones Commercial College and studied bookkeeping, but the city's economy was depressed. George couldn't find work, was offered a teaching job back home, and in October took the steamship *Denmark* to Muscatine, Iowa. He taught school that winter, but it wasn't long before he became restless, irritable with his students, and wanting to do more with his life. He studied law in Muscatine for a few months with C. G. Hayes and Brothers, and fell in love with Miss Carolyn Barrows, a Muscatine school teacher. George soon recruited and became captain for the Muscatine German American Company C Sigel Rifles, 35th Iowa Infantry. His brother, Henry, 20, enlisted in the company. George and Carolyn (Carrie) planned to marry when George got leave from duty, when he was to be promoted to the rank of major.

---

554 Burmeister, 08-11-1861 to 08-28-1861; Ware, 344–347. Eugene's account differs on the dates of arrival into St. Louis and receiving uniforms; William Branson returned to Muscatine by train. Branson, 08-23 to 08-24-1861.

555 Shortly after learning about the Battle of Wilson's Creek, General Frémont declared martial law in St. Louis and appointed Major Justus McKinstry as provost martial. Frank Blair furiously spoke and wrote about Frémont's failures until he placed Blair under arrest orders. "General Frémont's Column: Arrest of Frank Blair," New York Times, September 17, 1861. https://www.nytimes.com/1861/09/17/archives; "Francis Preston Blair, Jr. – Facts," American History Central, https://www.americanhistorycentral.com/entries/francis-preston-blair-jr-facts/. When Frémont arrived in Missouri July 25, he reported being shocked by the Missouri secessionists who were in active rebellion against the Federal Government (Cutrer, 44); "… later Frémont stated that because Lyon 'had saved Missouri from secession' he had left Lyon's movement to his own discretion. 'To any other officer in his actual situation, I should have issued peremptory to fall back upon the railroad at Rolla.'"(Cutrer, 45). Frémont added that he had made every possible effort to reinforce Lyon.

George Burmeister (after reenlistment)
Captain, Muscatine 35th Iowa Infantry.
From copy of a family photograph, with permission of Dolores Rawson, April, 2024.

There was little time for the First Iowa Infantry soldiers to reunite and reminisce before they returned to the war. Although the diary selections here tell us only about their short three-month terms in the summer of 1861, like most of the soldiers in the First Iowa Infantry, both Burmeister and Ware re-enlisted. George continued to write in his diary until shortly before his death. He received a bullet wound May 18, 1864, at Yellow Bayou, Louisiana, and died in Jefferson Barracks Hospital, Missouri, June 16, 1864.[556]

---

556 Information obtained from April 12, 2024 interview with Dolores Rawson and from her copy of Eugene Burmeister's brief biography, written for the family, and from John Davis, "Complete List of Civil War Veterans of German Descent of Muscatine County," Iagenweb.org/civilwar/county/mus_ger.html. Retrieved 4/10/2020.

"Capt. Geo. C. Burmeister wounded at Yellow Bayou, LA. Died June 16th 1864." George Burmeister Memorial image and ribbon made for the eleventh reunion of the 35th Iowa Infantry by Whitehead and Hoag Co., Newark, New Jersey.
Collection Muscatine Art Center, Muscatine, Iowa.

After his re-enlistment, Eugene Fitch Ware served in the war with the 4th Iowa Calvary. Four months after the Wilson's Creek battle, he rode with his cavalry unit from Rolla to Springfield and through the Wilson's Creek battlefield: "I went over the whole scene with as strange feelings as a mortal ever felt."[557] Near the end of the war, he served as Captain of the 7th Iowa Calvary. For a short while, after the war, he was a journalist for the *Burlington Hawkeye* before moving to Kansas, where he was editor of the *Fort Scott Monitor*. Eugene married Miss Jeanette P. Huntington

---

557 Ware, 353.

in 1874. The Wares also lived in Topeka and Kansas City. Eugene studied and practiced law, served two terms in the Kansas legislature, and published several books. Two schools were named after Eugene Ware: Eugene Ware Elementary in Kansas City and Eugene Ware Elementary School in Fort Scott. He died July 1, 1911.[558]

---

558 Ware, xx–xxiii, Clark Kenyon's "Introduction to the Camp Pope Edition;" Digital information transcribed from William E. Connelly, *A Standard History of Kansas and Kansans* (Chicago: Lewis Publishing Co. 1918). https://ksgenweb.org/archives/1918/ks/biow/wareef.html; kshs.org/p/eugene-fitch-ware-papers/14133. Retrieved 4/10/2020.

CONCLUSION

Neither the flaccid coercive mechanisms of Civil War armies nor charismatic leadership could alone or together have kept these armies in existence or made them fight.
—James McPherson (*For Cause and Comrades*)

Although they were in rags, looked like bums, and were perceived as bums by Lyon and by the Regulars, soldiers in the First Iowa Infantry earned dignity by outmarching other regiments. Despite having been poorly outfitted with outdated equipment; commanded by inexperienced non-military regimental officers; surprised and frightened when surrounded by angry secessionists; and often not knowing where they were headed or why; they followed orders in a context of buzzing harsh conditions. Soldiers endured the hardships while living in close companionship with men in their companies, but Eugene and George experienced and expressed feelings individually.

George Burmeister was somewhat of a pensive loner and only hinted at his feelings. He showed concern for cleanliness, foraging and food, and sharing it with friends.[559] George told us why he put up with such brutal

---

[559] Burmeister mentions George Aylsworth, William Eckles, Charles Esgate, and Michael Menz, and Alfred Colliers. There were other friends who enlisted in Company K: Benjamin Whisler, Isaiah VanMeter, John VanArsdel, and Erastus Soper.

treatment: "All this we bear knowing that we are serving our country."[560] Eugene seems like a young, cocksure teenager. He was prone to rambunctious fighting, jokes, and pranks with friends. Eugene described those closest to him who were from Company E, Burlington.[561] He boasted about their singing, the unit's accomplishment of challenging tasks, and his own swimming across the surging Grand River. He told of his company's exceptional drilling and how the Boonville residents asked for an exhibition. Eugene proudly wrote in his diary about how the soldiers learned "Land of Canaan" and included a few verses of their marching song.

The extreme march to help Sigel's regiments when it was too late was surely exhausting and depleting. The soldiers' efforts at Forsyth and Dug Springs under Lyon seemed in vain. Why did soldiers in the First Iowa Infantry fight to exhaustion for a man they claimed to hate? Why didn't they express fury?

McPherson wonders why the armies had not disintegrated before 1864, when soldiers were near collapse, when "many a man has gone crazy since this campaign began from the terrible pressure on mind and body."[562] He finds that even near the end of the Civil War, many Northern soldiers continued to be sustained by the same early factors of pride and conviction, duty, courage, and belief in their cause.[563] Eugene and George reveal company community as a dynamic, ebb and flow process that was central to their commitments to the Union cause in the summer of 1861.

As the values and commitments of the First Iowa soldiers were challenged, they became more tangible and the soldiers were inspired to act. Above all, Eugene and George expressed an expectation to fight for the Union. They wanted to "face the enemy." Lieutenant Colonel

---

560 Burmeister, 07-26-1861.
561 Ware mentions Bill Heustis, Charlie Stypes, Fletch Brandebury, Bill Fuller, James Drealard, William Syester, and James H. Guthrie. He told of marching beside Samuel Chapman, taking turns holding each other's muskets.
562 McPherson, 165, quoting Captain Oliver Wendell Holmes, Jr.
563 McPherson, 168.

Merritt asked soldiers in the First Iowa what they would do if mustered out before battle. Eugene Ware answered, "Want out, unless there is a fight." The soldiers wanted a voluntary, more honorable, decision. After dispute and debate, they voted. United, they did not want to let their comrades down. Wilkie confirmed this: "Our men, ragged, dirty, and ill fed as they are, will fight to the last moment."[564]

Group cohesion came with enlistments and expanded within the soldiers' respective military companies. Groups of close comrades shared experiences when foraging, cooking, talking and performing tasks. Face-to-face contact (propinquity) was inherent in the daily operations of men whenever they were eating, drilling, marching, or sleeping within company boundaries. Social trust, a bonding agent, was built from being responsible for each other during guard and picket duties, the interdependence necessary for accomplishing difficult tasks together, helping each other, and sharing resources (mutuality). They needed each other for problem solving, for camping, wagon and mule tending, procuring food, cooking, and river crossings.

The men were committed to each other, carrying each other's muskets, propping up falling comrades, cheering, and hugging each other as tired soldiers stumbled into camp. Soldiers felt pride from hacking it. They had to trust each other: "Confederates at our rear and rode around us all day"; "Fear attacks coming"; "Changed camp locations three times to keep enemy off guard." The soldiers had to rely on each other for safety whenever they expected an assault or took turns at dangerous guard or picket duty.

The sense of belonging to a company (what Piston and Hatcher term "company-level identity") came early from enlistments, from sharing a company name, flag, officers, and a company supply wagon. Even deteriorating uniforms, made by hometown women, became company symbols,

---

[564] Banasik (Wilkie), 128.

each set of rags a quirky reminder of where a man belonged. Wilkie wrote how the regiment started singing early in training camp when the boys were rowdy and boisterous, when the songs calmed petty jealousies and started to produce a "union of sentiment and purpose."[565] The circle of belonging enlarged to include the larger regiment whenever the soldiers drilled together, marched, sang "Land of Canaan," and lined up for battle together as the First Iowa Infantry. When Colonel Bates used "Iowa" to call them out, it was a unifying regimental source of pride. Lyon recognized the First's inner force and persistence and so renamed them the Iowa Greyhounds. Although their sense of belonging together was most intense within a group of closest comrades, their bonds extended whenever they worked with the larger brigade to include other soldiers, regiments, and officers.

The soldiers had woven blankets of endurance while experiencing something unnamed in their diaries. Sense of belonging, willing mutuality, and sharing of resources were critical in developing community. However, these are not sufficient under extreme duress. It requires commitment to shared ideology, a common cause. The ongoing lack of information and abundant misinformation which led to exaggerated camp rumors took a severe toll on the soldiers and created "buzzing" confusion. The diarists repeatedly wrote how they didn't know where they were marching, tell of their disappointment from orders to march south when they thought they were headed home, and of their fear of attacks without knowing when or how many enemy troops were coming. Eugene admitted that rumor magnified worries. We know little about the trickledown of information, how it was obtained or shared by General Lyon. What were the sources of misinformation? Even minimal information was significant in threatening situations. Fact or rumor, soldiers shared what was known. Poor information-sharing, severe deprivations,

---

[565] Banasik (Wilkie), 58.

and the lack of government support were weak links in maintaining company community. Uncertainty waged war on their commitments, but "there became the greatest fraternity among them."[566]

Leadership

Community is not formed as solid matter: it can wane. Community needs to be sustained and renewed. Leadership emerged here as an important strand in preserving it, especially as stressful conditions worsened. Little is known about leadership within company ranks and how it links to community. Eugene noted that enlistees had identified peer leaders from within their companies. He believed that leadership of his company and regiment was earned from decency, gumption, and bravery, and said the first two qualities were scarcer. The boys in his company had confidence in their First Lieutenant John C. Abercrombie (36) and Orderly Sergeant Jo Utter (28).[567] Eugene thought that the real leaders were the musket bearers: "They were the ones who made up the mind of the company and gave it excellence." Was Eugene Ware or George Burmeister an essential leader?

After years of adulation following press promotion of General Lyon as a Union martyr, it is small wonder that historians needed to make corrections to the record. However, recent accounts might be unduly critical of Lyon. It is fair to ask if Nathaniel Lyon, faulty as he was, became a strong leader of the Iowa soldiers. Leadership requires the ability to make decisions and to employ resources. General Lyon relied on the strong support of his officers, like General Thomas Sweeny, who was commanding troops at the Arsenal before Lyon's arrival in St. Louis. Lyon depended on him at Camp Jackson and throughout the Missouri

---

566 Ware, 157
567 Ware, 307, 308; Banasik (Wilkie), "Appendix A Roster of the First Iowa Infantry," 280–345.

campaign.[568] Sweeny was important in uniting soldiers of the First Iowa. Eugene described him when he was leading soldiers towards Forsyth as a "typical" Irishman, full of fun, but one who also expected strict discipline. Lyon was disappointed at any officer who had failed to hold a U. S. arsenal or fort against Southern secessionists takeovers, but two of those surrenders resulted in loyal officers for Lyon: Captain James Totten (forced to surrender at Little Rock Federal arsenal), and Captain Samuel D. Sturgis (surrendered Fort Smith, Arkansas).[569]

After the Iowa soldiers saw leadership in action, they developed growing confidence in the Regular Army officers and decided to trust Lyon. Although the soldiers complained that Lyon seemed always to be looking for fault; was too "Regular" army; required too much discipline; and paid too much attention to small infractions, the officers and Regular soldiers respected him. Eugene recounts this image of General Lyon:

> Lyon was a small man, lean, active and sleepless. He was not an old man, although he had wrinkles on the top of his nose. He had a look of incredulity; he did not believe things...He looked like a man who knew absolutely that he knew...His beard was worn full; it was a...meager, reddish, unattractive beard, and he pulled on it and jerked on it when he was talking decisively...His eyes seemed to look each separately...He believed in every man knowing his duty and doing it strictly...He was a man capable of grasping great occasions and doing great things, and at the same time a wasp to those around him.[570]

A Civil War leader had to organize the many parts of a campaign. They could be thwarted by bad luck, reduced resources, or lack of information.

---

568 Banasik (Wilkie), 117n200. Sweeny was a Regular Army captain who was elected (unofficially) a brigadier general of Missouri Militia.
569 Banasik (Wilkie), 364–365 and 102n161. Totten and Sturgis were graduates of West Point.
570 Ware, 339, 340.

Almost everything went wrong for Lyon after winning the skirmish in Boonville, starting with no wagons for transportation, then heavy rain, deep mud, and raging rivers. Rombauer noted how Lyon acquired strict discipline after years in the army and comprehended all phases of a given situation: "He didn't need subterfuge."[571] Lyon tried and failed to get the supplies and reinforcements he needed to make their fighting chances fair. Lyon was handicapped by conditions, but he was not handcuffed. He was determined and adapted his plans. Even Confederate Thomas Snead recognized Lyon's keen mind: "He had not, however, been a mere soldier in those days but had been an earnest student…and he comprehended the matter as well as any man."[572]

Governor Jackson, too, accomplished near-success in the Civil War, but he used different leadership styles. He was a politician, and Lyon was a military leader. Many citizens supported Claiborne Jackson because he represented their secessionist cause. Jackson's biographer profiles him as a man who sought control and dominance in his personal and political life.[573]

Many gaps remain in what I learned about these soldiers in the summer of 1861. At times, this project was like staring into an eddy. For every answered question sent swirling downriver, another, unanswered, foamed up in its place. Was Nathaniel Lyon a mentally unstable religious zealot whose purpose was to punish the enemy? Did he launch the Civil War in Missouri? What drives a man like Claiborne Jackson to do whatever it takes to achieve self-serving goals with little regard for the majority of his constituents? Did the Missouri government authorize the development of a state *secessionist* militia? Was the militia at Camp Jackson legally authorized by the state for a coup against the federal government as incited by General Frost and Governor Jackson? Can government acts

---

571 Rombauer, 152, 226.
572 Snead, 199.
573 Phillips, *Missouri's Confederate*, 159, 162–163. "Wire-pulling" is a term used for the use of secret influence.

be considered valid if they pass laws under illicit conditions for treasonous purposes? Was General William S. Harney a devoted Unionist or an elusive secessionist-leaning placeholder?

Although George Burmeister briefly reveals his religious conviction and Eugene Ware mentions his Congregational upbringing, there is little information about how religion played a role in their commitments. Were the Iowa enlistees influenced by the "Iowa Band" of ministers who held such important roles in the early churches, schools, and politics in eastern Iowa?[574] How did the Iowa women form groups and make decisions when sewing uniforms and flags for enlistees? What did they sew onto the flag made for Burmeister's Company K? How did they receive news about their local companies and loved ones? Did Franc Wilkie share his reports with newspapers other than the Dubuque *Herald*, and what role did the telegraph play in reporting news to Iowans in the summer of 1861? How did the families who were eagerly awaiting news of the soldiers most often learn about them?

George's and Eugene's beliefs were much like Lyon's battle plans, clear and direct. Lyon didn't dodge and dart but went straightforward to attack, though sometimes finding abandoned posts. Iowa soldiers and the Union soldiers mustered in St. Louis believed that if the Union lost the war they would no longer live in a worthy country: "Far better would it be if the war should continue until every home should be made desolate [than]…to surrender to those despots who are trying to destroy our country."[575] The unifying force of community needed to be renewed under conditions of stress, uncertainty, and fear. Lyon subjected his troops to deprivation and risk, but he "kept one mark in view," and

---

574 Douglas, *Pilgrims of Iowa*. A group of American Home Missionary Congregational and Presbyterian ministers, led by Asa Turner, built many of the earliest churches and schools in southeastern Iowa and strongly influenced early politics in the state.

575 McPherson, *For Cause and Comrades*, 99, quoting a soldier's 1862 letter which sounds surprisingly similar to Lyon's declaration at the Planters' House Meeting, June 11, 1861. Many German soldiers hated autocracy and fought against what they thought was a tyrannical South.

the soldiers knew it. Like Lyon, Eugene and George believed the Union represented the best government ever made and was worthy of their sacrifice.[576] Leadership emerged here as an important strand in bolstering community by maintaining hope for the Union cause.

The soldiers willingly followed leaders who would fight for their cause. Community, formed by soldiers and sustained by leadership, inspired the First Iowa Infantry to follow General Lyon from Boonville into the Wilson's Creek Battle.

The First Iowa soldiers were not ordinary. They fast-outmarched other regiments and kept a sense of humor. They overcame. They sang. They made two songs famous for other Civil War campfires across America. They wrote. Eugene wrote that Lyon took dreadful chances and never expected to rout the armies of McCulloch and Price, but his "raw" soldiers fought better than he expected. After Lyon discovered inner force and dedication beneath the rags worn by the First Iowa regiment, perhaps their commitments to the Union contributed to his decision to stay and fight at Wilson's Creek.

---

576 Peckham, 392, quoting a phrase used by Sherman.

ACKNOWLEDGMENTS

> Evidence is always construed and it is always liable to being misconstrued…At best our understanding of any historical moment is significantly wrong.
> —Marilynne Robinson (*The Death of Adam*)

The Civil War was fought and the outcome decided for a struggling Union of diverse people from different regions and economies, people who held contrasting ways of life, identities, and beliefs. Very different interpretations of the war have trickled down over time. It must have been easier for each side to blame the other for launching into the horrors of Civil War, and, perhaps not strangely, the finger-pointing continues. Just as there was no common accord between the North and the South which might have avoided the war, there may be no future grounds for consensus by Civil War historians. Hopefully, chroniclers will continue to search Civil War records, because in the rocky river of history floats a desire to learn from it even if "truths" are murky. I am deeply thankful for the accounts written by first-hand observers as well as those by later historians who, regardless of their differing viewpoints, provide careful research and thoughtful analysis.

Historians try to fit together the many illogical, irrational, and confusing pieces of a larger war puzzle, though it's not always a perfect fit.

Brian M. Jordan noted how soon after the war ended, the desire to bring closure intimidated the nation into expunging its causes and crucial details about how the war was fought. A Gettysburg survivor believed that a complete history of the battle could never happen because it was "a dizzying mosaic of human experiences."[577]

Diaries are pieces of the mosaic, even if the whole remains unfinished. Eugene Ware's and George Burmeister's diaries provide valuable insight into the daily grind of soldiering. This book began with access to George Burmeister's diary in the University of Iowa Libraries' collections of digitalized Civil War Diaries, followed by reading Eugene Ware memoir, republished by Camp Pope. I was smitten by the diaries, but I had to study Michael Banasik's 2001 edition of Franc Wilkie's reports and relevant secondary sources in order to understand the context of the soldiers' experiences. I had much to learn about General Nathaniel Lyon, Governor Claiborne Jackson, General Harney, and Missouri's entry into the Civil War.

I needed reinforcements to complete this work, including repeated readings by Clark Kenyon. His careful editing and Civil War expertise, especially his knowledge of the First Iowa Infantry, was my lifeline. James Hallman, WriteWorks Editing, was my final filter. I doubt that I could have completed the work without Polly Leftosky at MyWord Publishing, and Asya Blue Design, who pulled me through the final stages.

In my case, having a supportive husband is no cliché. For years, John Fieselmann took on many of my usual tasks and lovingly listened to my torments. For my earliest ramblings, Gail Zlatnik provided gentle guidance and diligent reviews. Julie Gammack told me that my work could be important and that I needed to see it through. Our daughter, Emily, other family members, and dearest friends said they wanted to read the book, and I believed them. Over the past seven years I've had countless

---

577 Jordan, 218, 224, 235–236.

serendipitous moments of discovery, but the afternoon I'll never forget was spent with Dolores Rawson shortly before her death. Dolores, 98, kept careful guard over a family history and hand-typed copies of her Great Uncle George Burmeister's diary, his books, and trunk.

I feel fortunate for having had faculty in the University of Iowa's Department of Sociology who, years ago, taught me about contrasting worldviews, their underlying assumptions, the importance of recognizing my own, and the role these play in creating knowledge. I am especially grateful to Stephen G. Wieting, who kept boundless faith in students like me. Sociology suggests looking carefully at trajectories of scholarship, then probing why they differ. In this case, a too-simple explanation for discrepancies in Civil War histories is that they are written by people who have greater empathy with either the secessionist or the Union cause. But history is much more complicated.[578] Different clarifying beliefs lead to different attributions, regardless of the facts. Historians grow up with different family stories, loyalties, disciplines, perspectives, and for many years, with very different history textbooks.[579] We shouldn't expect that Civil War historians would consistently come to similar conclusions.

---

578 Douglas Scott et. al., 2009. This study, while trying to accurately report the early skirmish between Jackson's State Guard troops and Lyon's army, June 17, 1861, at Boonville, Missouri, demonstrates the complexity of drawing conclusions from historical records which offer dozens of very different accounts of that single event.

579 "United Daughters of the Confederacy," *Encyclopedia Virginia, Virginia Humanities.* https://encyclopediavirginia.org/entries/united-daughters-of-the-confederacy; *Encyclopedia Britannica;* https://www.britannica.com/topic/United-Daughters-of-the-Confederacy. The United Daughters of the Confederacy (UDC) did much to ensure that Southern textbooks conformed to their selective narrative of the Civil War, which downplayed slavery as a cause and emphasized states' rights. Generations of students were taught southern Lost Cause lessons in an effort to highlight the services of Confederate soldiers and to honor the homes and women who supported them; See also Greg Huffman, "Twisted Sources: How Confederate Propaganda ended up in the South's Schoolbooks," *Facing South: The Online Magazine of the Institute for Southern Studies*, April 10, 2019. https://www.facingsouth.org/2019/04/twisted-sources-how-confederate-propaganda-ended-souths-schoolbooks. The United Daughters of the Confederacy raised money for monuments, Confederate veterans' families, and benevolences for the poor. In some states they continued their most effective tool of censoring Southern textbooks until the 1970s.

AFTERWORD

We live in a time when forgetting is the norm, but remembering is the key to understanding ourselves.
—Marilynne Robinson

When Southern extremists broke up the Union to create a new, next-door country, it was a huge gamble. Confederate politicians knew before the war that odds were against them, but they remained obstinate and callous. The first seven deep-south states to secede held less than one-third of the free population of the South. The decisiveness and persuasion of leaders in those secessionist states led to the outbreak of the Civil War. I am baffled as to why so many Southern citizens followed a minority of "Fire-eaters."

Why did too few Southerners listen to leaders who had the courage to warn about the risks of secession? Sam Houston called Lincoln's election unfortunate, "but no justification for rash action…The North is determined to preserve this Union. They are not a fiery, impulsive people as we are but once they begin to move in a given direction, they move with the steady momentum of a giant avalanche, and what I fear is that they will overwhelm the South with ignoble defeat."[580] Texas ratified the vote to secede on February 23, 1861. When Texas legislators overrode Houston's vetoes, he refused to take the oath

---

580 "Texas Civil War History," Retrieved 1/10/2021.

of the Confederacy and gave up his office. And sure enough, like Sam Houston predicted, the Fort Sumter boom triggered an "avalanche."

Before Alexander Stephens became the vice president of the Confederacy, he pleaded against secession: "This step, once taken, can never be recalled... When we and our posterity shall see our lovely South, desolated by the demons of war, which this act of yours will inevitably invite...who but this convention will be held responsible for it? Who but him...shall be held to strict account for this suicidal act?"[581] Why did the warnings not matter?

The "Fire-Eaters" (dubbed here as "Flamethrowers") made great efforts, at great expense, to convince non-slaveholders that secession was fully justified and to support it. Southern politicians understood the necessity of promoting defenses for the enslavement of others and organized rhetorical rationales from a variety of respected institutions. Compelling justifications began long before the rebellion. Starting in the 1860's, Alabama, Mississippi, Georgia, South Carolina and Louisiana sent commissioners to other slave states to "sell" the secessionist cause.[582] The commissioners gave speeches which were printed in newspapers and pamphlets. One official told audiences "I would rather see the last of our race, men, women, and children, immolated" (sacrificed), than subjugated to degradation (equality of the races).[583] Southern ministers often aided the cause, professing that abolition was atheistic. To substantiate the arguments, Southern churches used the Old Testament where (in the ancient cultures) slavery was condoned and claimed that the New Testament did not specifically condemn it.[584]

---

581 Rombauer, 159.
582 Charles Dew, *Apostles of Disunion: Southern Secession Commissioners and the Causes of the Civil War*. (Charlottesville: University Press of Virginia, 2001). 18–19, 38. The commissioners also claimed that, for example: They (white citizens) held the privilege of caste and could rejoice in being white; (Equality) would mean eternal degradation; The founding fathers made this government for the white man, not for negroes who (they said) were ignorant and inferior; There would be losses of billions of dollars to the South, and planters would be reduced to poverty. 45, 50, 54–56, 58, 77.
583 Ibid, 29, 101.
584 Gordon Rhea, "Why Non-Slaveholding Southerners Fought" American Battlefield Trust. https://www.battlefields.org/learn/articles/why-non-slaveholding-southerners-fought

Luther J. Glenn was sent to present his doctrines to the Missouri secession convention on March 4, 1861. The Commissioner from Georgia made several claims, saying how John Brown was an example of the hostile intentions of the North—that is, to start slave rebellions. He declared that Republicans are not true to the Constitution because they do not accept that slaveholders should be allowed to take their slaves into new territories. Glenn added that the South looks at the opinions of Mr. Seward, Mr. Sumner, Mr. Wilson and others to conclude that the object of Republicans is to make slavery extinct. He encouraged Missourians to join a Confederacy of homogenous people that would bring prosperity and happiness to its people. The Missouri delegates did not accept the invitation, and their hissing lasted for some time.[585]

After the attack on Fort Sumter, "Fire Eaters" called the North's reaction "subjugation" and the "war of northern aggression."[586] Many non-slaveholding citizens accepted the arguments of the persuasive commissioners, ministers, and politicians. For some their lands and slaves were birthrights, and any resistance to those rights was coercion. They were more loyal to their property and state than to the Union and believed that the North's stubborn refusal to acknowledge their needs was a disrespectful abolitionist stance. Robert E. Lee, who, despite his professed devotion to peace and to the Union, accepted command of the Army of Virginia saying, "I cannot raise my hand against my birthplace,

---

[585] "Speech of Luther J. Glenn to the Missouri Convention" under "Causes of the Civil War," https://civilwarcauses.org. Accessed 3/22/2025. Website text taken from *Journal and Proceedings of the Missouri State Convention, Held at Jefferson City and St. Louis, March 1861*, (St. Louis: George Knapp and Co., 1861); See also Dew, 78, who states the speech was March 2, 1861.

[586] Southern politicians dismissed key demographic factors about population and the industrial advantages of the North. Ward, *The Civil War*, 87. The Flamethrowers also appear to have been blind to the consequences of violence, as shown in "bleeding" Kansas. Slaveowners refused to acknowledge that slavery could not likely last much longer even if the South won war, because it relied on outdated agricultural practices and was abhorrent to non-slave holders. The U.S Act prohibiting Importation of Slaves was enacted 1808. Slavery was condemned by the Catholic Church, and banned in Denmark, Prussia, the United Kingdom, Spain, Sweden, Netherlands, France, Portugal, Mexico, Argentina, Brazil, Venezuela, Uruguay, Bolivia, Haiti, Peru, Chile, Greece;

my home."[587] As Sam Houston explained, "There comes a time when a man's section is his country."[588]

John McElroy believed the masses of Southern people yielded to the power of men who had an imperial breadth of view, who imagined their separate and equal status becoming among great powers of the earth as "nature and nature's God entitled them." Perhaps people followed the "Flame-throwers" because they fed on an emotional momentum of hatred and fear, not rationality. McElroy survived after spending fifteen months as a teenager in Confederate prison camps, where he witnessed the "rotting" deaths of thousands of soldiers. He asked that we "take abundant care that they (Civil War soldiers) shall not have died in vain."[589]

McElroy wrote that the best way to honor the dead is to remember that their sacrifices were made to ensure that our nation might live. I hope to honor the services of Eugene Ware and George Burmeister. This requires support for their beloved nation of participatory democracy which in turn requires trying to find win-win, and not "gloves off" solutions for opposing parties.[590] Democracy is the most challenging form of government because it depends on resolutions, not extortions, from citizens who are not prone to giving in. The struggle requires accepting the will of a majority, and this relies on social trust. Angry politics only increase the already fragile divides in our society. We too often allow the loudest, boldest, most aggressive voices to drown out the majority of reticent people. Some quiet folks are like those early Iowa settlers who carefully pondered what was right in a time of confusion and bitter divides.

---

587 Ward, *The Civil War*, 52.
588 "Texas Civil War History," Retrieved 1/10/2021.
589 McElroy, *Andersonville*, xiii, xvi. Internet Archive; McElroy, *The Struggle for Missouri*, 3, 23. McElroy was a young apprentice journalist in St. Louis before enlisting in in Company L, 16th Illinois Cavalry.
590 I wonder if Southern soldiers who survived the Civil War would have later displayed the Confederate flag that seems so popular today, which is not the same Stars and Bars flag carried into the Battle of Wilson's Creek by the brave rebels in 1861.

Citizens in pre-Civil War Iowa valued debate and were willing to listen and learn from different opinions. I hope never again to hear Civil War mentioned as a solution to our country's conflicts. It proposes that feral Americans will again torch the soul of our nation by killing fellow citizens.

APPENDIX A

Timeline of Key Events in St. Louis before Camp Jackson[1]

Setting the Scene for Camp Jackon: Spring, 1861	Correspondence and Actions, Secessionists: Governor Jackson, General Daniel Frost	Federal Government and U.S. Army Authorities: President Lincoln, General-in-Chief Winfield Scott, General Harney	Correspondence and Actions, Unionists: Francis Blair and Captain (later General) Lyon
January 22-24	General Frost to Jackson: Major Bell at Arsenal is on our side.	General Scott assigns Brevet Major Peter V. Hagner to replace Bell, and assigns Lieutenant Thomas W. Sweeney of 2nd Infantry to command infantry troops at arsenal.	Blair obtained evidence of secessionist plans for state militia to muster. Asks General Scott to garrison arsenal.

---

1 For dates and events I rely on Randy R. McGuire's use of original documentation in "Solving the Mystery of Arsenal Guns." https//:www.civilwarstlouis.com. (I would delete this information as unimportant, here and elsewhere.)But much of this information is also referenced in the following sources: Thomas Lowndes Snead, *Fight for Missouri* (1886), was a pro-Breckenridge (pro-Secession presidential candidate) newspaperman in St. Louis who became Governor Jackson's secretary, adjutant to General Sterling Price, and a congressman in the Confederate government. After the war he became an editor for the *Daily News* in New York City. James Peckham was a St. Louis Unionist and Republican member of the Missouri Legislature, with close connections to Francis Blair. He was listed on a roster of "parent company" of Union Home Guards in 1861 and later joined the Union Army as colonel of the 8th Missouri Infantry. His book, *Gen. Nathaniel Lyon and Missouri in 1861* (1866), although strongly biased in support of Lyon and the Union, is the earliest book on the Civil War in Missouri. Robert J. Rombauer was lieutenant colonel of the 1st Regiment of U.S. Reserve Corps (ninety-day enlistees), and commanded the First battalion at Camp Jackson. He wrote *The Union Cause in St. Louis in 1861* (1909). John McElroy wrote *The Struggle for Missouri* (1909), after serving in the Union army and writing about his imprisonment at Andersonville. More recent sources provide balance, expertise and perspective, for example, William Garrett Piston and Richard W. Hatcher III, *Wilson's Creek: The Second Battle of the Civil War and the Men Who Fought It* (Chapel Hill, 2000).

Date			
February 6			Lyon arrives to guard arsenal with 80 "seasoned" Company B, U.S. Infantry.
February 13		Scott to Harney: assign more men to protect Arsenal in advance of an emergency.	
			Under U.S. direction, Blair organizes Committee of Safety to oversee interests of Union. Started organizing patriotic, mostly German, volunteers across city for emergency defense.
February 18	Jefferson Davis inaugurated as president of the Confederate States of America.		
February 19		Harney reports to Scott that his information is inaccurate. The arsenal is secure under Major Hagner.	
February 21		Hagner reports to ordnance superiors that arsenal is perfectly secure.	
March 4		President Lincoln's inauguration.	Blair begins to petition for change in command at Arsenal.

APPENDIX A

March 11			Lyon is ordered to take charge of troops and defense of Arsenal.
March 20		Harney clarifies authority of Lyon to be in charge of defense and line troops, and Hagner to be in charge of ordnance stores.	
March 19			Convention of delegates elected for a decision on secession overwhelmingly vote to remain in the Union and establish possibility of a future meeting in case of emergency.
April 12	Attack on Fort Sumter.	Lincoln issues Proclamation to enlist troops.	
	Jackson refuses Lincoln's request, saying he will send not one man for such an unholy crusade.		
April 15	General Frost's advice to Gov. Jackson: obtain military legislation for legality and request arms from Jefferson Davis for attack on Arsenal.	On 16th Harney urgently requests advice. Arsenal may not be secure.	

April 17	Jackson follows Frost's advice. Sends dispatch with personal messengers to Jefferson Davis requesting arms.		
April 20	Secessionists take arsenal in Liberty, MO.		Harney gives Lyon no authority to muster troops.
April 21		Sec. of War recalls Harney to Washington and asks for Illinois regiments to support arsenal.	Lyon given command of Dept. of West with orders from Secretary of War to arm and protect loyal citizens, execute the laws and to muster four regiments.
April 23	Jefferson Davis responds, promising arms for attack on Arsenal.		
April 30		Under these "revolutionary times," President Lincoln and General Scott send authority to Committee of Public Safety to declare martial law in St. Louis, if deemed necessary.	Lyon is given authority to enlist 10,000 volunteers.

APPENDIX A

May 2	Governor Jackson continues to profess neutrality as he calls legislature into extraordinary session, orders state militias to assemble and requests $50,000 in bank loans.		
May 8	Crates of arms taken by southern secessionists from arsenal at Baton Rouge arrive into Camp Jackson.		Lyon was informed that arms from Confederacy have arrived in Camp Jackson. He has justification to capture secessionist encampment.
May 10	Frost sends note to Lyon claiming innocence, saying there is no plan to attack Arsenal.		Lyon captures Camp Jackson and while marching the prisoners, his troops are attacked by street mob and retaliate. Several soldiers, officers, and innocents ae killed.
May 11	Governor Jackson uses the violent outcome for propaganda to incite anger against the federals.	Harney returns from Washington with promise to restore peace and tries to disband Union Home Guards.	St. Louis Arsenal is secure.

APPENDIX B

Titles and themes from Lyon's Letters anonymously written to the *Manhattan Express* June 9, 1860–January 19, 1861[1]

The series of essays begins with Lyon's arguments for the Republican cause, support for Abraham Lincoln, and severe criticism of the other presidential candidates. Lyon believed that whatever contributes to the welfare for free laborers leads toward the happiness of all. He used caustic rhetoric to criticize pro-slavery Southerners and their political schemes. The U.S. Army captain called out the Southerners' use of derogatory terms like "niggerism," "Black Republicans," and "abolitionists" to chastise Northerners for being friends of slaves. He wrote that the Missouri Compromise was a binding contract akin to the Constitution and agreeing to change it was to "plunge into the pool of self-generated slime." Lyon believed that national sovereignty mattered more to the country than state sovereignty, given that citizens were not allowed to express their unbiased will without fears of fraud and violence. Lyon coined the term "Sovereign Squattereignty" and claimed that the true mission of Stephen Douglas was to find a trick (popular sovereignty) that allowed the government to serve the interests of the slaveholders.

---

1 Paraphrased themes with selected quotes From *The Last Political Writings of General Nathaniel Lyon*, 1861, 111–229.

APPENDIX B

Our Cause—Our Candidate I, June 9, 1860

These three letters announced the Republican cause: to honor labor and elevate the laborer, and to support Abraham Lincoln. He continued with a treatise on the economic philosophy of free labor.

Our Cause—Our Candidate II, June 16, 1860

Our Cause—Our Candidate III, June 23, 1860

Sovereign Squattereignty, June 30, 1860

Lyon wrote how, by calling us abolitionists, Southerners promote the false idea that we insist on the abolition of slavery all at once, and said that we (Republicans) are concerned for the white men of territories who risk the evils of becoming slaveholders or of being degraded by them. Northern support for the interests of laboring classes rests on the truth that whatever contributes to our welfare permanently leads toward the happiness of all, and ultimately to the negro.

Are We Subdued?, July 14, 1860

Lyon began by using the example of when, responding to Benjamin Franklin's personal appeal for justice in the colonies, the British Ministry said "We will subdue you." Lyon described how, when Benedict Arnold became a traitor against his people and native state, he adopted the motto, "We will subdue you." Lyon noted the middle name of Stephen Arnold Douglas to claim that Douglas, too, abdicated the rights of the people to self-government. Lyon believed that the indignation of these events would not be effaced from memory.

The Moral of the Question I, July 21, and II, July 28, 1860

Lyon argued that foreign slave interests harbored slavery here in the new country, when it was under the early general condemnation of the founders and the rest of the civilized world. He noted that the South's justification is that slavery has beneficial economic and physical benefits for our country, while the slavocracy in power is known for corruption and for giving contracts to money-making monopolies which support southern politicians.

The Southern philosophy of morality is that slavery benefits the prosperity of the South and therefore has to be as accepted as moral because of those beneficial effects. Lyon criticized the true mission of Stephen Douglas and his squatter sovereignty. He described a metamorphosis of our country into discontent at home and disgrace abroad, and the stupidity of the Know-nothing party and Breckenridge. Lyon argued the value of free labor and the role it played in advancing economy of the North. He wrote that the North has more enterprise, but the South has control of the government.

True to His Mission, September 11, 1860

Lyon wrote that Stephen Douglas has rendered himself "a squatter in the mire of self-humiliation" because of his acceptance of federal tyranny over Kansas. Lyon reminded readers that Missouri was denied admission to the Union for two years, because it allowed for slavery. After much debate, the Congressional solution was the Missouri Compromise. It ruled that the country west of Missouri would never have slavery. Lyon wrote that the true mission of Douglas was to find a trick such as his successful resolution (popular sovereignty) that allows the government to serve the interests of the slaveholders.

Fitness for The Presidency, September 22, 1860

Lyon declared for Lincoln.

The Secret of It, September 29, 1860

Lyon wrote how, in spite of the (hypocritical) sacred appreciation for "the ark of the covenant—our system of government—…we now find disunion of our government;" and that threats of disunion result from the possibility of having a government that does not advance the institution of slavery, "which carries in itself the elements of deterioration and weakness to those who tolerate it." Lyon claimed that "uneasy" politicians like Calhoun and Douglas, "traffic on the gullibility of people," using the cry of "niggerism" to portend disaster. He believed there is hope for a return to the true policy of our government.

Our Grievances, October 13, 1860

Lyon wrote that if the North dares to assert its constitutional right to vote against a Democratic candidate it would be an intolerable grievance for the South. Same as they threatened in 1856, the South threatens disunion if a Republican is elected. Threats of Southern wrath would bring rage, revenge, hate, blood, thunder dust, sword and destruction to overwhelm us (the North.) (President Buchanan) "whose visual obliquity corresponds to that of his moral sentiments," falsified his oath of office by complying with the demands of pro-slavery power. Lyon asked what would disunion solve, will South have more power to silence slave dissatisfaction, or will northern people more willingly return fugitive slaves? Can it silence longing for freedom?

Disunion, October 20, 1860

Lyon said that Northern resistance to the Fugitive Slave Law resulted from the aversion to doing violence to innocent citizens of the North and by executing the law with mob violence. There was no complicity or complaint from North about the treatment of John Brown. But we must overturn our time-honored policy (The Missouri Compromise) against the will of the people. Lyon encouraged people to resist the "bugaboo screechers" about the calamity of a Republican president, after all that "We have endured the Union under oppression" (following the repeal of the compromise). We can now vote with a moral obligation to abide by the result.

Our Political Summary, October 27, 1860

"In all matter of faith and purpose, whether initiated by political or religious associations, there is an assumed integrity of motive." Lyon wrote how they are told that the slavery system elevates the black race and that slaveholders are the true friends of the negro. At the same time "with emanations of malice" they charge us with being negro worshippers and Black Republicans. Lyon hates slavery but denied that their (Republican) efforts are not directed to elevate negroes, but to first elevate their own white race. "You may nurse a viper and get stung by it... but you shall not obtrude your viper on us." We hope to operate the (Republican) government according to its original construction and "we set ourselves at rest upon the final issue."

A Word to the Brethren, November 3, 1860

Lyon began by saying how they (fellow Republicans) are inspired by confidence in the ultimate prevalence of truth. You (Lyon's assumed reading audience in Kansas) fought against the unscrupulous measures of the Pearce administration to establish slavery in Kansas, and against James Buchanan's subservience to the slavery cause. Your principles have had practical results from their own inherent virtues. "Sufferings, sacrifices, and defeats could not deter you from your purpose." "Your Kansas struggle will prove to have been...an ominous indication of what may be expected...We salute you with gratitude and affection."

Republican Reflections, November 10, 1860

"The history of Kansas will...condemn to everlasting infamy the vile hordes of pro-slavery ruffians." Lyon asked how can anyone explain the strong opposition of the administration in 1856 to a public investigation of the offenses committed in Kansas, other than the need to protect their government complicity? Why did the Democratic senate repeatedly refuse to admit Kansas with her enlightened constitution? Although the reign of tyranny has continued, and "torn, and rent, and wrecked and precipitated it to ruin," her (Kansas) liberty "prepares to mount the throne of the nation."

Our Triumph, November 1860

"Our impulse is one of unbounded joy," wrote Lyon, and said that although the hopes of the people were meant to be sacrificed as a "holocaust to slavery" by the dominant powers, those who were "unswayed by bribes and unintimidated by threats" are now catching rays of deliverance. Their undeviating purpose was obstinance to cruelty and to the subversion of the framework of a national policy. He believed it was their duty to administer government with equal justice and to honor all parts of the country.

Lyon continued writing, that slavery is not extended by our Constitution over the territories unless as expressed by the will of the people without force or fraud; If a state accepts the advantages of the Union, that state should share the responsibilities of it; Under moral obligation "no state can of right withdraw from the Union, without the consent of the others, but by revolution."

Proposed Amendments to the Constitution, December 1, 1860

Lyon interpreted Mr. Buchanan's late message to Congress as an attempt to make slavery the "cohesive force which will bind these states in fraternal union."

Letter I, December 16, 1860; *Letter II*, January 19, 1861

Lyon's last letters to the newspaper spoke of observations from his assignments in various Kansas localities after Lincoln's election.

APPENDIX C

Events after Camp Jackson which led to The Planter's House Hotel meeting, and up to June 18, 1861

	Key Correspondence and Actions of Missouri Secessionists: Governor Jackson, and General Sterling Price	Key Correspondence and Actions of Federal Government and U.S. Army: President Lincoln, General Scott, General Harney	Key Correspondence and Actions of St. Louis Unionists: Francis Blair and General Lyon
After the Camp Jackson Affair	Governor Jackson (falsely) tells the Missouri legislature that Blair and Lyon are coming after them and successfully pushes for the Military Bill and loans, including transfer of funds from schools and charitable organizations	Missouri leaders pressure Attorney General Bates and President Lincoln for passivity, so as not to excite citizens who wanted neutrality.	Blair, Harney, and President Lincoln receive letters from across the state telling of the harassment of Union supporters and the assembling of secessionist troops.

214

APPENDIX C

May 14	Jackson repeatedly declares that Missouri should cast her fate with the South.	Harney condones U.S. military actions at Camp Jackson and condemns Jackson's Military Bill.	
May 18			Nathaniel Lyon is elected Brigadier General of the volunteers which is made official May 20. Blair receives orders from Washington to, when necessary, relieve Harney.
May 21		Price-Harney Agreement (truce) which obstructs Union activities.	Blair receives letters telling that Secretary of State Reynolds has gone to Richmond and is organizing forces and receiving arms from Arkansas.

Date			
May 27		Memo from U.S. Adj. General L. Thomas to General Harney: Authority of the U.S. is paramount. Outrages against citizens continue. Professions of loyalty by state authorities are not reliable.	
May 29	Jackson and Price organize State Guard troops in violation of the truce.	Gen. Harney informs Price of complaints. Price denies and warns Harney not to send out any forces.	
May 30	After Harney's removal from office, Price orders district commanders to hasten organizations of Missouri State troops. Gov. Jackson orders military commanders and arms moved to Boonville.	Blair, after holding permission to do so since May 18, delivers orders relieving Harney of command.	General Lyon is given command of the U.S. Army Department of the West.

APPENDIX C

Early June	Spokesmen call for a meeting with Governor Jackson, Price, Blair, General Lyon, to be held on or before June 12, 1861.		
June 11, 1861 Planters House Hotel Meeting	Price and Jackson reiterate their demands that U.S. troops must leave the state and not re-enter it. Price professes his adherence to the truce with Harney until Lyon produces a copy of the memorandum sent from Harney to Price stating that continued recruitment of secessionist troops could incite war and must stop. Price pleads ignorance. Price and Jackson leave by train for Jefferson City, giving orders to burn railroad bridges and cut telegraph lines.		General Lyon explains that Missouri remains a Union state and therefore it is the duty of the federal government to remain in Missouri to protect citizens, property, and civil authority. Lyon refuses Jackson's suggestion to continue by correspondence. He suggests that both parties write their views for immediate publication. Jackson refuses.

June 12	Jackson's Proclamation and Declaration of War is published in newspapers. Governor Jackson and General Price immediately abandon the state offices and leave Jefferson City.		Lyon and Blair read Jackson's published Declaration of war and learn that secessionists burned railroad bridges. Lyon orders troops from Iowa to guard railroads in northern Missouri.
June 13	Governor Jackson and General Price arrive in Boonville.	Major Horace Conant's account of the Planter's House Meeting is published in the *Missouri Democrat*.	General Lyon departs St. Louis in pursuit of Jackson and Price.
June 15			Lyon's troops arrive in the deserted state capital before leaving for Boonville.
June 17	After the Boonville skirmish, Jackson rides south to meet with Confederates in Arkansas.	Lyon's and Jackson's troops skirmish in Boonville. Lyon goes into camp.	

June 18			Lyon writes to Harding that he is expecting Col. Bate's First Iowa troops to join him. Lyon's Proclamation is published from Boonville. He refutes Jackson's falsehoods and reassures citizens.

APPENDIX D

Jackson's Declaration of War, June 12, 1861[2]

To the People of Missouri:

A series of unprovoked and unparalleled outrages have been inflicted upon the peace and dignity of this Commonwealth and upon the rights and liberties of its people by wicked and unprincipled men, professing to act under the authority of the United States Government. The solid enactments of your Legislature have been nullified, your volunteer soldiers have been taken prisoners, your commerce with your sister states has been suspended, your trade with your own fellow citizens has been and is subject to the harassing control of an armed soldiery, peaceful citizens have been imprisoned without warrant of law, unoffending and defenseless men, women, and children have been ruthlessly shot down and murdered, and other unbearable indignities have been heaped upon your State and yourselves.

To all these outrages and indignities you have submitted with a patriotic forbearance which has only encouraged the perpetrators of these grievous wrongs to attempt still bolder and more daring usurpations. It has been my earnest endeavor under all these embarrassing circumstances to maintain the peace of the State and to avert, if possible, from our borders the desolating effects of a civil war. With that object in view

---

[2] Banasik (Wilkie), 372-374.

I authorized Major-General Price several weeks ago to arrange with General Harney, commanding the federal forces in this State, the terms of agreement by which the peace of the State might be preserved. They came, on the 21st of May, to an understanding, which was made public. The State authorities have faithfully labored to carry out the terms of that agreement. The Federal Government, on the other hand, not only manifested its strong disapprobation of it by the instant dismissal of the distinguished officer who on its part entered into it, but it at once began and has unintermittingly carried out a system of hostile operations in utter contempt of that agreement and in reckless disregard of its own plighted faith. These acts have latterly portended revolution and civil war so unmistakenly that I resolved to make one further effort to avert these dangers from you. I therefore solicited an interview with Brigadier-General Lyon, commanding the Federal army in Missouri. It was granted, and on the 10th instant, waiving all questions of personal and official dignity, I went to St. Louis, accompanied by Major-General Price.

We had an interview on the 11th instant, with General Lyon and Col. F.P. Blair, jr., at which I submitted to them this proposition: That I would disband the State Guard and break up its organization; that I would disarm all the companies that have been armed by the State; that I would pledge myself not to attempt to organize the militia under the Military Bill; that no arms or munitions should be brought into the State; that I would protect all citizens equally in all their rights, regardless of their political opinions; that I would repress all insurrectionary movements within the State; that I would repel all attempts to invade it, from whatever quarter and by whomsoever made, and I would thus maintain a strict neutrality in the present unhappy contest, and preserve the peace of the State. And I further proposed that I would, if necessary, invoke the assistance of U.S. troops to carry out these pledges. All this I proposed to do upon the condition that the Federal Government would undertake to disarm the home guards which it has illegally organized and armed throughout the state, and pledged itself not to occupy with its troops any localities in the State not occupied by them at this time.

Nothing but the most earnest desire to avert the horrors of civil war from our beloved State could have tempted me to propose these humiliating terms. They were rejected by the Federal officers. They demanded not only the disorganization and disarming of the State militia and the nullification of the military bill, but they refused to disarm their own home guards, and insisted that the Federal Government should enjoy unrestricted right to move and station its troops throughout the State whenever and wherever that might, in the opinion of its officers, be necessary, either for the protection of the "loyal subjects" of the Federal Government or for the repelling of invasion, and they plainly announced that it was the intention of the Administration to take military occupation under these pretexts of the whole State, and to reduce it, as avowed by General Lyon himself, to the "exact condition of Maryland."

The acceptance by me of these degrading terms would not only have sullied the honor of Missouri, but would have aroused the indignation of every brave citizen, and precipitated the very conflict which it has been my aim to prevent. We refused to accede to them, and the conference was broken up. Fellow citizens, all our efforts at conciliation have failed. We can hope nothing from the justice or moderation of the agents of the Federal Government in this State. They are energetically hastening the execution of their bloody and revolutionary schemes for the inauguration of a civil war in your midst; for the military occupation of your State by armed bands of lawless invaders; for the overthrow of your State government, and for the subversion of those liberties which that government has always sought to protect, and they intend to exert their whole power to subjugate you, if possible, to the military despotism which has usurped the powers of the Federal Government:

APPENDIX D

Now, therefore, I, C.F. Jackson, Governor of the State of Missouri, do, in view of the foregoing facts and by virtue of the powers vested in me by the constitution and laws of this Commonwealth, issue this my proclamation, calling the militia of the State, to the number of 50,000, into the active service of the State, for the purpose of repelling said invasion, and for the protection of the lives, liberty, and property of the citizens of this State; and I earnestly exhort all good citizens of Missouri to rally under the flag of their State for the protection of their endangered homes and firesides, and for the defense of their most sacred rights and dearest liberties.

In issuing this proclamation, I hold it to be my solemn duty to remind you that Missouri is still one of the United States; that the executive department of the State government does not arrogate to itself the power to disturb that relation; that that power has been wisely vested in a convention, which will at the proper time express your sovereign will, and that meanwhile it is your duty to obey all the constitutional requirements of the Federal Government; but it is equally my duty to advise you that your first allegiance is due to your own State, and that you are under no obligation whatever to obey the unconstitutional edicts of the military despotism which has enthroned itself at Washington, nor submit to the infamous and degrading sway of its wicked minions in this State. No brave and true-hearted Missourian will obey the one or submit to the other. Rise, then, and drive out ignominiously the invaders who have dared to desecrate the soil which your labors have made fruitful and which is consecrated by your homes!

Given under my hand as Governor and under the great seal of the State of Missouri at Jefferson City this 12th day of June, 1861.

CLAIBORNE F. JACKSON

APPENDIX E

Lyon's Proclamation "To the People of Missouri", written June 18, 1861.

Upon leaving the city of St. Louis, in consequence of the declaration of war made by the Governor of this State against the government of the United States, because I would not assume in its behalf to relinquish its duties and abdicate its rights of protecting loyal citizens from the oppression and cruelties of secessionists in this State, I published an address to the people in which I declared my intention to use the force under my command for no other purpose than the maintenance of the authority of the General Government, and the protection of the rights and property of all law-abiding citizens. The State authorities, in violation of an agreement with General Harney, on the 21st of May last, had drawn together and organized upon a large scale the means of warfare, and, having made declaration of war, they abandoned the capital, issued orders for the destruction of the railroad and telegraph lines, and proceeded to this point to put in execution their purposes toward the General Government. This devolved upon me the necessity of meeting this issue to the best of my ability, and accordingly I moved to this point with a portion of the force under my command, attacked and dispersed hostile forces gathered here by the Governor, and took possession of camp equipage left and a considerable number of prisoners, most of them young and of immature age, who represent that they have been misled by frauds ingeniously devised and industriously circulated by designing leaders, who seek to devolve upon unreflecting and deluded followers the task of securing the object of their own false ambition. Out of compassion for these misguided youths, and to correct impressions created by unscrupulous calumniators, I have liberated them, upon condition that they will not serve in the impending hostilities against the United States Government. I have done this in spite of the known facts that the leaders in the present rebellion, having long experienced the mildness of the General Government, still feel confident that this mildness cannot be overtaxed even by factious hostilities having in view its overthrow; but if, as in the case of the late Camp Jackson Affair, this clemency shall still be misconstrued, it is proper to give warning that the Government cannot be always expected to indulge it to the compromised of its evident welfare.

Having learned that those plotting against the Government have falsely represented that the Government troops intended a forcible and violent invasion of Missouri for the purposes of military despotism and tyranny, I hereby give notice to the people of this State that I shall scrupulously avoid all interferences with the business, rights, and property of every description recognized by the laws of this State, and belonging to law-abiding citizens; but that it is equally my duty to maintain the paramount authority of the United States with such force as I have at my command, which will be retained only so long as opposition shall make it necessary; and that it is my wish, and shall be my purpose, to devolve any unavoidable rigor arising in this issue upon *those only who provoke it*.

All persons who under the misapprehensions above-mentioned, have taken up arms, or who are now preparing to do so, are invited to return to their homes, and relinquish their hostile attitude to the General Government, and are assured that they may do so without being molested for past occurrences.

Brigadier-General U. S. Vols, Com'g
(Peckham, 274–276)

BIBLIOGRAPHY

Books

Adams, George Rollie. *General William S. Harney: Prince of Dragoons*. Lincoln, NE: University of Nebraska Press, 2001.

Adamson, Hans Christian. *Rebellion in Missouri: 1861*. Philadelphia: Chilton Company, 1961.

Baker, Thomas R. *The Sacred Cause of the Union: Iowa in the Civil War*. Iowa City: The University of Iowa Press, 2016.

Banasik, Michael E. *Missouri in 1861: The Civil War Letters of Franc B. Wilkie, Newspaper Correspondent*. Iowa City: Camp Pope Publishing, 2001.

Benet, Stephen Vincent. *John Brown's Body*. New York: Farrar and Rinehart, 1936.

Billings, John D. *Hardtack and Coffee or the Unwritten Story of Army Life*. Boston: Smith and Co.,1888.

Boatner, Mark Mayo. *The Civil War Dictionary*. New York: Vintage Books, 1991.

Brewer, Luther A., and Barthinius L. Wick. "Linn County in War." In *History of Linn County Iowa*, 470–478. Cedar Rapids, IA: The Torch Press, 1911.

Brooksher, William Riley. *Bloody Hill: The Civil War Battle of Wilson's Creek*. Washington, DC: Brassey's, 1995.

Brown, Joshua. *Beyond the Lines: Pictorial Reporting, Everyday Life, and the Crisis of Gilded Age America*. Berkeley, CA: University of California Press, 2006.

Carmichael, Peter S. *The War for the Common Soldier: How Men Thought, Fought, and Survived in Civil War Armies*. Chapel Hill: The University of North Carolina Press, 2018.

Clark, Dan Elbert. *Samuel Jordan Kirkwood*. Iowa City: The State Historical Society of Iowa, 1917.

Clark, John S. *Life in the Middle West: Reminiscences of J.S. Clark*. Chicago: Advance Publishing Company, n.d.

Cutrer, Thomas W. *Theater of a Separate War: The Civil War West of the Mississippi 1861–1865*. Chapel Hill: The University of North Carolina Press, 2017.

Denny, James, and John Bradbury. *The Civil War's First Blood: Missouri, 1854–1861*. Boonville, MO: Missouri Life, Inc., 2007.

Dew, Charles B. *Apostles of Disunion: Southern Secession Commissioners and the Causes of the Civil War*. Charlottesville: University of Virginia Press, 2001.

Douglas, Truman Orville. *The Pilgrims of Iowa*. Concord, NH: The Rumford Press, 1911.

Dretske, Diana L. *The Bonds of War: A Story of Immigrants and Esprit de Corps in Company C, 96th Illinois Volunteer Infantry*. Carbondale, IL: Southern Illinois University Press, 2021.

Elson, Henry William. *History of the United States*. New York: The Macmillan Company, 1929.

Geiger, Mark W. *Financial Fraud and Guerilla Violence in Missouri Civil War 1861–1865*. New Haven, CT: Yale University Press, 2010.

Grant, Ulysses S. *Personal Memoirs of U. S. Grant*. 2 vols. New York: Charles L. Webster & Co., 1885.

Ingersoll, Lurton Dunham. *Iowa and the Rebellion*. Philadelphia: Lippincott, 1866.

Jordan, Brian Matthew. *A Thousand May Fall: Life, Death, and Survival in the Union Army*. New York: Liveright Publishing Corporation, 2021.

Larimer, Charles, ed. *Love and Valor: Intimate Civil War Letters Between Captain Jacob and Emiline Ritner*. Western Springs, IL: Sigourney Press, 2000.

Lathrop, H. W. *The Life and Times of Samuel J. Kirkwood, Iowa's War Governor*. Iowa City: Published by the Author, 1893.

Lyftogt, Kenneth L. *Iowa and the Civil War, Volume I: Free Child of the Missouri Compromise 1850–1862*. Iowa City: Camp Pope Publishing, 2018.

[Lyon, Nathaniel]. *The Last Political Writings of General Nathaniel Lyon, U.S.A.:With a Sketch of His Life and Military Services*. New York: Rudd and Carleton, 1861.

McElroy, John. *Andersonville: A Story of Rebel Military Prisons*. Toledo: D.R. Locke, 1879.

———. *The Struggle for Missouri*. Washington, DC: The National Tribune Company, 1909.

McPherson, James M. *Battle Cry of Freedom: The Civil War Era*. New York: Oxford University Press, 1988.

———. *For Cause and Comrades: Why Men Fought in the Civil War*. New York: Oxford University Press, 1997.

Matson, Daniel, *The Life Experiences of Daniel Matson*. Published posthumously by Mary H. Matson, March 18, 1924.

Military History and Reminiscences of the Thirteenth Regiment Illinois Volunteer Infantry in the Civil War in the United States, 1861–1865, prepared by committee of the regiment. Chicago: Woman's Temperance Publishing Association, 1892.

Parrish, William E. *Turbulent Partnership: Missouri and the Union 1861–1865*. Columbia, MO: University of Missouri Press, 1963.

Parsons, Talcott. *The Social System*. Glencoe, IL: Free Press, 1964.

Patrick, Jeffrey L. *Campaign for Wilson's Creek*. Abilene: State House Press, 2018.

Peckham, James. *Gen. Nathaniel Lyon and Missouri, 1861: A Monograph of the Great Rebellion*. New York: American News Company, 1866.

Phillips, Christopher. *Damned Yankee: The Life of General Nathaniel Lyon*. Baton Rouge: Louisiana State University Press, 1996.

———. *Missouri's Confederate: Claiborne Fox Jackson and the Creation of Southern Identity in the Border West*. Columbia, MO: University of Missouri Press, 2000.

Piston, William Garrett, and Richard W. Hatcher II. *Wilson's Creek: The Second Battle of the Civil War and the Men Who Fought It*. Chapel Hill: University of North Carolina Press, 2000.

Potter, David M. *The Impending Crisis: America Before the Civil War 1848–1861*. Edited by Don E. Fehrenbacher. New York: Harper Perennial, 2011.

Reavis, L. U. *The Life and Military Services of General William Selby Harney*. St. Louis: Bryan, Brand and Company, 1878.

Robinson, Marilynne. *The Death of Adam*. New York: Picador, 2005.

Rombauer, Robert Julius. *The Union Cause in St. Louis in 1861: An Historical Sketch*. St. Louis: Nixon Jones, 1909.

Roster and Record of Iowa Soldiers in the War of Rebellion, Together with Historical Sketches of Volunteer Organizations, 1861–1866. 6 vols. Des Moines: Iowa General Assembly, 1908–1911.

Schofield, John M. *Forty-Six Years in the Army*. New York: The Century Company, 1897.

Shalhope, Robert E. *Sterling Price: Portrait of a Southerner*. Columbia, MO: University of Missouri Press, 1971.

Shanks, John P. C. *Vindication of Major General John C. Frémont Against the Attacks of the Slave Power and Its Allies*. Washington, DC: Scammell & Co., 1862.

Snead, Thomas L. *The Fight for Missouri: From the Election of Lincoln to the Death of Lyon*. New York: Charles Scribner's Sons, 1886.

Tönnies, Ferdinand. *Fundamental Concepts of Sociology (Gemeinschaft und Gesellschaft)*. Edited by Charles Loomis. East Lansing, MI: Michigan State University Press, 1957.

U.S. War Department. *The War of the Rebellion: A Compilation of the Official. Records of the Union and Confederate Armies*. 128 vols. Washington, DC: Government Printing Office, 1880–1901.

Ward, Geoffrey C., Ric Burns, and Ken Burns. *The Civil War: An Illustrated History*. New York: Alfred A. Knopf, 1992.

Ward, Henry Winfield. *Western-Leander Clark College, 1856–1911*. Dayton, OH: Otterbein Press, 1911.

Ware, Eugene Fitch. *The Lyon Campaign in Missouri, Being a History of the First Iowa Infantry*. 1907. Reprint. Iowa City: Camp Pope Bookshop, 1991.

Woodward, Ashbel. *Life of General Nathaniel Lyon*. Hartford, CT: Case, Lockwood and Company, 1862.

Young, Dannagal Goldthwaite. *Irony and Outrage: The Polarized Landscape of Rage, Fear, and Laughter in the United States*. New York: Oxford University Press, 2021.

Articles

Borderwich, Fergus M. "Congress Fights the Civil War." *American Heritage*. Spring 2020. Amercanheritage.com.

Briggs, John E. "Enlistment of Iowa Troops During the Civil War." *Iowa Journal of History and Politics* 3 (1917): 323–392.

Cook, Robert. "The Political Culture of Antebellum Iowa: An Overview." *The Annals of Iowa* 52, no. 3 (1993): 225–250.

Fine, Gary Alan. "Agency, Structure, and Comparative Contexts: Toward a Synthetic Interactionism." *Symbolic Interaction* 15, no. 1. (1992): 87–107.

———. "The Sociology of the Local: Action and its Publics." *Sociological Theory* 28, no. 4 (December 2010): 355–376

Geiger, Mark W. "Indebtedness and the Origins of Guerilla Violence in Civil War Missouri." *The Journal of Southern History* 75, no. 1 (February 2009): 49–82.

Hammond, William. "Recollections of General Nathaniel Lyon." *Annals of Iowa* 4, no. 6 (1900): 414–436.

Hicks, John D. "Organization of the Volunteer Army in 1861 with Special Reference to Minnesota." *Minnesota History Bulletin* 2, no. 5 (February 1918): 324–368.

Lumpkin, Ben Gray." 'The Happy Land of Canaan': An Unpublished Civil War Song." *Civil War History*, 11:1 (1965).

Marshall, Gordon. "Community." In *A Dictionary of Sociology*, edited by Gordon Marshall, 97–98. New York: Oxford University Press, 1998.

Moeller, Herbert L., and Hugh C. Moeller. "Lincoln and Grant in Iowa." In *Our Iowa, It's Beginning and Growth*, 269–275. New York: Newsome and Company,1938.

O'Connor, Henry. "With the First Iowa Infantry." *The Palimpsest* 3, no. 2 (February 1922): 53–61.

Parrish, William E. "General Nathaniel Lyon, A Portrait." In *The Civil War in Missouri: Essays from the Missouri Historical Review, 1906–2006*, 11–29. Columbia, MO: The State Historical Society of Missouri, 2006.

Piston, William Garrett. "The 1st Iowa Volunteers: Honor and Community in a Ninety Day Regiment." *Civil War History* 44 (March 1998): 5–23.

Pollock, Ivan L. "Iowa Civil War Loan." *Iowa and War* 3 (September 1917).

Price, Hiram. "Paying the First Iowa." *Palimpsest* 3 (February 1922): 62–65.

Robinson, Marilynne, "One Manner of Law, the Religious Origins of American Liberalism," *Harpers*, 08/2022. https://harpers.org/archive/2022/08.

Scott, Douglas, Steven J. Dasovich, and Thomas D. Thiessen. "Archaeology of the First Battle of Boonville, Missouri, June 17, 1861." In *From These Honored Dead: Historical Archaeology of the American Civil War*, 26–41. Gainesville, FL: University Press of Florida, 2014.

Stevens, Walter Barlow. "Lincoln and Missouri." *Missouri Historical Review* 10 (January 1916): 65–119.

Swanberg, W. A. "Was the Secretary of War a Traitor?" *American Heritage*, February 1963. Amercanheritage.com.

Urry, John. "Sociology of Time and Space." In *The Blackwell Companion to Social Theory*, edited by Bryan S. Turner. Malden, MA: Blackwell Publishers, 2000.

Upham, Cyril B. "Arms and Equipment for the Iowa Troops in the Civil War," *Iowa Journal of History and Politics* 16 (January 1918): 3–52.

Williams, Ora. "Lincoln and Iowa." *The Annals of Iowa* 34, no. 2 (Fall 1957): 142–146.

Woodward, C. Vann. "What the War Made Us." In *The Civil War: An Illustrated History*, 398–401. New York: Alfred A. Knopf, 1992.

Newspapers

"Report from Rolla, August 13." *The Clinton Herald*, August 17, 1861.

Internet Resources

"1860 Census: Population of the United States." *United States Census Bureau*. www.census.gov.

"About the Wabash Railroad." *Wabash Railroad Historical Society*. http://www.wabashrhs.org/p/wabash-railroad.html.

"Abraham Lincoln, Stephen Douglas, and the Election of 1860." *Worldhistory.us*. https://worldhistory.us/American-history/Abraham-lincoln-stephen-douglas-and-the-election-of-1860.php.

"Alexander Clark Organizes African Americans in Iowa to Fight in the Civil War," *Iowa PBS*. https://www.iowapbs.org/iowapathways/artifact/1571/alexander-clark-organizes-african-americans-iowa-fight-civil-war.

"Artist-Journalists of the Civil War," 02/17/1961. https://TIME.com/archive/6623040/the-press-artist-jounalists-of-the-civil-war.

"The Battle of Wilson's Creek: The Camp Jackson Affair." *National Park Service*. nphistory.com/publication/civil_war_series/26/sec2.htm.

"Claiborne Fox Jackson." *State Historical Society of Missouri: Historic Missourians.* https://historicmissourians.shsmo.org/claiborne-fox-jackson.

"Daniel Marsh Frost (1823–1900)." *Missouri Encyclopedia.* https://missouriencyclopedia.org/people/frost-daniel-marsh.

Davis, John. "Complete List of Civil War Veterans of German Descent of Muscatine County," *IA GenWeb Project.* https://iagenweb.org/muscatine/CivilWar/civilwar2.htm.

"Francis Preston Blair, Jr.—Facts." *American History Central.* https://www.americanhistorycentral.com/entries/francis-preston-blair-jr-facts/.

"Frost Family." *ArchivesSpace Public Interface.* https://archives.slu.edu/agents/people/341.

"The Generals and Admirals: Winfield Scott (1786–1866)." *Mr. Lincoln's Whitehouse.* https://www.mrlincolnswhitehouse.org/residents-visitors/the-generals-and-admirals/generals-admirals-winfield-scott-1786-1866/.

Grau, Scott R. "Turner, Asa," *The Biographical Dictionary of Iowa.* https://uipress.lib.uiowa.edu/bdi/DetailsPage.aspx?id=383.

Holzer, Harold. "Election Day 1860." *Smithsonian Magazine.* November 2008. https://www.smithsonianmag.com/history/election-day-1860-84266675/.

Hudziak, Mark. "The Battle of Boonville, Missouri, June 17, 1861." *The Iron Brigader.* https://ironbrigader.com/2018/10/26/the-battle-of-boonville-missouri-june-17-1861/.

Huffman, Greg. "Twisted Sources: How Confederate Propaganda ended up in the South's Schoolbooks." *Facing South: The Online Magazine of the Institute for Southern Studies.* https://www.facingsouth.org/2019/04/twisted-sources-how-confederate-propaganda-ended-souths-schoolbooks.

"John S. Phelps Papers," Community and Conflict: The Impact of the Civil War in the Ozarks. https://Ozarkcivilwar.org/archives/3549.

BIBLIOGRAPHY

"July 11, 1861: Senate Expels Ten Southern Members." *United States Senate*. https://www.senate.gov/artandhistory/history/common/civil_war/July10_TallySheet_FeaturedDoc.htm.

"Major Horace A. Conant and the Planter's House Hotel Meeting." *Missouri's Civil War Blog*. https://mocivilwarblog.wordpress.com/tag/horace-conant/.

"Map of Yellow Springs Township Kossuth, Northfield, Pleasant Grove, Mediapolis, Danville, and Middletown Cities," Cadastral Maps. An Illustrated Historical Atlas of Des Moines Country, Iowa, 1873. https://digital.lib.uiowa.edu/node/436504.

McGuire, Randy R. "Solving the Mystery of the Arsenal Guns: The St. Louis Arsenal in the Years Leading up to the Civil War, Parts 1 and 2." *Civil War St. Louis*. http://www.civilwarstlouis.com/arsenal/.

"Meeting at the Planters House." *Civil War St. Louis*. www.civilwarstlouis.com/articles/meeting-at-the-planters-house/.

"Missouri-Kansas Border War." *Missouri Encyclopedia*. https://missouriencyclopedia.org/events/missouri-kansas-border-war.

"On This Day." *National Constitution Center*. https://constituioncenter.org/blog/on-this-day-lincolns-emancipation-proclamation-changes-history/.

Phillips, Christopher. "Claiborne Fox Jackson." *The Kansas City Public Library: Civil War on the Western Border*. https://civilwaronthewesternborder.org/encyclopedia/jackson-claiborne-fox.

———. "Montgomery, James." *The Kansas City Public Library: Civil War on the Western Border*. https://civilwaronthewesternborder.org/encyclopedia/montgomery-james.

"Planters House Hotel Meeting." *The Kansas City Public Library: Civil War on the Western Border*. https:/civilwaronthewesternborder.org/timeline/planters-house-hotel-meeting

Rhea, Gordon, "Why Non-Slaveholding Southerners Fought." Address to the Charleston Library Society, January 25, 2011. American Battlefield Trust. https://www.battlefields.org/learn/articles/why-non-slaveholding-southerners-fought

Roe, Jason. "The Contested Election of 1855." *The Kansas City Public Library: Civil War on the Western Border*. https://civilwaronthewesternborder.org/blog/contested-election-1855.

Rule, G. E. "The 140-year Debate Over the Number of Guns at the Arsenal." *Civil War St. Louis*. www.civilwarstlouis.com/articles/guns-at-the-arsenal/

"Samuel R. Curtis." *Iowa in the Civil War, Biographies and Obituaries*. https://Iagenweb.org/civilwar/biographies/biographies_c.htm.

"Speech of Luther J. Glenn to the Missouri Convention," under "Causes of the Civil War," https://civilwarcauses.org. Website text attributed to *Journal and Proceedings of the Missouri State Convention, Held at Jefferson City and St. Louis, March 1861*, (St. Louis: George Knapp and Co., 1861).

"The Congregational Christian Tradition." *Congregational Library and Archives*. https://www.congregationallibrary.org/congregational-christian-tradition.

"Timeline." *Civil War St. Louis*. https://www.civilwarstlouis.com/cwstltimeline/.

Trout, Kristen M. "Fallen Leaders: Brigadier General Nathaniel Lyon." *Emerging Civil War*. https://emergingcivilwar.com/2021/08/10/fallen-leaders-brigadier-general-nathaniel-lyon/.

Urofsky, Melvin I. "Dred Scott decision." *Encyclopedia Britannica*. https://www.britannica.com/event/Dred-Scott-decision.

"Ulysses S. Grant's Experiences During the Camp Jackson Affair." *National Park Service*. https://www.nps.gov/articles/000/ulysses-s-grant-s-experiences-during-the-camp-jackson-affair.htm.

"United Daughters of the Confederacy." *Encyclopedia Virginia, Virginia Humanities*. https://encyclopediavirginia.org/entries/united-daughters-of-the-confederacy

The Ohio State University digitalized eHistory. *The War of the Rebellion: A Compilation of the Official Records of the Union and Confederate Armies* (Washington, DC: Government Printing Office, 1880–1901.) https://ehistory.osu.edu>books>war-rebellion-official-records-civil-war.

"William James." *Stanford Encyclopedia of Philosophy*. https://plato.stanford.edu/entries/james/.

"United States Presidential Election of 1860." *Encyclopedia Britannica*. www.Britannica.com/event/united-states-presidential-election-of-1860.

Manuscripts and Special Collections

Claiborne Jackson, 1861. Office of Governor, Record Group 3.15, Missouri State Archives.

George C. Burmeister Diaries 1861–1862. Civil War Collection, Special Collections and Archives, The University of Iowa Libraries.

William Branson Diary. The State Historical Society and Western Historical Manuscript Collection, a Joint Collection of University of Missouri and the State Historical Society SHOM.

Theses and Dissertations

Geiger, Mark "Missouri's Hidden Civil War: Financial Conspiracy and the Decline of the Planter Elite, 1861–1865." PhD Dissertation, University of Missouri, Columbia, 2006.

_____. "Missouri Banks and The Civil War: The End of a Pro-Southern Entrepreneurial Southern Elite" master's thesis, University of Missouri, Columbia, 2000.

INDEX

Abercrombie, John C. 35, 119, 190
Abolition 61, 84, 199, 209
    Abolitionists 30, 38, 53, 55, 83-85, 106, 208-209
Accidents 135, 137
Almstedt, Henry 70
American Home Missionary Society 3
Arkansas 11, 47, 63, 68, 78, 97-99, 114, 121, 126, 133, 135, 138, 141, 155-157, 160, 177-179, 191
    Arkansas Rangers 141
    Camp Walker 160
    Fort Smith 68, 133, 191
Arrow Rock 104
Arsenal 9-10, 19, 51-52, 58-60, 62-67, 69-75, 77, 79, 83, 97, 110, 121, 124, 126, 182, 190-191, 203
    Secessionist takeovers 67
    See St. Louis Arsenal 9-10, 52, 59, 62-63, 65-66, 69, 72, 74, 110, 121, 124
Aylsworth, George 130, 186
Baker, Thomas 1, 4, 7-8, 17, 25, 27, 41, 137
Banasik, Michael E. 2, 14, 31, 35, 37, 39-45, 47, 52, 103-104, 107-109, 112, 114, 116-118, 120, 122, 126, 128-129, 133-134, 139, 141-142, 145, 147-148, 150-151, 153-154, 157, 160-161, 163, 165, 167, 170-171, 175, 179, 188-191, 196, 220
Barrows, Carolyn 182
Bates, Edward 61-62, 75
Bates, John F. 40-42, 46, 75, 104, 110, 113-114, 118, 129, 131-132, 145, 169, 189
Baton Rouge 7, 74, 92, 176

Battle of Carthage 135
Beardsley, Captain James 166, 176
Bearss, Ed 178
Bell, Major 59, 67, 73
Billings, John D. (note) 148
Blair, Francis Preston 10, 52, 59, 60, 61, 62, 64, 68, 69, 75, 77, 78, 113, 156, 182
Blair, Montgomery 60, 62-63
Blandowski, Captain 71
Boernstein, Colonel Henry 69, 114
Booming, Buzzing, Confusion 15, 124
Boon's Lick 80-82, 89, 97
Boonville 20, 47, 52, 73, 90, 97-99, 103, 109-114, 116, 118-120, 122, 124-128, 130, 132-134, 137, 143, 145, 187, 192, 194, 197
    Banks 45, 73, 82, 84-86, 91, 113, 121-122, 135
    Skirmish 109, 118-119, 154, 161, 164, 192, 197
    Camp Cameron 20, 113-115
    First Iowa Infantry and 2, 4-6, 8, 10-12, 14, 16, 18-19, 31-32, 40, 47, 52, 100-101, 104, 110-111, 114-115, 120, 123, 126-127, 131, 141, 162, 168, 176, 178-183, 186-187, 189-190, 194, 196
Border Wars (Kansas) 55, 72
    Atchison and 83-84
    Jackson and 7, 53, 59, 69, 73, 75, 78, 84-86, 90, 92, 96-99, 113, 134, 141, 190
    Lyon and 6-8, 11, 14-15, 19-20, 51-55, 57-58, 64, 67, 73-75, 91, 93, 119-120, 126, 134, 145, 163, 167, 186, 203, 221

Harney and 19, 54, 56-59,
    64-69, 76-79, 90, 93, 95, 97,
    193, 196, 221, 224
Brandebury, Fletch 115, 187
Branson, William 5, 109, 133, 139,
    141, 155, 157, 161, 165-167,
    182
Breckenridge, John C. 31, 56, 59, 210
Brown, B, Gratz 7, 12, 28, 51, 61,
    108, 179, 200, 211
Buchanan, James 9, 25, 30, 56-57, 59,
    65-66, 88, 211-213
Bull Run (See Manassas) 10, 156
Burlington, Iowa 27, 38
    Douglas's Speech 29
    Lincoln's speech 29-30
    Zouaves 2, 34-35, 37, 39-40
Burmeister, Charles 181
Burmeister, George 2, 6, 19, 26-27,
    33, 46, 123, 128, 180, 183-
    184, 186, 190, 193, 196-197,
    201
Burmeister, Henry 182
Burrit, Elijah H. 150
    Geography of the Heavens
    150
Butternut (clothing and confusion)
    144, 158, 163
Cabell, Edward C. 78, 97
Cairo 75, 134-135, 145, 156
Cameron, Simon 31
Camp Cameron 20, 113-115
Camp Creek 130
Camp Ellsworth 19, 40, 47
Camp Jackson 6, 8, 19, 52, 57, 68-69,
    71-77, 79, 83, 88, 90, 92,
    96-97, 113, 119-121, 190,
    192, 203, 214, 225
Camp Mush 145, 157
Camp Walker 160
Carthage 135
Carmichael, Peter S. 17
Cause 1, 4, 8, 12, 15, 18, 20, 33, 35,
    41, 54, 58, 66, 68, 71, 74, 80,
    85, 88, 99, 108, 120, 124,
    136, 144, 186-187, 189, 192-
    194, 197, 199, 203, 208-209,
    212
Cedar Rapids 2, 27, 32-34, 39, 41
Chambers, Captain 118
Chapman, Samuel 139, 187
Churchill, Thomas 178
"Churubusco", Corporal 167
Clark, Ezekial 37, 118
Clinton, Iowa 34, 130
Clinton, Missouri 122
Clique (the secret) 73, 81-83, 90, 99,
    192
Colliers, Alfred 41, 186
Commissioner of Banking (Missouri)
    73, 85, 166
    Jackson 84-86
    Price 73, 85-86
Community, Local 15
Company Community 18, 20, 115,
    124, 141, 187, 190
Company E 2-3, 5, 34-36, 40, 43-44,
    46, 105, 112, 115, 118-119,
    123, 128-129, 139, 144, 150,
    157, 174-175, 187
Company K 2, 33-34, 36, 41, 105, 132,
    137, 150, 186, 193
Conant, Major Horace 7, 92-95
Congregational 53-54, 193
Cook, Thomas Z. 25, 33, 42, 44, 169
Copperheads 30
Cornyn, Florence M. 172
Corporal Bill (see William J. Fuller) 7,
    95, 105, 144, 147, 187
Cowskin Prairie 141
Curtis, Samuel R. Colonel (see also
    Second Iowa Infantry) 47,
    103
Cutrer 179
Davis, Jefferson 26, 56, 67-69, 73, 83,
    91, 97, 99, 160, 183
Denmark (the steamboat) 182
Diaries 2, 4-6, 11, 15-18, 20, 148, 155,
    189, 196
Double-Quick 45, 129, 153
Douglas, Stephen A. 3, 15, 29-30,
    42-43, 57, 59, 61-62, 72, 145,
    151, 193, 197, 208-211

Drealard, James 144, 187
Dred Scott vs Sanford 3, 25, 30-31
Dretske, Diana L. 16-17
Dubuque (See Governor's Grays) 2, 27, 39, 43, 108, 131, 160, 193
Dug Springs 160-162, 164, 187
Duke, Basil 67, 74
Easton, Captain Langdon 68
Eckles, William 41, 139, 186
Ellsworth, Col. Elmer E. 19, 40, 47
Emotional intimacy 201
Enlistments 15, 17-19, 37, 47, 188
Erving, William 34
Esgate, Charles, 44, 186
Espirit de corps 17
Ethnic Strife 103
Extended Military families 17
Falstaff's (Sic) Recruits 129
Family 4, 17, 26, 28-29, 53, 60, 78, 83, 123, 139, 155, 181, 183, 196-197
Fast Marching 141
Fifth Missouri 121, 180
Fine, Gary 15, 17, 45, 107, 128, 133, 139
Fire Eaters 29, 107, 198-199, 200
First Iowa Infantry 2, 4-6, 8, 10-12, 14, 16, 18-19, 31-32, 40, 47, 52, 100-101, 104, 110-111, 114-115, 120, 123, 126-127, 131, 141, 162, 168, 176, 178-183, 186-187, 189-190, 194, 196
    Boarding steamboat for Hannibal 100
    Boonville 20, 47, 52, 73, 90, 97-99, 103, 109-114, 116, 118-120, 122, 124-128, 130, 132-134, 137, 143, 145, 187, 192, 194, 197
    Giving Speeches 105
    Greyhounds 189
    Guarding Bridges 47, 105
    Retreat 12, 135, 155, 162, 165, 167-168, 170-173, 177-179, 181
    Training Camp 18-19, 34, 38-39, 43, 46-47, 100, 189
    Uniforms 14, 34, 37, 45-46, 110, 112, 116, 157, 181-182, 188, 193
    Wilson's Creek 2, 5-6, 8, 10-14, 16, 18, 20, 92, 99, 160, 166, 169-172, 174, 178, 180, 182, 184, 194, 201, 203
Floyd, John Buchanan 9-10, 56-57
Forsyth 150, 153-154, 157, 187, 191
Fort Leavenworth 56, 122, 132
Fort Riley 54-55, 114
Fort Scott 58, 185
Fort Smith (see Arkansas) 68, 133, 191
Fort Sumter 1-2, 10, 18, 31, 40, 42, 62, 66, 90, 199-200
Fowler, Leonidus (See "Hard Times") 148
Free Soil 25
Frémont, John C. 29, 134-135, 143, 148, 156, 170, 182
French Jo 108
Frost, Daniel 52, 57, 67, 69, 71-73, 83, 193
Fugitive Slave Act 3, 24-25, 106
Fuller, William J. (Corporal Bill) 7, 95, 105, 144, 147, 187
Gemeinschaft 16
German Company (Burlington, Iowa, Missouri) 123, 139
German Home Guards 121, 158, 163
Glenn, Luther J. 200
Gesellschaft 16
Gottschalk, F. 39
Governor Jackson (see Jackson, Claiborne) 7-8, 11, 47-48, 52-53, 59, 64, 66-68, 71-75, 77-79, 86, 91, 93-95, 97-98, 100, 103, 107, 109, 192-193, 203
Grand River 122, 132-133, 187
Granger, Capt. Gordon 178
Grant, Nathaniel 66-67
Grant, Ulysses S. 10, 28, 30, 69, 74

Green, Colton 67, 78
Grey Hounds 131, 135
Grimes, James 24
Guelich, Quartermaster of First Iowa (note) 151
Gypsies 14
Hammond, William A. 55, 104
Hannibal 19, 47, 100, 104-105, 151
"Happy Land of Canaan" 108-109, 131-132, 135, 139, 187, 189
"Hard Times" 147-148
Hardee's Manual of Arms 41
Harding, Chester 103, 110, 124, 135, 143-146, 156
Harney, William Selby 19, 54, 56-59, 64-69, 76-79, 90, 93, 95, 97, 193, 196, 221, 224
Harney-Price Truce 90
Hatcher, Richard W. 6, 10-11, 16-17, 39-40, 58, 63, 67-68, 79, 89-92, 95, 109, 121-126, 128, 133-134, 153, 160-161, 163, 165-166, 171-180, 188, 203
  See Piston, William 6, 10-11, 16-17, 39-40, 58, 63, 67-68, 79, 89-92, 95, 109, 121-126, 128, 133-134, 153, 160-161, 163, 165-166, 171-180, 188, 203
Hay, John 61-62
Heustis, Bill 115, 128, 139-140, 157, 164, 187
Home Guards 52, 155, 166, 172, 203, 222
Hometown community 15, 37
Houston, Sam 198-199, 201
Huntington, Jeanette 184
Illinois, Thirteenth Volunteer Regiment 103, 166
Iowa 1-8, 10-14, 16-21, 24-41, 43-47, 52, 55, 60-61, 84, 97, 100-101, 103-115, 117-118, 120, 122-124, 126-127, 129, 131-133, 135-136, 139, 141-142, 144-148, 150-153, 155, 157, 161-163, 165, 167-168, 174-184, 186-191, 193-194, 196-197, 201-202
  Militia 29, 32-35, 37, 40, 46, 57, 69, 71-73, 75-76, 83, 90, 98, 133, 191-192, 221-223
  Politics 1, 3, 7, 14, 24-25, 29, 73, 81-84, 86, 89, 193, 201
Jackson, Claiborne Fox 6-8, 10-11, 19, 47-48, 52-53, 57, 59, 62-69, 71-100, 103, 106-107, 109, 113-114, 116, 119-121, 125, 134-136, 138, 140-141, 147, 150, 157, 159, 161, 166, 173, 190, 192-193, 196-197, 203, 214, 220, 223, 225
  Boon's Lick 80-82, 89, 97
  Boonville 20, 47, 52, 73, 90, 97-99, 103, 109-114, 116, 118-120, 122, 124-128, 130, 132-134, 137, 143, 145, 187, 192, 194, 197
  Camp Jackson 6, 8, 19, 52, 57, 68-69, 71-77, 79, 83, 88, 90, 92, 96-97, 113, 119-121, 190, 192, 203, 214, 225
  Commissioner of Banking 73, 85, 166
  Marriage 57, 81
  Politics 1, 3, 7, 14, 24-25, 29, 73, 81-84, 86, 89, 193, 201
  Military Bill 76, 78, 93, 221-222
  Proclamation 31, 47, 76, 80, 90, 95-97, 99, 103, 106, 110, 114, 223-224
  Secession Convention 62-63, 200
Jefferson Barracks 58, 126, 183
Jefferson City 73, 75-76, 95-98, 100, 200, 223
Jennie Deane 47
Johnston, Joseph E. 56, 68
Johnson, Mason 44
Jordan, Brian M. 1-2, 17, 23, 26, 31, 70, 196
Kansas 3-5, 19, 24, 26, 54-58, 63, 65, 68, 73-74, 77, 82-84, 92, 114, 122-123, 132-133, 149, 152, 160, 172, 175-176, 180, 184-

185, 200, 210, 212-213
Border Wars 55, 72
Kansas City storehouse 68, 77
Kansas-Nebraska Act of 1854 3
Kansas soldiers 123, 132-133
Second Regiment 152

Kate Cassel 38

Keokuk 19, 27, 34, 38, 40-41, 47, 100, 104, 111, 119

Kirkwood, Samuel 10, 14, 31, 36-37, 47

Leadership 190-192, 194

Lee, Robert E. 68, 200, 201

Liberty Arsenal 66-67, 73, 77

Link 45, 67, 140

Linn County 27, 33

Little Baldy 110, 163

Little Dixie 73, 80, 82

Lincoln, Abraham 1, 7-10, 14-15, 27-31, 34-35, 43, 45, 51-52, 55-57, 59-62, 64-65, 67-68, 70, 78, 87-88, 90, 106, 146, 151-152, 155-156, 198, 208-210, 213
Lincoln Douglas Debates 29-30
Lincoln and Missouri 51, 60
request for enlistments 47

Little Rock 99, 126, 191

Lovie, Henri 12, 178-179

Lyon, Nathaniel 2, 6-8, 10-11, 46-47, 51-56, 58, 60, 63, 65, 75, 79, 92, 98, 100, 113, 120, 141-142, 169, 190, 192, 196, 203, 208
Description by Wilkie 39
Description by McElroy 201
Description by Ware 25, 105, 177
Letter to Col. Bates, letter to Keokuk training Camp 34
Missouri Campaign 2, 5, 18, 101, 190

Lyftogt, Kenneth 8, 11, 14, 23, 25, 32, 34-35, 41, 46, 118, 122, 131, 134, 144, 172, 174

McClellan, George B. 14, 109, 114, 145

McCulla's Store 161-164

McCulloch, General Benjamin 11, 97, 114, 121, 135, 141, 157, 159-160, 162-163, 165-166, 171-174, 179, 194

McElroy John 7, 52, 54, 60, 67-68, 71, 74, 76-77, 90, 92-95, 145, 170, 180, 201, 203

McGuire, Randy 9, 59, 72, 121, 203

McKee, Edwin 41

McKinstry, Justus 124, 143-144, 182

McPherson, James M. 7, 15, 31, 35, 43, 74, 84, 89-90, 92, 124, 136, 186-187, 193

Mace (See also Johnson, Mason) 44-45, 137, 156, 167

Macon (City) 47, 104-105, 107-110

Manassas 156

Marshall, Gordon 4, 16

Marvin (or Marven), John C. 33

Matson, Daniel 5, 31, 123, 139, 156

Matthies, Charles Leopold 35, 39, 123, 139

Maynard Rifles 133

Melville 139

Mentz, Michael 44, 186

Merritt, William 40-41, 145, 147, 150, 174, 176, 188

Military Bill 76, 78, 93, 221-222

Minority Coercion 7, 100

Mississippi River 3, 10, 19, 27, 34, 40, 51, 60, 92, 133-134
Riverboat traffic 3

Missouri Compromise of 1820 25, 61

Missouri 2-8, 10-11, 13, 18-20, 23-25, 28, 31, 34, 44, 46-49, 51-68, 70-78, 80-101, 103-107, 109-116, 120-122, 125-128, 130, 133-136, 138, 140-146, 150, 153, 155-158, 160, 162-163, 166-167, 169-170, 172-173, 175-177, 179-180, 182-183, 190-192, 196-197, 200-201,

203, 208, 210-211, 220-225
Federal troops, First
Missouri Volunteers, Third
Volunteers, Fourth Reserves
77, 96, 126
Demographics 51, 81, 88-89
Commissioner of Banking
73, 85, 166
Convention 59, 61-63, 88-89,
98, 199-200, 223
Kansas City (MO)
Storehouse 68, 77
Presidential Election 1860
31, 87
Missouri Democrat 61, 93-94
Missouri Register 107
Missouri River 59, 80, 82, 91, 97, 112-113, 115, 120, 122, 126
Missouri State Guard 11, 52, 76-77, 94, 109, 160, 163, 166, 173, 175, 177, 179
Montgomery, James 57
Motley Crew 120
Mount Pleasant 5, 7, 131
Grays 34, 39, 43, 131
Mudsills 104
Muster (See terms of duty) 36, 67, 146-147
Nebraska-Kansas Act, see Kansas-Nebraska Act 24
Neosho 141
Northern Missouri Railroad 103-104, 120
O'Connor, Henry 5, 40, 114, 125, 131, 134, 136, 151, 154
O'Shannon 115
Osage River 135-137
Osceola 136
Oxford Dictionary of Sociology 16
Ozark 97, 153
Ozarks 154-155
Palmyra 105
South River Bridge 105
Peace Policy 62
Pearce, Nicholas B. 160, 179
Peckham, James 53-55, 57-58, 64, 75-77, 79, 92-96, 99, 104, 109-110, 122, 124, 135, 143-146, 156, 168, 170-172, 174, 178, 194, 203, 225
Pelican Rifles 176
Phelps, John S. 155
Phelps, Mary Whitney 155
Phillips, Christopher 7, 51-56, 59, 61-63, 65, 67-68, 71-73, 75-76, 80-85, 87-92, 96-97, 100, 110, 114, 143, 171, 192
Pierce, Franklin 56-57
Pillow, Gideon 173
Pioneers (See Voerster's Sappers and Miners) 126
Piston, William Garrett 6, 10-11, 16-17, 39-40, 58, 63, 67-68, 79, 89-92, 95, 109, 121-126, 128, 133-134, 153, 160-161, 163, 165-166, 171-180, 188, 203
Planter's House 91-92, 94-95, 214
Plummer, Joseph B. 171, 178, 180
Pond Springs 144
Popular Sovereignty 24, 30, 208, 210
Porter, Asbury B. 41
Porter, Dr. Frank 143
Price, Hiram 118
Price, Sterling 11, 52-53, 67, 72-73, 85, 90, 92-93, 98-99, 166, 173, 203
Commissioner of Banking 73, 85, 166
General, Missouri State Guard 11, 52, 76-77, 94, 109, 160, 163, 166, 173, 175, 177, 179
Governor 7-8, 11, 47-48, 52-53, 59, 64, 66-68, 71-75, 77-79, 86, 91, 93-95, 97-98, 100, 103, 107, 109, 192-193, 203
McCulloch 11, 97, 114, 121, 135, 141, 157, 159-160, 162-163, 165-166, 171-174, 179, 194
Politics 1, 3, 7, 14, 24-25, 29,

244

73, 81-84, 86, 89, 193, 201
Price-Harney Agreement
76-77
Wilson's Creek 2, 5-6, 8,
10-14, 16, 18, 20, 92, 99,
160, 166, 169-172, 174, 178,
180, 182, 184, 194, 201, 203
Primary Groups 15, 120
Proclamation 31, 47, 76, 80, 90,
95-97, 99, 103, 106, 110,
114, 223-224
    See Governor Jackson's 7-8,
47-48, 68, 79, 91, 97, 100,
103, 203
    See Lyon's 2, 7-8, 11-13,
18-19, 25, 48, 53-56, 60,
62-63, 65-66, 69-72, 75,
90-91, 93-94, 96, 98-99, 101,
103, 107, 109-110, 114-117,
119-121, 125-126, 131-133,
135, 137-138, 141, 143-146,
150, 155, 157, 160, 163-166,
169-174, 176-178, 180, 182,
190, 192-193, 197, 208, 212-
213, 224
Rains, James S. 160, 162, 172
Regulars (official U. S. military
soldiers) 116, 117, 118, 120,
122, 129, 131
Renick 104, 109, 112
Republicans 9, 25, 30, 62, 72-74, 88,
200, 208-209, 212
    Iowa 1-8, 10-14, 16-21,
24-41, 43-47, 52, 55, 60-61,
84, 97, 100-101, 103-115,
117-118, 120, 122-124, 126-
127, 129, 131-133, 135-136,
139, 141-142, 144-148, 150-
153, 155, 157, 161-163, 165,
167-168, 174-184, 186-191,
193-194, 196-197, 201-202
Reynolds, Thomas C. 52, 59, 64,
97-98
Ritner, Jacob 28, 29, 112, 129, 132,
133
Robinson, Marilynne 53, 195, 198
Rolla 14, 121-122, 124, 135, 143-144,
155, 160-161, 166-167, 170-
173, 176, 179-182, 184
    RR Terminus 121, 166
    See also Sigel and Sweeney
69, 121
    Union Retreat 177, 181
Rombauer, Robert Julius 43, 58, 64,
69-71, 77-79, 88, 91, 93, 161,
165, 169, 192, 199, 203
Salomon, Charles 121
Sappington, John S. 81
Saxton, Rufus 70
Schofield, John M. 145, 147, 172, 176
Scott, Winfield 3, 25, 30-31, 57-58,
65-66, 68, 73, 109, 146, 160,
184-185, 197
Secesh 35, 44-46, 105, 114, 163, 167
Secession 7, 10-11, 19, 25, 29, 31,
46-47, 57, 62-64, 69-72,
74-75, 85, 87-91, 97-100,
105, 107, 135, 145, 182,
198-200
    Convention 59, 61-63, 88-89,
98, 199-200, 223
Second Artillery (See Totten) 126
Second Iowa Infantry (see Samuel
Curtis) 47, 103
Shannon, Joseph O. 115
Sharps Rifles 128
Shueyville, Iowa 26
Schuster 155, 181
    H. E. 181
    Adolph 155
    Hugo 155
St. Joseph 47, 103-104
St. Louis 6, 8-10, 12, 19, 26, 44,
51-53, 58-63, 65-70, 72-77,
82, 85, 89-91, 93, 96-98,
100, 110, 112, 114, 116-117,
119-121, 124, 126, 128, 131,
134-135, 145, 155-156, 167,
169, 181-182, 190, 193, 200-
201, 203, 221, 224
    Arsenal 9-10, 19, 51-52,
58-60, 62-67, 69-75, 77, 79,
83, 97, 110, 121, 124, 126,
182, 190-191, 203

Safety Committee 77
Sigel 69, 121-122, 134-135, 138, 141, 159, 170-171, 173, 177-179, 182, 187
Slavery 10, 23-25, 27-28, 30-31, 41, 46, 54, 57-58, 60-61, 70, 73, 81-82, 84, 86, 88, 106, 145, 167, 197, 199-200, 209-213
Snead, Thomas L. 7, 30, 65, 67, 69, 88, 91-98, 121, 135, 160, 174, 192, 203
Southern ancestry 3
Springfield 8, 11, 13-14, 20, 45, 61, 121-122, 124-126, 135-136, 141-145, 148, 150-151, 154-155, 158, 160-161, 164-167, 169-175, 177, 179, 184
Springfield Rifles 45
State Guard Troops (See Missouri State Guard) 11, 52, 77, 110, 153, 163, 179, 197
Steele, Frederick 176
Stephens, Alexander 199
Stevens, Walter 51-52, 61-62, 67, 106
Stewart, Charles 44
Streaper, George 35, 43, 46, 119
Sturgis, Samuel D. 68, 122-124, 128, 131-134, 176-178, 191
Stypes, Charles 115, 187
Suicides 137
Swan Creek 153
Sweeny, Thomas 69, 121-122, 150, 153-154, 172, 190-191
Terms of Duty 141, 146-147, 181
Texas 11, 63-64, 157, 160, 198, 201
    Secession 7, 10-11, 19, 25, 29, 31, 46-47, 57, 62-64, 69-72, 74-75, 85, 87-91, 97-100, 105, 107, 135, 145, 182, 198-200
    See McCulloch 11, 97, 114, 121, 135, 141, 157, 159-160, 162-163, 165-166, 171-174, 179, 194
    See Sam Houston 198-199, 201
    See Twiggs 64
Thirteenth Illinois Regiment 166
Thomas, Lorenzo 1, 7-8, 11, 33, 52, 56, 59, 66-67, 69, 75, 78, 91-92, 95, 121, 124, 154, 178-179, 190, 192, 203
    Adjutant-General of U.S. Army 78, 143, 146, 179
Tönnies, Ferdinand 16
Totten, James 114, 126, 175-176, 178, 180, 191
    Totten's Battery 114, 126, 176
Townsend, Edward D. 146
Training Camp (see Keokuk) 18-19, 34, 38-39, 43, 46-47, 100, 189
Typhoid 145
United Brethren in Christ 26
U.S. Army of the West 91
Utter, Joseph 15, 190, 221
VanArsdel, John M. 41, 186
Veal 36, 115, 128
Voerster, John D. (see Pioneers) 126
Walker, Leroy Pope 141, 160, 179
Ware, Eugene 2-6, 9-10, 14-15, 18-19, 25, 27-32, 34-38, 40, 43-47, 90, 104-120, 122-123, 125, 127-133, 135-140, 143-144, 147-158, 160-167, 170, 172, 174-185, 187-188, 190-191, 193, 196, 201
    Burlington 27, 38
    Description of Lyon 191
    Enlistment 16, 18, 27, 29, 35, 38, 46, 146-147
    Militia 29, 32-35, 37, 40, 46, 57, 69, 71-73, 75-76, 83, 90, 98, 133, 191-192, 221-223
    R.R. Guard Duty 43-44, 104, 110, 112, 140, 149, 155
    Wilson's Creek 2, 5-6, 8, 10-14, 16, 18, 20, 92, 99, 160, 166, 169-172, 174, 178, 180, 182, 184, 194, 201, 203
Wentz, Augustus 39

Whisler, Benjamin 41, 186
Western College 26-27, 32-34, 41
       Western Light Guards 33
Wilkie, Franc B. 2, 14, 19, 31, 35, 37,
       39-45, 47, 52, 103-104, 107-
       109, 112, 114, 116-118, 120,
       122, 126, 128-129, 133-134,
       138-139, 141-142, 147-148,
       150-151, 153-154, 157, 160-
       161, 163, 165, 167, 170-171,
       174-175, 179, 188-191, 193,
       196, 220
Wilsons Creek Battle 6, 11, 14, 18,
       184, 194
Zouave 34, 37, 40

www.ingramcontent.com/pod-product-compliance
Lightning Source LLC
Chambersburg PA
CBHW030105170426
43198CB00009B/505